Gender and Leisure

What role do leisure, culture, sport and tourism play in shaping gender relations?

The highly contested nature of both 'gender' and 'leisure' encapsulates many of the most critical social and cultural debates of the early twenty-first century. Drawing on a wide range of theoretical perspectives, as well as extensive original empirical research, *Gender and Leisure* offers new insights into social and cultural explanations of the theories, policies and practices that serve to produce, legitimise, reproduce and rework gender and leisure in everyday life.

The book begins by introducing and evaluating the key social and cultural ideologies, philosophies and beliefs that have underpinned our theoretical understandings of gender and leisure. Theoretical perspectives developed in structural and poststructural theory, feminist and gender studies, cultural sociology and social and cultural geography then inform subsequent analyses of leisure policy and practice.

Part two of *Gender and Leisure* develops a series of case studies of leisure sites and processes to explore gender relations embodied in contemporary leisure policies and practices. These include leisure places, leisure education, leisure management and the relationships between leisure, sport and tourism.

Cara Carmichael Aitchison is Professor in Human Geography, University of the West of England.

Gender and Leisure

Social and cultural perspectives

Cara Carmichael Aitchison

Routledge
Taylor & Francis Group

LONDON AND NEW YORK

First published 2003
by Routledge
11 New Fetter Lane, London EC4P 4EE

Simultaneously published in the USA and Canada
by Routledge
29 West 35th Street, New York, NY 10001

Routledge is an imprint of the Taylor and Francis Group

Typeset in Sabon by
Florence Production Ltd, Stoodleigh, Devon
Printed and bound in Great Britain by
TJ International Ltd, Padstow, Cornwall

British Library Cataloguing in Publication Data
A catalogue record for this book is available from the
British Library

Library of Congress Cataloging in Publication Data
A catalog record for this book has been requested

ISBN 0–415–26155–4 (hbk)
ISBN 0–415–26156–2 (pbk)

Contents

4   Gender and leisure places   62

5   Gender and leisure policy   86

6   Gender and leisure education   118

Figures and tables

Figures

Tables

Acknowledgements

The seeds of this book were sewn many years ago and I would like to acknowledge the support of those who have helped see it through to fruition. Particular thanks go to Celia Brackenridge, Karla Henderson, Ken Roberts, Sheila Scraton, Betsy Wearing and Diana Woodward for their unstinting support of my research journey in gender and leisure over the last decade.

I would also like to thank other colleagues, students and 'teachers' who have provided inspiration and invitations to develop my ideas: Hossein Alizadeh, Kay Biscomb, Liz Bondi, Kath Browne, Josephine Burden, Peter Burns, Fred Coalter, Garry Chick, Mike Crang, David Crouch, Liz Cunningham, Nigel Curry, Anne Dunnet, Malcolm Foley, Tim Hall, Jennifer Hargreaves, Faezeh Hashemi, Barbara Humberstone, Mohammad Ehsani, Heather Gibson, Fiona Jordan, Tess Kay, Teus Kamphorst, Gerry Kenyon, Jan te Kleus, Lesley Lawrence, Francis Lobo, Nicola MacLeod, Mags Mernagh, Carol Morris, Alison Oram, Joanna Orsman, Stephen Owen, Kim Polistina, Stephen Shaw, Peter Taylor, John Tribe, Gill Valentine, Tony Veal and Garry Whannel.

A special thanks goes to the Routledge Sport and Leisure team and, in particular, to Samantha Grant, Editor of Sport and Leisure for her patience.

I acknowledge the following for permission to use copyright material that I have previously authored.

Taylor and Francis for excerpts from 'A decade of Compulsory Competitive Tendering (CCT) in UK sport and leisure services: some feminist reflections', first published in 1997 in *Leisure Studies* 16(2), 85–105; 'New cultural geographies: the spatiality of leisure, gender and sexuality' first published in 1999 in *Leisure Studies* 18(1), 19–39; 'Poststructural feminist theories of representing others: a response to the crisis in leisure studies' discourse', first published in 2000 in *Leisure Studies* 19(3), 127–144; 'Women in leisure services: managing the social–cultural nexus of gender equity', first published in 2000 in *Managing Leisure* 5(4), 81–91; 'Gender and leisure research: the "codification of knowledge"', first published in 2001 in *Leisure Sciences* 23(1), 1–19.

Sage for excerpts from 'Theorising Other discourses of tourism, gender and culture: can the subaltern speak (in tourism)?', published in 2001 in *Tourist Studies* 1(2), 133–147.

The Learning and Teaching Support Network Subject Centre for Hospitality, Leisure, Sport and Tourism for permission to reprint material from 'Engendered education: adapting models from the sociology of education for leisure, sport and tourism in higher education', first published in 2003 in the *Journal of Hospitality, Leisure, Sport and Tourism Education* 2(1), 93–104.

The Australia and New Zealand Leisure Studies Association for excerpts from 'Young disabled people, leisure and everyday life: reviewing conventional definitions for leisure studies', first published in 2000 in *Annals of Leisure Research* 3(1), 1–20.

The Women's Sports Foundation for excerpts from *Women and Sport: A Syllabus Guide* first published in 2001.

1 Introduction

Introducing the social–cultural nexus of gender and leisure

'Gender' and 'leisure' are highly contested terms. Previously understood as nouns, 'gender' and 'leisure' have come to be seen as possessing the multiple identities of nouns and verbs. Within recent social and cultural discourses poststructural feminist writers such as Judith Butler (1990, 1993) have spoken of 'doing gender', symbolic interactionist leisure theorists such as Jack Kelly (1983) have talked of 'experiencing leisure' and cultural theorists such as Chris Rojek (2000) have drawn attention to 'performing leisure'. In attempting to uncover the meanings of gender and leisure, and the power relations constructed in and through gender and leisure, these discourse encapsulate many of the most critical social and cultural debates of the late twentieth and early twenty-first century. This book seeks to explore these discourses and debates in relation to gender and leisure as mutually informing sites and processes, as nouns and verbs and as structures and cultures.

A central focus of the book is the development of a theoretical critique that integrates social and cultural perspectives. This critique draws on structuralist and poststructuralist accounts of gender and leisure in recognition of the interconnections between social and cultural relations. This accommodation of the social and the cultural, or the material and the symbolic, is articulated here through the conceptualisation of the *social–cultural nexus*. The social–cultural nexus is explained as both a site and process of construction, legitimation, reproduction and reworking of gender and leisure relations. In this regard, the book demonstrates the development of feminist leisure studies from what Karla Henderson *et al.* (1989) described as a single '*Feminist Perspective on Women's Leisure*' to a multiplicity of '*Feminist Perspectives on Women's Leisure*' (Henderson *et al.* 1996) through to an approach that seeks to synthesise elements of these different perspectives by highlighting the significance of the social–cultural nexus. In this way, the book engages with poststructural theory to explore the cultural workings and reworkings of gender and leisure relations in everyday life while simultaneously acknowledging the value of structuralist analyses of patriarchy and capitalism or patriarchal capitalism in shaping the power relations that construct, legitimate and reproduce gender and leisure relations, often on a global scale. Elshtain (1981) has described these grand global theories of structuralism as 'narratives of closure' and this book seeks to open these narratives to cultural critiques of gender, leisure and difference in both structural relations and 'experiential diversity' (Brah 1991).

In discussing contested meanings of gender and leisure, we are therefore required to ask ourselves questions of epistemological difference: what we know of and what we consider as leisure, how we come to know about gender–power relations within leisure sites and processes, how our beliefs and values shape what we know, what 'evidence' there is to support or refute our claims to knowledge, and how we come to have this knowledge rather than or in addition to other kinds of knowledge (Oakley 2000, Stanley 1997). This book seeks to address these questions by contextualising the subject field of leisure studies in relation to other areas of social sciences that have informed feminist and gender leisure studies.

It is well over ten years since the last book on gender and leisure was written by anyone in the UK and the text introduced here now provides a new set of questions to accompany Eileen Green, Sandra Hebron and Diana Woodward's question *Women's Leisure, What Leisure?* (1990). Whereas the 1980s saw the publication of a series of feminist studies of leisure in the UK, we had to look to other parts of the globe for critical insight to gender and leisure in the 1990s. In Australia, Besty Wearing has been instrumental in refocusing leisure studies' attention from the sometimes homogenising category of women to the more nuanced relations of gender discerned through poststructural and postcolonial critiques (Wearing 1996, 1998). I remain acutely aware, however, that the subject field of leisure studies is a predominantly western discourse where white voices speak in many volumes as author and authority over 'Other' voices.

However, this book is not just concerned with forming alliances between social and cultural theory or colonial and postcolonial discourses; it also seeks to build bridges between theory and policy. An underpinning theme throughout the book is the way in which particular leisure policies and practices are the outcome of equally particular leisure perspectives and philosophies. The book is structured to progress from a discussion of the perspectives, philosophies, ideologies, values and beliefs that inform theories of gender and leisure to an evaluation of the leisure policies and practices that are informed by and, in turn, reinform and reform such theories. The first half of the book is thus largely theoretical whereas the second half of the book explores gender relations in leisure policy, education and management. The sites and processes of policy, education and management are acknowledged here as central in the production, normalisation, reproduction and reworking of gender and leisure-related knowledge, power and relations and thus informed by and informing of the theoretical perspectives outlined in the first half of the book.

Each chapter of the book reflects my own academic background and research experience and draws on different disciplines or subject fields to shape an interdisciplinary account of gender and leisure. Chapter 2 'Gender and leisure theory', is informed by social, cultural and gender theory and each subsequent chapter builds on these social, cultural and feminist critiques alongside further critiques from leisure studies. In addition, Chapter 3 'Gender and leisure studies', is informed by sociology; Chapter 4 'Gender and leisure places' by geography; Chapter 5 'Gender and leisure policy' by social and public policy, Chapter 6 'Gender and leisure education', by the sociology of education, and Chapter 7 'Gender and leisure management', by management studies. Although each chapter can be read as a relatively self-contained critique of gender and leisure in a specific arena, together the chapters build a cumulative account of the interplay between social and cultural power in the construction of gender and leisure relations such that the whole of the critique is greater than the sum of the parts.

Structure and outline of the book

Chapter 2 'Gender and leisure theory', aims to explore the ways in which different kinds of knowledge have been constructed within social science in general and gender studies in particular. The critique then seeks to appraise how these ways of knowing have shaped our understandings of gender and leisure. The chapter therefore introduces the theoretical foundations upon which more detailed discussions of gender and leisure are developed throughout the subsequent chapters. The chapter first seeks to identify and explain a series of social science perspectives that has served to shape our understanding of social relations including leisure relations. These are defined broadly as positivism, phenomenology, structuralism and poststructuralism. The second half of the chapter then seeks to identify and explain a range of perspectives from feminist and gender theory that has fashioned our understanding of gender relations as a key component of wider social relations. Feminist perspectives discussed include liberal feminism, socialist and Marxist feminism, radical feminism, poststructural feminism, and postcolonial and black feminism. Instead of viewing these perspectives as forming a coherent typology of neatly defined classifications, the chapter reveals the complex and competing nature of knowledge and understanding, the multiple ways of knowing about social and cultural relations including gender relations, and our different understandings of social and cultural phenomena including leisure. The chapter thus seeks to draw attention to the interface between structures and cultures or the interconnections between material and the symbolic realities to reveal the dynamic nature of power at the site of the social–cultural nexus.

Chapter 3 'Gender and leisure studies', chronicles the development of leisure studies as a subject field within the social sciences. The chapter discusses the major schools of thought within the subject field including the constructed dichotomy of pluralist and neo-Marxist critiques and distinct approaches to the study of leisure in Europe and North America. It then appraises the ways in which these discourses have informed competing definitions of leisure as time, activity, function and freedom and revisits these definitions from feminist and gender perspectives that are deemed to be lacking in the early leisure studies literature. In chronicling the development of the leisure studies literature the chapter examines the role of different disciplines and subject fields in the evolution of the leisure studies canon. Here, the influence of sociology in informing both leisure studies and gender studies is particularly significant and is discussed in relation to the sociology of leisure and leisure sociologies. The impact of sociology and socialist feminist research within leisure studies is then evaluated through a review of a series of major case studies of women's leisure that were researched in the UK during the 1980s. The chapter then concludes by introducing more recent feminist leisure research undertaken from poststructuralist perspectives that have embraced studies of leisure and culture and have turned our attention to the interconnections between structures and cultures of gender and leisure.

Chapter 4 'Gender and leisure places', supplements and complements the previous chapter's sociological critiques with geographical perspectives. This discussion is developed by *placing* gender and leisure in relation to a series of geographical discourses that have developed over the course of the last century. The first discourse outlined is that of 'geographies of leisure and leisure geographies' which evaluates the origins and development of the relationships between geography and leisure studies. The second phase of the chronological account introduces structuralist theories and the concept of spatialised feminism through an exploration of the rise of structuralist interpretations of space and place within geography and the subsequent development of spatialised feminism as an explanatory framework developed by socialist feminist geographers. The next phase introduces social and cultural geographies and the concept of gendered leisure space to explore the impact of geography's 'turn to culture' and the incorporation of studies of leisure, including gendered leisure space, in recent social and cultural geography. The following sections of the chapter then examine the place of 'the gaze' within these more recent geographies of gender and leisure, the increasing visibility of poststructural perspectives and theories of sex and gender together with the place of 'the dualism' in the production and reproduction of gendered power relations and, hence, gender–leisure relations. The penultimate phase in the chronology of geography, gender and leisure then explores the legacy of colonial geographies and the development of postcolonial geographies where a discussion of the place of 'the Other' further informs our understanding of gender and leisure relations.

Chapter 5 'Gender and leisure policy' evaluates the importance of policy as a vehicle for implementing different perspectives or value systems in practice. The origins of contemporary leisure policy are placed in a historical context of public sector intervention in leisure from the eighteenth century. The chapter then moves on to examine the development of contemporary leisure policies designed to address social exclusion, including women's marginalisation in leisure. The chapter highlights the influence of socialist feminism and structuralist perspectives more generally in the development of policies that have sought to adopt leisure-related strategies as a means of addressing social exclusion. The focus of the chapter then moves from these wider contextual discussions to an illustration of policy development in the area of sport and the role of national bodies such as Sport England and the Women's Sport Foundation in implementing policies designed to promote gender equity in sport. The chapter moves from national policy debates to the implementation of leisure-related policy at a local level where the changing nature of local authorities and their impact on leisure provision and participation is examined in a discussion of UK local authority leisure policy spanning the last two decades. The role of strategic approaches and public–private alliances in the delivery of gender equity through leisure and sport policy is explored and the recent development of equity and inclusion within local cultural strategies is discussed.

Chapter 6 'Gender and leisure education', then seeks to explore the ways in which leisure studies knowledge is formed within higher education and research. The chapter evaluates leisure studies education as a series of sites and processes that are significant in the production, legitimation, reproduction and reworking of perspectives on gender and leisure and, therefore, on gender–power relations per se. Two models of 'gender scholarship' in generic higher education are reviewed and three further models of gender scholarship within leisure, tourism and sport studies are introduced and evaluated in relation to broader feminist sociologies of education. The models are tested in relation to one site of engendered education; that of academic journals. The findings of empirical research reveal that, while the models do provide a generalised trend towards gender scholarship, their rather structuralist approach masks the nuances of gender–power relations in higher education. Poststructuralist analysis, or a combination of structuralist and poststructuralist analysis, is therefore advocated as a more sophisticated approach towards developing a critique of engendered education in leisure, tourism and sport studies and thus enhancing gender equity that can inform leisure practice.

Chapter 7 'Gender and leisure management', explores the translation of theory, policy and education into leisure management practice. It seeks to identify and explain the origins and nature of terms, concepts and theories that address the interrelationships of gender, sexuality, organisations and organisation in relation to leisure management. The chapter introduces Hearn *et al.*'s (1989) concept of 'the sexuality of organisation' to emphasise a shift in thinking from structural constraints to cultural relations. Similarly, theories of gender relations that distinguish between gender as a variable, standpoint feminism and poststructural feminism are outlined and evaluated to demonstrate the shift in feminist theory from liberal to socialist to poststructural. The concepts of sex role spill-over and sex-role stereotyping are also introduced and explained together with illustrations of vertical and horizontal sex-segregation within organisations. The shift in research philosophy and the conceptualisation of gender relations in the workplace is mirrored by a shift in the focus of research methodology from distributive to relational research and a commensurate shift in research methods from quantitative to qualitative. The chapter then explores research into gender equity in the service sectors of health, retail, finance, hospitality and tourism to contextualise research of gender and leisure management within the wider service sector. This section also serves to complement and supplement the earlier accounts of gender equity in the educational sector that were provided in the previous chapter. The research findings from the Institute of Leisure and Amenity Management project entitled *Gender Equity in Leisure Management* (Aitchison *et al.*, 1999) are introduced and the chapter focuses upon structures *and* cultures of (un)equal opportunities in leisure services and career progression in leisure management. Throughout the discussion of gender equity in UK leisure management comparative data from international studies of gender equity in sport and leisure management are used to evaluate the findings in a wider context. Of particular note here is the study of gender equity in sports organisations in Australia, New Zealand and Canada conducted by Jim McKay (1996), the work of Bialeschki and Henderson (1984) and Henderson and Bialeschki (1993, 1995) examining the status of women and their career development in leisure management in the US, and Shinew and Arnold's (1998) study 'Gender equity in the leisure services field', again in the US. Across all of these research studies there was strong evidence to demonstrate that women's experience of leisure management was shaped by both structural and cultural factors. Indeed, there was evidence to show that the inter-relationship between structures and cultures was often what consolidated or maintained gender inequity within leisure management organisations.

In summary, this book seeks to offer a critical appraisal of a range of different perspectives on gender and leisure and to then explore these perspectives in relation to leisure policy, education and management. The book concludes that it is at the site and process of the social–cultural nexus that gender and leisure relations are often formed and reformed within leisure theory, leisure studies, leisure spaces, leisure policy, leisure education and leisure management. As befits a project that has drawn on poststructural accounts, there is no final closure to these discussions in the form of a concluding chapter that provides one answer to a clearly defined problem or set of issues. Instead, the conclusion seeks to summarise the social and cultural critiques developed throughout the book and to leave the reader with a series of questions related to each of the discussion chapters.

2 Gender and leisure theory

Introduction: ways of knowing, seeing and believing

This chapter seeks to provide the theoretical foundations upon which more detailed discussions of gender and leisure are developed throughout the subsequent chapters of the book. Social and cultural theories offering contested and sometimes overlapping perspectives on gender are introduced and explained. An appreciation of these perspectives will inform the subsequent discussions of different ways of seeing and explaining gender and leisure relations introduced in the next chapter and then revisited throughout the remainder of the book.

A continuing assertion throughout the book is that particular leisure policies and practices are the outcome of equally particular leisure perspectives and philosophies. In other words, our view of the world, and leisure's place within the world, shapes the way in which our leisure relations are produced and understood. To understand leisure relations, including the gender dynamics of such relations, requires an understanding of the perspectives, philosophies, values and beliefs upon which these relations are based. This chapter first seeks to identify and explain a series of social science perspectives that has served to shape our understanding of social relations including leisure relations. The second half of the chapter then seeks to identify and explain a range of perspectives from feminist and gender theory that has shaped our understanding of gender relations as a fundamental component of wider social relations. What the chapter reveals is the complex and competing nature of knowledge and understanding, the multiple ways of knowing about social and cultural relations including gender relations, and our different understandings of social and cultural phenomena including leisure. The chapter concludes by stressing the importance of social *and* cultural critiques of gender and leisure relations. The importance of developing theoretical critiques that integrate social and cultural perspectives is, indeed, the central focus of the book. This recognition of the mutually informing nature of social and cultural relations is articulated through the conceptualisation of the *social–cultural nexus*. Here, the social–cultural nexus is perceived as both a site and process in the construction, legitimation, reproduction and reworking of gender and leisure relations.

Research philosophy is concerned with the examination of the nature of knowledge and the links between theory and data in the construction of knowledge (Mannheim 1952). In relation to gender and leisure this means asking ourselves what we know, how we come to know, how our beliefs and values shape what we know and what evidence there is to support or refute our claims to knowledge (Oakley 2000, Stanley 1997). Discussions of research philosophy are central to this book's investigation of the interrelationships between social and cultural relations in defining what we consider as leisure, what we know about gender–power relations within and around leisure sites and processes, and how we come to have this knowledge rather than or in addition to other kinds of knowledge.

Discussions of research philosophy usually attempt to address two sets of overlapping considerations. First, epistemological issues, which refer to the nature of knowledge and theories of knowledge construction, need to be considered. Second, ontological issues, which refer to theories of being or existence and the ways in which our existence is shaped by the nature of knowledge, require consideration.

The aim of this chapter is to explore the ways in which different kinds of knowledge have been constructed within social science in general and gender studies in particular and to appraise how these ways of knowing have shaped our understandings of gender and leisure. The chapter is therefore concerned with identifying and analysing how such knowledge is produced, legitimated, reproduced and reworked within both dominant and emergent paradigms in social science broadly and gender studies more specifically. As such, discussions of research philosophy, and a concern with epistemological and ontological issues, form a continuous thread throughout the chapter. Subsequent chapters reiterate and develop the pivotal points of these discussions. For example, poststructural theory is explored in depth in Chapter 4 where contemporary social and cultural geography offers new insights into gender and leisure places. Chapter 5 discusses the limitations of structural theory in relation to gender and leisure policy and Chapters 6 and 7 consider the ways in which structural *and* poststructural theories have informed our understandings of gender and leisure education and gender and leisure management respectively.

A central function of any discussion of research philosophy is, therefore, to lay the foundations for the subsequent evaluation of methodology, collection, analysis and presentation of primary data in the form of empirical research. Within this book, however, discussion of research philosophy has a second but equally important purpose. This book is not just concerned with presenting existing or even new accounts of feminist and gender leisure research. It is also concerned with re-evaluating fundamental epistemological issues within the social sciences in general and leisure studies in particular. This re-evaluation of epistemological paradigms within leisure studies therefore goes beyond the simple rejection of existing or dominant epistemological perspectives. Rather, the chapters within the book attempt to engage with, to learn from, and to develop, emergent and competing epistemological perspectives within social science and leisure studies.

A feminist epistemology cannot be directly equated with any of the more established epistemological perspectives of positivism, phenomenology or structuralism discussed in this chapter. Instead, different feminist perspectives align themselves more readily with one epistemology or another. For example, there is clear affinity between socialist or Marxist feminism and a structuralist epistemology. However, it is not the intention of this book to align with one of these established epistemologies and to reject the others out of hand. Rather, it is intended to evaluate each perspective in turn, to assess the presence and impact of each within leisure studies, to appraise the relevance of each epistemology to gender analyses, and to evaluate the suitability of each to gender analyses of leisure studies.

This chapter therefore seeks to identify the major social science paradigms and to evaluate feminist epistemologies within the social sciences. The relationships between feminist epistemology(ies) and the more established epistemologies of positivism, phenomenology and structuralism are reviewed and the ways in which these and other theoretical perspectives have influenced the development of leisure studies is then appraised in the next chapter.

Social science and the philosophy of knowledge: contested ways of knowing

For the purposes of this discussion, it is important to identify general epistemological trends within the social sciences, the relative influence of each of the main epistemological positions, and the relevance of these to the development of alternative feminist epistemologies. Such a discussion emphasises that neither science nor social science remain static. Instead, change, development, transformation and 'progress' are seen to be the driving forces behind and the outcomes of both intellectual endeavour and scientific inquiry. The extent to which academic enquiry seeks to discover or uncover 'the truth' lay at the heart of many debates in social science during the twentieth century and remains central to discussions in social and cultural theory at the beginning of the twenty-first century. Searching for the truth, whether at a universal or individual level, is perhaps the essence of the human condition and discussions of the way in which the truth is discovered were also central to the work of social philosophers Karl Popper and Thomas Kuhn.

> Popper wants to say that despite local vagaries and perturbations, the choice between theories, between paradigms even, is, or can be, made

on rational scientific criteria. It is the effort to develop these criteria in a process of criticism, trial and error, that results in the slow progress towards truth as weaker offerings are discarded. Kuhn, on the other hand, seems to suggest that such choices are not rational in this sense, but the outcome of non-rational, extra-scientific considerations and factors, such as the distribution of power and reputation within disciplines, within society itself, personal commitments, wider cultural and political circumstances, and so on. The 'facts' cannot decide the matter because what the 'facts' are is dependent upon the particular paradigm they belong to, as do the standards in force for judging which theories are better than others.

(Hughes 1990: 74)

The debate between Popper and Khun is significant in revealing not only the contested nature of truth but also the contested nature of the search for truth in the form of scientific inquiry. For the purposes of the discussions set out in this book, Kuhn's acknowledgement of the significance of interdisciplinary knowledge and the role of power in the *Structure of Scientific Revolutions* (Kuhn 1975) is key to our understanding of the development of social scientific enquiry related to gender and leisure and the production, legitimation, reproduction and reworking of particular kinds of knowledge over others. Throughout Kuhn's work he reiterated the significance of arbitrary and accidental cross-disciplinary, multidisciplinary and interdisciplinary developments in offering new ways of seeing what he termed the 'particular constellation' of received beliefs within a previously established paradigm. According to Kuhn it is:

in these and other ways besides, normal science repeatedly goes astray. And when it does – when, that is, the profession can no longer evade anomalies that subvert the existing tradition of scientific practice – then begin the extraordinary investigations that lead the profession at last to a new set of commitments, a new basis for the practice of science. The extraordinary episodes in which that shift of professional commitment occurs are the ones known in this essay as scientific revolutions. They are the tradition-shattering complements to the tradition-bound activity of normal science.

(Kuhn 1975: 6)

Kuhn was also important in identifying the role of power as a means of safeguarding the authority of particular paradigms or perspectives within scientific communities. However, he clearly alerts us to the instability of such power and the possibilities of contesting perceived wisdom and therefore of initiating 'scientific revolutions'. Such change is, in part, rendered possible as a consequence of the inability to close the boundaries around a scientific community and the inevitable influence of scientific discovery from other disciplines. Power, interdisciplinarity and the power of inter-disciplinarity are key within our understanding of gender and leisure relations and, perhaps more significantly, in our understanding of the changing nature of theorising gender and leisure relations.

Drawing on Kuhn's theory, it is possible to contend that epistemological and methodological debate underwent a polarisation during the 1960s with positivism, in the form of the scientific method, being contrasted against both phenomenology and structuralism. During this period, the increasing respectability of science over social science led to an emphasis on the scientific methods of objectivity and deduction, the use of experiments, quantifiable data, verification procedures and the formation of scientific laws. The social sciences, many of which were still relatively young disciplines at that time, adopted and adapted methods from the sciences to enhance their credibility. The use of scientific methods to investigate social science phenomena has therefore been a paradox that has both challenged and divided social scientists for the last half-century or more.

The 1960s, however, did not represent the first period of epistemo-logical challenge or change. The origins of the empiricist orthodoxy seen in the natural sciences of the twentieth century can be traced back to Plato (427–347 BC) and his development of rationalist, mathematical principles and, marginally later, to Aristotle (384–322 BC) and his empiricist legacy. The more recent origins of the positivist orthodoxy can be traced to yet another group of European philosophers when Bacon (1561–1626) and Descartes (1596–1650) founded modern philosophy in the sixteenth and seventeenth centuries. Bacon continued the Aristotelian legacy and its focus on empiricism and Descartes followed the Platonic tradition of rationalism, although both were concerned with the search for a new certainty of knowledge that would overcome medieval scepticism and superstition and provide a scientific approach to knowledge for the modern era.

The sixteenth and seventeenth centuries are identified by attempts to create universal principles of intellectual authority that seek to denote a universal source of knowledge or truth fixed for all time. This rather rigid or certain view is in sharp contrast to the notion that knowledge is relative to the contemporary society within which it is created and legitimised. Moreover, and importantly for this book, the history of the philosophy of science is largely a history of men, recorded by men, where women are either Othered or rendered invisible. Feminist critiques of what counts as knowledge and who creates knowledge are therefore fundamental to feminist ideology, feminist politics and the academic discussions of gender relations that are developed throughout this book.

Feminism is an applied field of study and instrumental to political activism, decision-making, policy-making, planning and management. It is also an academic field of enquiry that seeks to increase knowledge, understanding and appreciation of gender–power relations. In both of these endeavours, a reappraisal of traditional epistemologies has been a necessary prerequisite for change. Within the academy there has been substantial criticism by feminist academics of rigidly defined academic disciplines which, it is argued, have served to prevent a comprehensive analysis of women's oppression by compartmentalising aspects of that oppression rather than joining the pieces of the jigsaw to form a whole picture. For this reason, multidisciplinary fields of study such as cultural studies, media studies and leisure studies should, in theory, be more accommodating to feminist analysis, albeit in relation to a particular field of study rather than any one discipline. However, the parameters of the field of study, and the definition and demarcation of topics worthy of study within the field, may already have been defined in patriarchal terms. Prior to evaluating feminist epistemologies, then, it is first necessary to identify and assess the characteristics and relative weaknesses of each of the more established epistemologies that shaped social science and leisure studies during the latter half of the twentieth century: positivism, phenomenology and structuralism.

Positivism: a functional legacy

Positivism is central to the methodology of the natural sciences and has its roots in many of the scientific developments from the fifteenth century onwards. However, the modern origins of the approach and its application to the social sciences are most closely identified with the nineteenth-century French philosopher August Comte. The approach investigates phenomena through the testing of hypotheses and is commonly referred to as the *scientific method*. These hypotheses are made from empirical generalisations, by accepted procedures, about observable phenomena. Comte believed that this method, which was already proving its worth within the natural sciences, could be used just as successfully in the social sciences. The value of the scientific method, he asserted, was in its ability to discover the truth by undertaking empirical research based on the principles of rationality and objectivity. Such principles had been central to the work of Plato and Aristotle and then Bacon and Descartes as outlined above and the influence of these earlier philosophers was central to Comte's philosophy. Although Comte admitted that not all social questions could be answered using positivism, he emphasised that if a question could not be answered using the positivist approach then it could not be answered at all, and therefore there was no point in asking it. He emphasised that 'there could be no real knowledge but that which is based on observed facts' (Easterby-Smith *et al.* 1991: 22). Comte's view emphasised the objective nature of reality and paved the way for the development of quantitative methods of research within the social sciences: 'his spirit was carried forward in the work of J.S. Mill, Herbert Spencer and Emile Durkheim, and is diffusely represented in the style and manner of the social sciences today' (Hughes 1990: 19).

Positivist epistemology is underpinned by a series of propositions and, although these are not always combined in all positivist research, they present a comprehensive picture of the broad characteristics of positivism. Easterby-Smith *et al.* (1991) have summarised these characteristics of positivism under eight headings. First, they identify the importance of *independence* where the observer is independent of the phenomenon being observed; second, *value–freedom* where the choice of what to study, and how to study it, can be determined by objective criteria rather than by personal values, politics and beliefs; third, *causality* where the aim of the social sciences is to identify causal explanations and fundamental laws that explain patterns and regularities in human behaviour and action; fourth, *hypothetico-deductiveness* where science proceeds through a process of hypothesising fundamental laws and then deducing what kinds of observations will demonstrate the truth or falsity of these hypotheses; fifth, *operationalisation* where concepts need to be put into action or operation in a way that enables facts to be measured quantitatively; sixth, *reductionism* where problems as a whole are better understood if they are reduced into the simplest possible elements; seventh, *generalisation* where it is necessary to select samples of sufficient size in order to be able to generalise about regularities in behaviour, and, finally, *cross-sectional analysis* where such regularities can most easily be identified by making comparisons of variations across samples (quoted and adapted from Easterby-Smith *et al.* 1991: 23).

However, these eight characteristics are at odds with many of the underlying principles of both feminist and poststructuralist research. Positivism's reductionist approach, which sees parts of systems as unrelated elements, uninfluenced by external societal and environmental factors, promotes the reification of individuals. Moreover, this emphasis on objective research assumes that objective information always exists and can be gathered and analysed in an objective manner. There are many areas of women's lives, of leisure, and of tourism, sport and culture where objective data are limited, primarily because much of women's lives is 'hidden' and leisure, tourism, sport and culture involve relationships between people which cannot always be measured objectively. However, even if such objective data did exist, treating research subjects as 'objects' would not necessarily provide meaningful results and, as Stanley and Wise (1993: 168) stress: 'treating people as objects – sex objects or research objects – is morally unjustifiable'. Lack of objective data has meant that those areas of leisure that can be quantified, such as sport participation figures, numbers of countryside visits, and distance travelled to participate in leisure or tourism, have been studied in detail. Other areas of leisure such as informal socialising, home-based leisure, the 'everyday' nature of leisure and the leisure servicing of men and children have remained under-researched (Bennett and Watson 2002, de Certeau 1984). Moreover, detailed research of more formal leisure participation has been undertaken at the expense of research into leisure's cultural relations with areas such as leisure consumption addressed more explicitly by scholars in subject fields such as media studies and cultural studies than by leisure researchers per se (Roberts 1999). Indeed the complex and changing interrelationships between leisure and culture have remained marginal to the leisure studies research agenda and the more complex social and cultural relations that both shape and are shaped by leisure relations remain underresearched and under-theorised within leisure studies (Aitchison 2000a, Rojek 2000).

Feminist critiques of the use of positivist approaches in leisure and tourism studies have focused on the inadequacy of relying on statistical information to present a picture of gender relations that are informed by deeper structural and cultural constraints within society. Feminist epistemology emphasises that even when objective data do exist, they cannot be investigated in a truly objective manner as both the research and the researcher are imprinted, to some degree, by the nature and workings of gender–power relations of society. Habermas (1971) provided one of the strongest critiques of the 'objectivity' and 'value-freedom' proposed by positivism. He associated the creation of knowledge with power and self-interest among the knowledge-producing groups and this controversial issue is explored in Chapter 6 where the production, legitimation and reproduction of leisure studies education and research are discussed in more detail.

In summary, positivism cannot provide an underpinning epistemology in feminist research and analysis because feminism does not claim to be value free or objective (Oakley 1998, Stanley 1997). At most, positivist approaches can be used to supplement interpretive, structuralist and post-structuralist epistemologies thereby providing an additional perspective and a means towards greater understanding rather than an end in itself.

Phenomenology: a more meaningful approach

> There is no absolutely 'objective' analysis of culture or ... of 'social phenomena' independent of special and 'one-sided' viewpoints ... All knowledge of cultural reality, as may be seen, is always knowledge from particular points of view.
>
> (Weber 1949: 72–81)

Phenomenological epistemology states that knowledge is obtained subjectively in a world of meanings created by individuals. Phenomenology's ontology, or theory of reality, states that what exists is that which is perceived to exist, and its methodology emphasises individuality and subjectivity. Husserl (1970) stressed that reality is given meaning by people following its construction in the social world, rather than in the natural or physical world. Phenomenology is therefore more concerned with *interpreting* the world than with *explaining* it and attempts are made to interpret social processes by establishing what these processes mean for the individuals involved. This can be achieved through unique case studies, in-depth discussions or interviews and participant and non-participant observation involving interpretative analysis often referred to as *hermeneutics* and intuitive and empathic understanding summarised by the German term *verstehen*. Thus, phenomenological approaches focus on people as thinking individuals, emphasising meaning, experience and interpretation, as well as the subjectivity of both observer and observed. The aim is not necessarily to increase explanation or predictive power but to improve understanding.

A range of social theorists has used phenomenological approaches and it has been argued that there is little in common between the theories of such researchers other than a sceptical view of positivism. Many of the branches of phenomenology, such as humanistic sociology and symbolic interactionism (Berger 1963, Berger and Luckman 1966), interpretative sociology (Habermas 1962), and ethnomethodology (Garfinkel 1967), were influenced by the work of Weber (1949). Weber emphasised the behavioural responses of individuals within what he defined as modern bureaucratic and rational society where the emphasis is upon continual demonstration of the work ethic through standardisation, punctuality, precision and 'being busy' in constructing 'society' rather than thinking of society as a more blatant controlling, punitive and repressive system (Durkheim 1895).

Within the multiplicity of phenomenological perspectives, at least four common features can be identified. First, *intentionality*, which emphasises that the world exists as a series of mental constructions created in intentional acts; second, *verstehen*, which emphasises interpretative and empathic understanding rather than explanation; third, *hermeneutics*, which attempts to explicate meaning behind action through interpretation; and, finally, *bracketing*, which emphasises that individual situations should be studied free of preconceived ideas and that to do this researchers need to be aware of their own biography and the ways in which this might impact upon the research process and outcome. Phenomenology has been criticised by positivists for being subjective and non-scientific in that its theories cannot be verified by testing hypotheses. Indeed, it is difficult to evaluate the contribution of phenomenological research as it is not cumulative in the sense that much traditional scientific work is. However, it should be recognised that there can be no such thing as definitive qualitative *or* quantitative social science research, as neither can be replicated exactly or verified completely.

As phenomenological investigation is dependent upon communication and intersubjectivity, the importance of language is paramount. Language always introduces a subjective element into research as language and labels for concepts may not always be understood identically by people speaking the same language, and are frequently understood in different ways following translation. However, the concept of 'man-made language' may be a greater barrier to overcome than any caused by national linguistic boundaries and frontiers:

> But even with the abolition of the dichotomy of female/male, private/ public, with the elimination of the double standard, the end of male control of the printed word and the beginning of comparable working conditions for women and men writers, the problem *of man-made language* still remains.
>
> (Spender 1980: 224)

Spender draws attention to the phenomenon of 'the male-as-norm' and feminists have contested this view by disputing the ways in which core bodies of knowledge have served to render women invisible. In contrast to Kuhn's scientific revolution and Popper's advocacy of conjecture and refutation as the route towards social scientific discovery, Lakatos suggested that theoretical development is made through the process and outcome of a *research programme* in which there is an agreed core of knowledge and a disputed periphery. Such a view would state that theoretical revolutions are accomplished slowly through simultaneous competing research programmes, rather than through full-scale overthrow of theoretical paradigms as envisaged by Kuhn (1975) or by conjecture and refutation as advanced by Popper (1959). But much feminist theory and, more recently, postmodern and poststructural theory disputes the existence of an agreed core of knowledge or a single truth or grand narrative that is understood universally. If knowledge and power are socially and culturally specific, then there can be neither a universal core nor even a static periphery as social and cultural change will inevitably lead to changes in the nature of knowledge and power, the knowledge of power, the power of knowledge and a myriad of other interrelationships between the two. Massey, writing about gender and geography, illustrated only too well the feminist challenge to the disputed core when she stated:

> The language of geography is often still remarkably archaic. We all know the patiently-pained expression from across the table at the meeting when we've just, hesitatingly or ironically, interjected '. . . or she . . .'. The look which says 'OK, OK, do you have to point it out every time? . . .'. (Why not: we are excluded every time?) . . . 'You know when I say "he" I include women'. Such breathtakingly inadequate conceptualisation would be jumped on in any other context.
>
> (Massey 1984: 13)

The power of 'man-made language' manifests itself in a variety of ways and at many different levels. These range from titles of textbooks referring to 'mankind', to patterns of conversation, the use of language to manipulate and demonstrate authority, and the use of language as an inclusive or exclusive form of communication. Like Massey's colleagues referred to above, many would claim that such use of language is not intentionally exclusionary but, as the subsequent discussions in this book illustrate, it is often the social action of naming and the cultural manifestation of power that serve to exclude.

Structuralism: constructing social critiques

Structuralists have criticised phenomenologists for their failure to recognise fully the more obvious societal constraints that exclude individuals and groups from social and economic activities and power. It is therefore worth examining these criticisms by looking at structuralism and by debating ways in which structuralism and phenomenology have been integrated within feminist analyses.

Structuralism seeks explanations for observed phenomena in general structures that underpin all phenomena but are not identifiable within them. With the *structure as construct* theory, observed phenomena are seen as representations of deep structures genetically imprinted on human consciousness, for example, the linguistic theories of Chomsky (2003), the social anthropological theories of Levi Strauss (1968), and the psychological theories of Piaget (1958). However, structuralism can also be viewed as *structure as process* where phenomena are seen as representations of underlying social structures. Here, it is the transformation of structure at *societal* rather than *neural* level that is significant. Such theory has formed the basis of Marx's work, of the Marxian humanism of the Frankfurt School, the critical theory of Habermas (1989) and Giddens' theory of structuration (1984).

Marxist theory explains social and cultural relations as the products of the dominant economic relations within society. According to Marx (1844) industrial capitalism, as the emerging dominant global economic system in the eighteenth and nineteenth centuries, resulted in alienation and estrangement as the working classes were divorced from the true value of their labour and therefore their sense of true worth as individuals. Capitalism depended upon those in power – the capitalists – being able to profit from the surplus value of workers' labour by selling the products of their employees' labour for more than the cost of the labour. In other words, where the cost of labour is less than the true value of the labour an economic profit can be made and capitalism sustained. As the labour costs of the western working classes increased in relative terms during the twentieth century so capitalism sought new sources of cheaper labour in the form of men, women and children in poorer countries thus transforming industrial capitalism into global capitalism.

The Frankfurt School developed Marxist theory to explain relations of cultural production and consumption. Adorno and Horkheimer (1944) and Marcuse (1964) developed the concept of instrumental reason from Weber's sociology of rationalisation to explain the ways in which culture had increasingly come to be seen in terms of economic and bureaucratic efficiency rather than simply as art, cultural production or performance. Industrial capitalism, they argued, had begun to entrap the working classes into a system of consumer culture that was simultaneously developed by and dependent upon capitalism for its continued growth. Thus, through the new cultural apparatus of mass media and advertising the working classes were to become as much defined by what they consumed as by what they produced. Locked within such a consumer culture of commodification and commercialisation, capitalism would remain secure as the only struggles working people would engage in were struggles within capitalism rather than struggles to overcome capitalism.

Traditional structuralist theory therefore emphasises the importance of societal structure and constraint, while phenomenological theory emphasises the importance of human agency. In contrast to this seeming polarisation, social theorists such as Berger (1963) and Giddens (1984) point to the mutual dependency of both structure and agency, such that a dialectic is formed between individuals and society, with each influencing the other in a continuous process. Thus the individual both shapes and is shaped by society. So, although culture can be created through the interaction of subjective meanings shared by individuals and communities this subjectivity can be also take on an objective appearance as cultural meanings are often built into the structures of institutions, and the symbols and cultural artefacts of society.

Poststructuralism: deconstructing cultural power

Poststructuralism has been given a variety of labels including postmodern, deconstructionist, linguistic, or French theory, and has been heavily influenced by French philosophy. Much of the work draws on the psychoanalytic, linguistic and cultural theories of male writers such as Derrida, Lacan and Foucault but has been articulated in feminist poststructural theory by feminist writers such as Cixous, Kristeva and Irigary. While each of the labels cited above denotes a slightly different theoretical perspective they have much in common. Language and communicative practices are central to poststructural critiques which often employ discourse theory and discourse analysis to read between the lines of social and cultural relations and to identify and make sense of the power relations inherent within social and cultural processes. Flax (1990: 41) has emphasised this point by stating that 'Postmodern discourses are all deconstructive in that they seek to distance us from and make us sceptical about beliefs concerning truth, knowledge, power, the self, and language that are often taken for granted within and serve as legitimation for contemporary Western culture'. Hughes (1990: 117), for example, has stated that 'meaning is profoundly to do with language considered not as a system of grammatical or syntactical rules but as social interaction. To adapt a statement from Austin: language does not merely report on the world but is itself performative of action in that world'.

Hughes' use of the term 'performative' alerts us to the poststructural discourse of Butler (1990, 1993) and others, where meaning and identity are seen as fluid and enacted processes. This focus on language and meaning also resonates with many of the theories of phenomenology, including ethnomethodology and interpretative sociology. While some parallels can be drawn between postmodernism and phenomenology, 'postmodernists have gone beyond earlier historicist claims about the inevitable "situatedness" of human thought within culture to focus on the very criteria by which claims to knowledge are legitimised' (Nicholson 1990: 3). One of the main concerns of poststructuralism is therefore to refute the notion of one single theory or 'grand narrative' capable of explaining social, cultural and power relations throughout time and across space. In particular, poststructuralism denies the existence of one single truth or logical reason; logocentric constructs that have been so important in western philosophy since the Enlightenment. As Bryson (1992) states:

> the search for a single all-encompassing theory is therefore rejected in principle, as is the very possibility of objectivity. Western philosophy's quest for truth and certainty (described as logocentrism) is therefore abandoned and is seen as the product of a particular historical era that is becoming inappropriate in a postmodern society that is increasingly characterised by fragmentation, diversity and diffuseness in all spheres of life. Existing theories, particularly Marxism, which claim to embody certainty and objectivity are rejected as totalitarian; here it is not simply the conclusions that are rejected, but the quest for truth itself.
>
> (Bryson 1992: 225–226)

This acknowledgement of the uncertainty of truth renders regimes of truth unstable and modern bureaucracies and economic systems open to question. According to Foucault (1979, 1980), one of the most influential poststructural theorists, power therefore has to be exercised in everyday discourses to maintain such regimes of truth. In addition to exercising power through punitive and penal social codes and practices evident in the material realities of our social institutions, power is also exercised in cultural practices 'dispersed throughout society, and exercised at a micro-level' (Bryson 1999: 37). Foucault's identification of the 'panoptican' provides an insightful illustration of the way in which macro-level social structures can be maintained through micro-level cultural practices. The panoptican was a prison designed to afford the prison guards views into all the prison cells but without enabling prisoners to see which cells were being watched at any one time. This form of surveillance resulted in a corresponding form of self-surveillance as prisoners policed their own behaviour for fear of being seen and therefore caught if they behaved in any way deemed to be outside the behavioural codes enforced within the prison. The concept of self-surveillance therefore emphasises the relationship between structural power, in the form of the prison and prison guards, and cultural power in the form of self-surveillance and self-policing.

Surveillance can also serve to influence our behaviour in everyday life where we are subject to the gaze of others and where we can be 'Othered' by the gaze. These concepts are discussed in more detail in Chapter 4 but it is important to recognise the ways in which the gaze of others often results in self-policing of behaviour within everyday life. The fundamental fear of being 'Other', of being marginal, an outsider, or just different is played upon from the playground to the workplace to encourage conformity to the dominant codes and behaviours of society (Lorde 1984). Subsequent chapters within this book will illustrate that, according to a structuralist perspective, the dominant codes of society are generally constructed, legitimated, normalised and reproduced by and in the interests of those with power. Poststructural theory, however, provides a lens through which to view the potential for the reworking, disruption, contestation, transgression and transformation of the dominant codes and behaviours of society such that change is possible over periods of time and across different spaces.

Feminist epistemology within the social sciences

This section introduces a series of theoretical contexts for the study of gender within social science by identifying and evaluating a range of distinct and sometimes competing feminist perspectives. The next chapter extends this evaluation to an exploration of the contribution of different feminist perspectives to leisure research. These two chapters therefore attempt to outline dominant and emergent paradigms and discourses within the subject fields of gender studies and leisure studies respectively. Subsequent chapters integrate these studies of gender and leisure to explore forms of feminist resistance, contestation and negotiation of dominant discourses or what Spender (1981) referred to as challenges to the 'patriarchal paradigm' (Aitchison 1997a). In addition to drawing on gender studies and leisure studies these later chapters draw on a series of other subject fields and subdisciplines that have developed rapidly over the last two decades and include social and cultural geography, social policy, the sociology of education and management studies. In this way the chapters seek to bring multi and interdisciplinary feminist analyses to the study of the social and cultural sites and processes that inform leisure theory, policy and practice.

Extensive debate has taken place within feminist circles about the nature of feminist epistemology or epistemologies; the relationships between epistemology, methodology and methods; and the existence of feminist research methods (Dyck 1993; Gray 1997; Harding 1987; Jackson and Scott 2002; Jackson and Jones 1998; Katz 1994; Madge *et al.* 1997; Oakley 1998; Roberts 1981; Stanley and Wise 1993). It is important to review these debates at the outset so that the reader can make informed judgements about the epistemological and methodological underpinning to research discussed in each of the subsequent chapters and topic areas. The debates concerning the existence and nature of a feminist epistemology have been documented clearly elsewhere (Jackson and Jones 1998; Stanley 1990; Stanley and Wise 1983, 1993). Stanley and Wise contend that previous criticism of feminist research is founded largely on a semantic misconception whereby many academics have assumed that feminist researchers have been calling for a radical change to research methods rather than research epistemologies. To emphasise this point, Stanley (1990: 26), in *Feminist Praxis*, notes that many reviewers of *Breaking Out: Feminist Ontology and Epistemology* (1983) interpreted the book 'as a discourse on either method or methodology, while it was produced as a discussion of epistemology'.

Both feminist research and poststructural research are more concerned with a re-evaluation of epistemology rather than methodology. Waugh (1998: 179) states that 'feminists as well as poststmodernists have long recognised the need for a new ethics responsive to technological changes and shifts in the understanding between the relations of power and knowledge'. Stanley and Wise have also advocated the need to revisit and re-evaluate epistemological issues:

> An 'epistemology' is a framework or theory for specifying the constitution and generation of knowledge about the social world; that is, it concerns how to understand the nature of 'reality'. A given epistemological framework specifies not only what 'knowledge' is and how to recognise it, but who are the 'knowers' and by what means someone becomes one, and also the means by which competing knowledge-claims are adjudicated and some rejected in favour of another/others. The question of epistemology, then, is crucial, precisely fundamental, for feminism, for it is around the constitution of a feminist epistemology that feminism can most directly and far-reachingly challenge non-feminist frameworks and ways of working.
>
> (Stanley and Wise 1993: 188–189)

A feminist epistemology can be defined as a set of concepts that rejects traditional epistemological theories for their empiricism and rationalism (Coward 1977). This emphasis on empiricism and rationalism is associated primarily with post-Enlightenment thinking, with modern science, and with positivism. Such an approach is also manifest in research that has been constructed to explain social phenomena where men's experiences are viewed as 'the norm' and women's experiences are viewed as secondary, as deviant from the norm, or as Other. Feminists have rejected these interpretations of their lives because they have been made by undertaking research within a patriarchal framework that neglects or negates women's experiences. Stanley and Wise, for example, criticise such research as demonstrating 'fictitious sympathy', and, using Woolf's (1931) term, they go on to say:

> The basis of our objections to social science attempts to deduce or predict feelings and emotions is that these derive from 'fictitious sympathy' of people who remain outside of the experience they write about and claim competence in. Instead of writing about how they know what they claim to know (which would necessitate locating the social scientist within the research process) they write about the experiences of others as though these were directly available to them. That these are necessarily transformed in a researcher's construction of them is ignored.
>
> (Stanley and Wise 1993: 165)

Feminist research therefore acknowledges the significance of the researcher or writer in shaping the research process and written outcomes. Moreover, the relationship between the researcher and the research subject(s) has received scrutiny from a number of feminist researchers (Code 1981; Farran 1990; Gilligan 1982; Oakley 1981; Seller 1994; Stanley and Wise 1983, 1993). From here on, this book will refer not to research subjects but to research participants. This attempt to create a less hierarchical relationship within the research process is in line with what Morris *et al.* (1998: 221) see as the 'third tenet of feminist methodology which is the rejection of hierarchical relationships within the research process by making those being researched into partners or collaborators'. The other tenets of feminist methodology, outlined by Morris *et al.* (1998: 220–222) include: a 'commitment to feminist principles' in the purpose, conduct and reporting of the research; a commitment 'to doing feminist research *for* women, and not just *on* them; and a 'commitment to reflexivity, based on notions of openness and intellectual honesty'. Each of these tenets is derived from generic feminist philosophy and their research application is discussed more fully in relation to gender and leisure research outlined in this and subsequent chapters.

The relationship between the researcher and the researched is clearly one aspect of the research process where ethical issues are highlighted. Such ethical issues relate to both research philosophy and to research methodology. Oakley (1981, 1998) and Farran (1990) both give detailed accounts of their own experience of interviewing for research purposes and of the constraints that the traditionally defined research interview places on both feminist analysis and feminist practice as a result of the predetermined relationship between researcher and researched. But ethical concerns in feminist research also relate to more fundamental issues than the practice of specific research methods or techniques. The very purpose of feminist research itself has an ethical dimension in that feminist research is a political project undertaken in order to highlight, and subsequently improve, conditions for women within society. Feminist research is therefore research undertaken from a particular perspective or epistemology: a feminist perspective or feminist epistemology. Just as it is difficult to separate philosophical and methodological issues from ethical issues, so it becomes difficult to separate ethical issues from political issues. Feminist research has an explicit political purpose and distinct schools of thought within feminism have placed political significance on different power relations that are seen to subordinate women. For example, whereas liberal feminism sees the lack of equality of opportunity within organisations and institutions such as education and work as being a major cause of inequality, socialist and Marxist feminism view the very structure of such institutions as inherently patriarchal. Radical feminism, in a further contrast, directs attention towards the institution of the family, sexuality and the oppression of women through unpaid domestic labour and reproduction. Poststructural feminism would view such a perspective as essentialist and overly homogenising of women and postcolonial and black feminism might also emphasise the cultural diversity of women and the legacy of colonial power in shaping gender relations.

Liberal feminism: reform from within

Liberal feminism has the longest but perhaps the least clearly articulated history of all feminist perspectives. Indeed, Evans (1995: 28) has stated that 'liberal theorists are scarce, while empirical writers, apparently of liberal persuasion, abound'. Tong (1989: 13) introduced her history of liberal feminism with an appraisal of the feminist writings of Mary Wollstonecraft (1759–1799) including *A Vindication of the Rights of Women* (1792). Bryson, however, states that: 'Contrary to popular opinion, feminist theory did not begin with Mary Wollstonecraft at the end of the eighteenth century, but goes back at least to medieval times (and no doubt found private expression much earlier)' (Bryson 1992: 11).

Like the majority of liberal feminist writers, Wollstonecraft contended that women's inferior position within society was the result of inequality of opportunity. The liberal feminist position therefore locates the locus of women's subordinate status in society within public structures such as the education system and the legal system and does not accept that deeper structural and cultural oppression exist within both the public and private spheres. Consequently, liberal feminists have contested the more radical view that the 'personal is political' and do not view the public–private dichotomy as necessarily problematic. Campaigns by first wave feminism, centred round the suffragette movement, therefore concentrated on women's position in the public sphere with calls for voting reform. In a similar way Bryson contends that:

> the years after the Second World war contained the seeds of the discontents that were to erupt in the 1960s; this Second wave of feminism was to develop rapidly in all kinds of directions, but it began in America as an essentially liberal protest against the failure of that society to deliver to women the promises of independence, self expression and fulfilment that seemed central to the American dream.
>
> (Bryson 1992: 159)

Liberal feminism, concerned with reform rather than wholesale change, seeks to improve opportunities for women within existing structures and systems rather than by challenging the foundations upon which these systems and structures are based. It could be argued that liberal feminism cannot provide an appropriate or complete feminist perspective from which to address the issue of knowledge construction, legitimation and reproduction as it gives insufficient recognition to the structures and cultures that sustain gendered knowledge and power. For example, a liberal feminist analysis might focus on employment patterns within education or on educational achievement patterns between the sexes. This concentration on quantifiable and measurable assessment could be seen as positioning liberal feminism too close to positivism to be an appropriately challenging perspective for research into the complexities of the interrelationships between gender, power and knowledge.

This section goes on to outline alternative feminist perspectives and to offer some criticisms of liberal feminism but there are two inherent difficulties in undertaking such a critique. First, as Eisenstein (1982) emphasises, while liberal feminism is not a radical philosophy per se it is a radicalising force in that the majority of mainstream feminist demands and campaigns are derived from a liberal feminist perspective. Second, liberal feminism is not a clearly articulated political philosophy in the way that socialist or radical feminism are and therefore any political critique of liberal feminism runs the risk of being rather one-sided. As Bryson states, liberal feminism 'has seldom been expressed as a self-conscious political theory, but more as a "common sense" application of pre-existing values to women's situation' (Bryson 1992: 160).

As Chapters 3 and 5 illustrate, the liberal feminist approach has under-pinned much of the academic leisure theory in addition to dominating leisure policy and practice. The main emphasis of liberal feminist policies has been on *Catching Up The Men* (Dyer 1982) and on identifying and overcoming visible barriers to women's leisure participation. Barriers or constraints to women's participation have been described under the head-ings of biological, social, physical, legal and financial but these all tend to concentrate on the symptoms of gender–power relations within society rather than the underlying structures and cultures which might be chal-lenged by socialist/radical and poststructural feminism respectively. This concentration on effect rather than cause has been particularly prevalent within research dominated by a liberal feminist perspective which could be accused of providing a rather partial and superficial explanation and resulting in equally partial and superficial measures advocated to address inequality. For example, while many liberal feminist policies and campaigns have been relatively successful in attracting women into sport, there is evidence to show that increases in participation are not sustained and that there is a bias towards middle-class women. Overall, the results from campaigns such as the English Sports Council's Milk in Action for Women in 1988 began to show signs of diminishing returns, indicating deeper structural and cultural constraints (Aitchison, 1997b). As Chapter 5 demonstrates, in spite of Sports Council efforts to attract more women into sport during the 1980s, the numbers participating in outdoor sport actually fell between 1983 and 1988 thus suggesting that there may be wider structural and cultural barriers to women's sport and leisure participation (Sports Council 1989).

Socialist and Marxist feminism: the constraints of patriarchal capitalism

A socialist feminist perspective argues that many of the barriers which prevent women from participating in leisure are the result of capitalism's private–public patriarchal dichotomy, women's unpaid domestic and child-rearing role, and their status as a reserve army of labour. Socialist and Marxist feminists assert that it is these underpinning structural constraints that must be challenged if social policy interventions are to have any significant impact on women's position in leisure, both as participants and providers.

In contrast to liberal feminism, Marxist, socialist and radical feminism all have clearly articulated political philosophies. A number of 'textbooks on feminist theory give the impression that feminists were split into two opposing camps: Marxist or socialist feminists versus radical feminists' (Jackson 1998: 13). Jackson goes on to contend that a more accurate account of feminist theory would refer to a continuum of different pers-pectives rather than a dichotomy 'between those who saw women's subordination as a consequence of capitalism and those who saw it as a consequence of patriarchy' (Jackson 1998: 13). In addition to differing emphases on capitalism and patriarchy by Marxist/socialist and radical feminist analyses respectively, differing explanations exist *within* each perspective. Jackson (1998: 15) provides illustrations of competing explanations which, she suggests, result from differing emphases being placed on production, reproduction or sexuality on the one hand and on culture or ideology on the other hand.

Marxist feminism locates gender relations within an explanation of economic and class relations. A central tenet of Marxist feminism is that any improvement in women's situation requires economic change as a precondition. The family is seen as propping up capitalist society by providing unpaid domestic work and a reserve army of labour to service its needs. As such, Marxist feminist theory is concerned with examining the material base of women's subordination in both employment and family relations. Although Marxism has been criticised for failing to address issues of gendered power, Marxist feminists emphasise that Marx referred to both *production* and *reproduction* in his theory of the creation of a surplus value of labour:

> The private sphere, so dear to the liberal feminist's heart, is a veritable prison to the Marxist feminist. It subordinates woman by permanently excluding her from the public, productive world and leaving her with a life comprising little more than the emotional support of man who engages in 'real' human activity.
>
> (Tong 1989: 67)

While Marxist and socialist feminism have a number of features in common, they are separated by the different relationships they identify between class and gender relations. Whereas Marxist feminism emphasises economic relations over patriarchal relations as the cause of women's oppression, socialist feminism sees both patriarchy and capitalism operating together as a 'dual system' of oppression with neither being dominant. Evans, for example, states that 'following the perception that the relationship between feminism and Marxism was fraught, marred by the primacy of capitalism and class, the distinctive socialist feminist project became the analysis of capitalism and patriarchy, and the relationship between the two' (Evans 1995: 108).

Socialist feminism emphasises the dual role of capitalism and patriarchy in the continued subordination of women and its epistemology states that knowledge is created in the interests of specific social groups. It can be argued that socialist feminism has been the acceptable face of feminism within academia as it provides a more clearly articulated theoretical and hence academic base than liberal feminism, but is not as unpalatable to a male-dominated establishment as radical feminism. Socialist feminism emphasises the 'dual system' of oppression brought about by both capitalism and patriarchy operating in unison without one system necessarily having primacy over the other. In this respect socialist feminism can be seen to occupy the middle ground between Marxist and radical feminism.

Radical feminism: the sexuality of oppression

MacKinnon (1983: 227) has asserted that 'sexuality is to feminism what work is to Marxism: that which is most one's own yet most taken away'. Because feminism takes sexuality as its starting point, and Marxism takes the economic relations of work and employment as its starting point, MacKinnon (1983: 227–228) has argued that the two philosophies are mutually incompatible. Moreover, she goes on to stress that attempts by socialist feminists to integrate the two theories 'have not recognised the depth of the antagonism or the separate integrity of each theory' (MacKinnon 1983: 236).

The radical feminist perspective states that neither a traditional liberal feminist approach nor a Marxist or socialist feminist approach provides an adequate analysis of the complex structures that interact to subordinate women. Unlike the liberal feminist perspective, which views the state as essentially neutral, radical feminism sees the state as but one of many manifestations of patriarchal power. This perspective is equally critical of Marxist feminism, which is seen to ignore the non-economic bases of male power and female subordination. Barrett (1988: 4) surmises that radical feminist 'ideas represent an irreducible core of truth and anger which forms the obstinate basis of feminist politics'.

Radical feminism therefore views patriarchy, rather than class or a combination of patriarchy and class, as the cause of women's subordination and oppression. Patriarchy is seen as being present in all structures and processes within society, in both the public and private spheres, and is seen to precede all other forms of oppression related to class and 'race'. Male sexual power is seen as the root of patriarchal power. Radical feminism has paid particular attention to patriarchal constructions of society through sex-role stereotyping, heterosexism and compulsory heterosexuality, the institution of marriage, and practices of pornography, prostitution, rape, sexual abuse of women and children, and other forms of abuse of power including 'domestic' violence (Daly 1973, 1978; Dworkin 1981, 1982; Firestone 1979; Griffin 1981; Jeffreys 1997; MacKinnon 1995; Millet 1970; Rich 1977).

However, radical feminist critiques of patriarchy tend to view power relations as a 'zero-sum game' in which power is gained by one side at the expense of the other. This dualistic view of power can also be seen in the writings of major social theorists such as Marx and in C. Wright Mills' *The Power Elite* (1957), criticised by Parsons shortly after its publication:

To Mills, power is not a facility for the performance of function in, and on behalf of, the society as a system, but is interpreted exclusively as a facility for getting what one group, the holders of power, wants by preventing another group, the 'outs' from getting what it wants.

(Parsons 1960: 221)

Walby (1990: 177) emphasises the all-pervasive power of patriarchal capitalism and suggests that a fuller explanation of women's subordination must take account of the interaction of patriarchal relations in both the public and private spheres by examining the mode of production, relations in paid work, in sexuality, in cultural institutions, and must also consider male violence. It could be argued that leisure, in both the public and private spheres, as an area of academic study, and of policy-making and practice, has the potential to provide an arena where all of the above patriarchal relations are manifested in some form or another. However, radical feminist analysis has been relatively absent within leisure, tourism and sport studies. There appears to be no radical feminist research in tourism although Enloe (1989) and Jeffreys (1999) do provide analyses that draw on both radical and socialist feminist theory to critique the political economy of international sex tourism. There are, however, a number of radical feminist critiques of sport, such as Brackenridge (2001), Lenskyj (1986, 1990) and Theberge (2000) who provide useful accounts of patriarchal constructions of sexuality in sport and child sexual abuse in sport. In relation to education and research, Stanley (1980) appears to provide the only radical feminist critique of leisure studies as an academic field of enquiry.

Critiques of the patriarchal construction of language have also played an important role within radical feminist analysis with the work of Spender (1980), referred to earlier, being particularly influential. But it is within poststructural feminism that the role of language in creating, maintaining and reproducing power has formed a central theme in feminist critiques.

Poststructural feminism: the cultural codes of modernity

The previous sections have demonstrated that each feminist perspective focuses on what it deems to be the major cause of women's oppression. Liberal feminists are largely concerned with male domination of public institutional structures, radical feminists are primarily concerned with male domination of private familial and sexual relations, Marxist feminists are concerned with male domination of economic relations and socialist feminists point to the duality of the social relations of the family and the economic relations of the market as being the cause of women's oppression by and for the benefit of men.

In contrast, poststructural feminism draws our attention to the way in which cultural relations serve to shape gender relations. Instead of focusing on the political, social and economic manifestations of the gender order, poststructural feminism seeks to uncover the very cultural codes by which such an order is constructed, legitimated and reproduced (Weedon 1997). This means that a 'poststructuralist feminist challenge for women [is] to subvert male colonisation of knowledge and theory' (Wearing 1998: 143) that informs the way we think about, construct and normalise political, social and economic relations in both the public and private sphere. Indeed, poststructural feminism calls into question the post-Enlightenment grand narratives that have served to construct the world into dualistic categories of public–private, male–female, work–leisure, nature–culture and self–other. Wearing, writing in relation to leisure studies, questions these dualistic categories, boundaries and hierarchies when she states that,

> Poststructuralist feminists such as Lloyd (1989) and Grosz (1989), have challenged and deconstructed many of the binary oppositions beloved of male post-Enlightenment rationality. They have sought, for example, to eliminate the feminisation and inferiorisation of terms such as feminine when set in opposition to masculine, body in opposition to mind, nature to culture, intuition to rationality. While some male writers on leisure have begun to apply poststructuralist theory to leisure in a questioning of the work/leisure and production/consumption dichotomies where the former are prioritised and latter inferiorised (e.g. Rojek, 1993a: 143), it has been left to poststructural feminists to suggest ways in which the deconstruction of these dichotomies may be specifically applied to women's experiences of leisure.
>
> (Wearing 1998: 148–149)

Writing about poststructural and postmodern feminism more generally, Haraway (1985: 191) has contended that such theoretical perspectives have developed, 'as an argument for pleasure in the confusion of boundaries and for responsibility in their construction'. Indeed, she goes on to identify the labelling of different types of feminism as a reaction to what has gone before rather than an indication of what might emerge in the future:

> It has become difficult to name one's feminism by a single adjective – or even to insist in every circumstance upon the noun. Consciousness of exclusion through naming is acute. Identities seem contradictory, partial and strategic. With hard-won recognition of their social and historical constitution, gender, race, and class cannot provide the basis for belief in 'essential' unity. There is nothing about being 'female' that naturally binds women. There is not even such a state as 'being' female, itself a highly complex category constructed in contested sexual

scientific discourses and other social practices. Gender, race or class consciousness is an achievement forced on us by the terrible histor-ical experience of the contradictory social realities of patriarchy, colonialism, racism and capitalism.

(Haraway 1985: 191)

Postmodernism and poststructuralism are frequently used interchange-ably and it is important to acknowledge that although they are overlapping and mutually informing they are also differentiated by their objects of study. Postmodernism is concerned with the critical study of modern-ity whereas poststructuralism is concerned with the critical study of the power relations inherent in, and resulting from, the structures and struc-tured order of modernity. Thus postmodernism seeks to deconstruct the meta-narratives and grand theories of modernist society whereas poststructuralism seeks to reveal the power relations upon which the construction, legitimation and reproduction of modernist society depends. This difference in object and method of study has resulted in postmodern accounts remaining largely within the realms of the humanities whilst poststructural critiques have crossed into the social sciences where critical engagement with theories of social, economic and cultural power is already established.

In relation to feminism, Evans (1995: 125) has identified postmodernism and poststructuralism as 'feminism's third difference: a difference *within women*'. For Evans, cultural feminism (not to be confused with the cultural emphasis of postmodern and poststructural feminism) was identified as 'feminism's first difference' and 'is distinguished from previous difference beliefs, within the second wave, by its insistence that women's charac-teristics and values are for the good, indeed are superior and ethically prior to men's and should be upheld' (Evans 1995: 76). This invokes a vision of women and 'women's characteristics' as innate and static, in turn implying that cultural feminism is both essentialist and universalist in its theorising. Evans distinguishes between the 'strong' cultural feminism of Daly and Rich and the 'weak' cultural feminism of feminist philoso-phers and psychologists such as Ruddick, Held and Gilligan. Whereas 'strong' cultural feminism has sometimes advocated separatism, for example through eco-feminist movements, 'weak' cultural feminism is less essentialist or universalist and views qualities devalued in women (caring and nurturing, for example) as virtues which could be developed by both men and women. But feminism's 'third difference', that of postmodernism, refutes the existence of these essentialist categories.

In *Deconstructing Equality-Versus-Difference: or, The Uses of Post-structuralist Theory for Feminism*, Scott (1994: 357) argues that, 'poststructuralism and contemporary feminism are late-twentieth-century movements that share a certain self-conscious critical relationship to established philosophical and political traditions'. Scott goes on to identify four concepts 'used by poststructuralists that are also useful for feminists' (1994: 358). These she defines as *language*, *discourse*, *difference* and *deconstruction*. It is the uses of such concepts, in relation to theorising what Flax (1990) has highlighted as *truth*, *knowledge*, *the body* and *the self*, which are seen as poststructuralism's contribution to developing understanding of the temporary and localised or historically and spatially specific nature of the relations of power, including gendered power.

According to Soper (1990) the deconstructionist approach of postmodernism has challenged conventional feminist and humanist theorists. Similarly, McNay (1992: 2) points to 'tensions' between poststructuralist theory and 'more politically engaged forms of critique'. While poststructural feminism shares some elements of radical feminism such as attacks on malestream philosophy and linguistics, the relativist nature of poststructuralism is perceived by many radical feminists as being one of the greatest current threats to the feminist political project. Moreover, it is argued that this threat is exacerbated by the increasing acceptance of postmodern feminism within academia. In refuting the existence of one underlying mechanism of oppression, postmodern feminism has been accused of weakening its critical analysis. Indeed, it has been argued that postmodernism may be a theory whose time has come, but only for men. As men have had their Enlightenment they are in a position of strength from which to deconstruct truths and to decentre themselves (Flax 1990; Nicholson 1990). 'On the other hand, for women to take on such a position is to weaken what is not yet strong' (Nicholson 1990: 6). Similarly, writing in relation to geography, Gregory *et al.* (1994) contend that:

> in prioritising the mapping of fragments and differences, a postmodern human geography runs the risk of ignoring the more systematic features and relations of social, political and economic structure: the geographical imagination may well be broadened in one direction, but it is simultaneously eclipsed in another.
>
> (Gregory *et al.* 1994: 10)

Hartsock (1990: 169) expresses similar reservations about the usefulness of Foucault's poststructuralist analysis of power for the wider feminist project claiming that 'Foucault has made it very difficult to locate domination, including domination in gender relations'. Hartsock therefore emphasises the difficulty of embracing wholesale the poststructuralist position because, she argues, poststructuralism's emphasis on social criticism as both contextually, temporally and locally specific negates theories of power as systemic phenomena. With no systemic power relations there can be no overall system of domination and oppression, only specific contexts of subordination, resistance and transformation. Clearly, one of the questions for this book to examine is the extent to which systemic male power (patriarchy) exists within leisure relations and/or the extent to which localised, contextualised and pluralised power relations exert their influence on, and in relation to, gender and leisure.

The challenge for this and other discussions of gender and leisure, then, is to provide a broad analysis of the cultural 'fragments and differences' in the inter-relationships between gender and leisure while simultaneously attending to the broader structural relations of power. Each of the following five chapters identifies the contribution of poststructuralist perspectives to identifying and explaining gender–leisure relations in specific social and cultural arenas. Chapter 8 then attempts to summarise and synthesise these contributions in a discussion that draws out the complementarities between social and cultural analyses such that they are revealed as mutually informing and balanced within the social–cultural nexus.

Postcolonial and black feminist theories: marking a difference

Postcolonial theory currently offers some of the most sophisticated accounts of power and identity to go beyond both the grand narratives of modernist theory and the deconstructionist critiques of postmodernism. Although (Brooks 1997) has noted that the terms 'postcolonial' and 'Black' have recently been criticised as being homogenising, writers such as Kanneh (1998) have stated that 'Black feminism' does have a crucial role to play in recognising difference both in relation to black women and in relation to black feminism. Such perspectives are vital to counter the first world-view from white feminism that has been accused by some black feminists of being inherently racist (Flax 1990; Simmonds 1992). Acknowledging difference is central to postcolonial feminist theories which also draw upon and develop many of the tenets of poststructural feminist theory. A discussion of postcolonial feminist theory provides a useful reference point from which to look back at historical constructions of women as Other, while simultaneously providing a critique of the gendered legacy of colonialism which is manifest in the everyday structures and cultures of contemporary society (Memmi 1967; Said 1978). Wearing (1998) summarises these points by stating, 'Feminist postcolonial criticism has been particularly concerned with the lived experiences of women who cannot be fitted into Eurocentric, Western middle-class white theorisation, as formulated by male theorists and their feminist counterparts (Wearing 1998: 162).

Postcolonial theory has its origins in writings from the early 1980s that sought to develop Gramsci's (1978) work on 'the subaltern classes' (Bhabha 1983, Prakash 1994). Postcolonial theorists sought to give voice to the colonised subaltern whose voice had been silenced by the colonialist author and authority. However, Spivak (1985), in her influential essay 'Can the subaltern speak?', warns against postcolonial attempts to 'uncover' the subaltern's voice which, she argues, has been rendered silent through the hegemonic forces of patriarchal capitalism. Using the example of sati (the burning of the Indian widow on her husband's pyre), Spivak illustrates the silencing of the colonised women as distinct from colonised men. Rather than attempting to give voice to the individual colonised female subject – a task which Spivak sees as impossible given the 'silenced' nature of such voices – postcolonial feminist intellectuals are encouraged to:

> adapt the Gramscian maxim – 'pessimism of the intellect, optimism of the will' – by combining a philosophical scepticism about recovering any subaltern agency with a political commitment to making visible the position of the marginalised. Thus it is the intellectual who must 'represent' the subaltern.
>
> (Loomba 1998: 234)

For example, Hargreaves has argued that 'Muslim women in sport who are forced to be silent in their own cultures should be able to secure some form of representation and support from outside without being reduced to 'the Other' (Hargreaves 2000: 76). Said's (1978) essay *Orientialism*, by focusing on the hegemonic domination of colonised people, emphasises a series of binaries of East–West, feminine–masculine, colonised–coloniser that offer little scope for agency on the part of 'the colonised' (Bhabha 1983). Indeed, Vaughan (1994) exposes a paradox whereby:

> at a theoretical level, then, Said appears to have placed himself in the position of denying the possibility of any alternative description of 'the Orient', any alternative forms of knowledge and by extension, any agency on the part of the colonised. The fact that this theoretical position runs counter to Said's professed political aim of effecting the dissolution of 'Orientialism' could be seen as an ironic validation of his own theory, since even he seems trapped within the frame of Orientialism, unable to move outside it.
>
> (Vaughan 1994: 3)

Said's work can be seen to be reflective of what Memmi (1967: 85), writing about 'the colonised', described as 'the mark of the plural' (all Others look the same). Loomba (1998) further exposes the essentialism inherent in those postcolonial theories which emphasise the totally 'silenced' or wholly 'speaking' subject:

> It is difficult (and in my view unnecessary) to choose between these two positions. Parry takes anti-colonial nationalism as emblematic of the native ability to question and counter colonial discourses. But 'natives' are divided by differences of gender, as Spivak so effectively points out, and by those of class, caste and other hierarchies. As we

have discussed earlier, anti-colonial nationalism can only be taken as representative of the subaltern voice if we homogenise the category 'subaltern' and simplify enormously our notion of 'speaking'. At the same time, too inflexible a theory of subaltern silence, even if offered in a cautionary spirit, can be detrimental to research on colonial cultures by closing off options even before they have been explored. Spivak's choice of the immolated widow as emblematic of the 'subaltern' is thus significant. Such a figure is in fact the most perfect instance of subaltern silence, since she is a conceptual and social category that comes into being only when the subject dies.

(Loomba 1998: 235–236)

In alternative postcolonial theories of gender and Othering, where greater agency has been given to actors, it is possible to identify input from, and development of, many of the tenets of wider poststructuralist and feminist theory (Aitchison, 2001a). Brooks (1997: 105) has commented that 'this intersection is an interesting one, as all three movements have in common the process of dismantling or subverting hegemonic discourses'. Such subversion, she argues, is achieved through the displacement of dominant discourses by marginal epistemologies. This process involves engagement and dialogue with dominant discourses rather than dichotomous opposition. Moreover, like postmodernism's relation to modernity, postcolonialism can be seen as signifying 'a critical engagement with colonialism, not to claim that colonialism has been overturned' (Spoonley 1995: 49). Reiterating these iterative theoretical developments Mills (1998: 98–99) contends that postcolonial feminist theory has had three distinct impacts. First, by focusing on the global rather than the western parochial, postcolonial feminism has challenged the authority and representativeness of white feminist theorising. Second, postcolonial feminism has challenged the masculinity of postcolonial theory and its lack of engagement with the dynamics of gendered power in colonial and imperial contexts (McClintock 1995). Third, rather than merely providing deconstructionist critiques of previous feminist theory or postcolonial theory, postcolonial feminist theorising has begun to build theory in its own right. These attributes offer a potentially significant contribution to leisure and tourism studies which, like the leisure and tourism industry itself, represents a global phenomenon dominated by the western, English-speaking world.

Dirlik (1994: 356) suggests, however, that 'Postcoloniality is the condition of the intelligentsia of global capitalism' and Appiah (1996: 62) pronounces postcolonialism as 'the condition of what we might ungenerously call a comprador intelligentsia' where western intellectuals become 'otherness machines'. Western academics may thus be guilty of compliance with the 'cultural logic' (Jameson, 1986) of late capitalism which has manifested itself in postmodernism. Here, the work of Spivak (1985, 1987, 1993) has been instrumental in questioning white western feminists' representations of 'Third World women' as Other through the homo-genising of the category 'women'. Like the postcolonial theories of Said (1978, 1993), Spivak and other postcolonial feminist theorists have paid particular attention to the role of language and discourse in creating and sustaining power relations. In this respect, there are clear parallels with poststructural feminist theory and these have been identified by a number of black feminist theorists (hooks 1990; Kanneh 1998; Mirza 1997). However, Evans (1995: 139) points out that, paradoxically, 'despite its status as the voice of heterogeneity and the decentred self, it [postmod-ernism] has ignored blacks' (Evans 1995: 139).

Postmodernism's rejection of identity politics has had the potential to deconstruct, and thereby dilute, oppositional black voices (hooks 1990). This very weakness, however, may also be postmodernism's contributing strength in that 'postmodernism's deconstruction of 'the subject', including 'the Black subject' can also be seen as liberating the diversity of Black lived experiences and subjectivities' (Kanneh 1998: 95). Evans (1995), however, takes a more cynical view of postmodernism's potential 'contri-bution' to social theory and to political change:

> Nancy Hartsock, for example, has asked why a cognitively relativist view has sprung up at exactly the time when 'the previously silenced had begun to speak for themselves' (1990: 163). Why is it at this precise moment that the notion of the subject, and the possibility of the truth, becomes suspect?
>
> (Evans 1995: 139)

Overview

This chapter has provided the theoretical foundations upon which more detailed discussions of gender and leisure are developed in the following chapters. The discussions above sought to offer generalist and feminist perspectives on social and cultural theory that will be developed further in the subsequent chapters and in relation to specific aspects of gender and leisure.

This chapter first sought to identify and explain a series of perspectives from social science that has served to shape our understanding of social relations, including leisure relations. These perspectives were broadly defined as positivist, phenomenological, structuralist and poststructuralist. The second half of the chapter then sought to identify and explain a range of perspectives from feminist and gender theory that has shaped our understanding of gender roles, relations and processes within the context of wider social relations. These feminist perspectives were acknowledged as overlapping in their view of gender relations but were presented as a typology for the purpose of clarity. The theoretical perspectives discussed included liberal feminism, socialist and Marxist feminism, radical feminism, poststructural feminism, and postcolonial and black feminism.

In spite of the presentation of theoretical perspectives in sanitised typologies the chapter reveals the complex and competing nature of knowledge and understanding, the multiple ways of knowing social and cultural relations including gender relations, and our different understandings of social and cultural phenomena including leisure. Such knowledge provides a firm theoretical foundation from which to approach the subsequent chapters of the book where discussions engage with both structural and poststructural critiques to explore the social–cultural nexus of gender and leisure relations.

3   Gender and leisure studies

Introduction: sociologies of leisure and leisure sociologies

This chapter introduces the subject field of leisure studies, outlines the major schools of thought within the subject field and reviews the impact of a series of socialist feminist studies of leisure published in the late twentieth century. It then examines the shifting focus from structural to cultural analyses of gender and leisure at the turn of the twenty-first century and explores some of the contemporary tensions within the subject field of leisure studies. The discussion of theoretical perspectives outlined in the previous chapter provides the theoretical insight into the social, cultural and gender theories that are developed here in relation to theories of leisure.

Veblen's (1925) *The Theory of the Leisure Class* and Huzinga's *Homo Ludens* (1947) can be highlighted as the first publications in the sociology and socio-psychology of leisure respectively. The subject field of 'leisure studies', however, really came into being during the 1960s and 1970s with the publication of a number of key texts in the sociology of leisure: de Grazia's (1962) *Of Time, Work and Leisure*; Dumazadier's *Toward a Society of Leisure* (1967) and *The Sociology of Leisure* (1974); Linder's (1970) *The Harried Leisure Class*; Parker's (1971) *The Future of Work and Leisure*; Rapoport and Rapoport's (1975) *Leisure and the Family Life Cycle* and Roberts' (1978) *Contemporary Society and the Growth of Leisure*.

The origins of leisure studies can be traced to a number of disciplines and subject fields that experienced increasing status within the academy during the 1960s and 1970s. These two decades were significant in laying the foundations for the development of the subject field and setting the parameters for the field of study by concentrating on definitions of leisure, the role of leisure in society and the growth of leisure. On both sides of the Atlantic the leisure studies writings of the 1960s and 1970s were informed by a period of economic growth and increasing consumption. In western societies 'the future' was approached simultaneously with a new kind of optimism and trepidation as forecasts were made of an increase in leisure and a decrease in work with technological advances predicted to offer savings in labour and opportunities for leisure. Examples of this interest in predicting the future of leisure within society are evident in the titles and content of books published at the time such as Bell's (1973) *The Coming of Post-Industrial Society*, Toffler's *Future Shock* (1971) and *The Third Wave* (1980), Veal's (1979) *The Future of Leisure*; Jenkins and Sherman's (1981) *The Leisure Shock*, Kelly's (1983) *Leisure Identities and Interactions* and Parker's (1983) *Leisure and Work*.

During the 1970s three multi-disciplinary areas in particular played an important role in the formation of leisure studies in the United Kingdom and can be seen in the origins of the Leisure Studies Association, formed in 1975, and the *Leisure Studies Journal*, founded in 1982. The sociology of work; physical education and human movement studies; and rural planning and countryside recreation were largely responsible for the development of the leisure studies canon.

As a subdiscipline of sociology, the sociology of work shed light on leisure as the corollary of work whilst also demonstrating the ways in which leisure patterns were, to a large extent, shaped by work and employment patterns (Roberts 1978). Green *et al.* (1990: 11) noted that 'The "Founding Fathers" of the sociology of leisure in Britain emerged with the publication of their textbooks on leisure in the early 1970s, most notably Stanley Parker and Kenneth Roberts. Before that, students and researchers in the area were limited to American material of a functionalist nature'. Parker (1995: 29) was instrumental in theorising the relationships between work and leisure. He devised a simplistic typology of work–leisure relationships in which he saw: the 'extension pattern' or spill-over of work into leisure as 'having leisure activities which are often similar in content to one's working activities and of no sharp distinction between what is considered as work and what as leisure'; the 'opposition pattern' where 'leisure activities are deliberately unlike work and there is a sharp distinction between what is work and what is leisure'; and the 'neutrality pattern' consisting of 'leisure activities which are generally different from work but not deliberately so, and of appreciating the difference between work and leisure without always defining the one as the absence of the other'. Roberts (1995: 42) had earlier emphasised the duality of work and leisure but cautioned against focusing on work at the expense of other influences: 'To understand leisure we certainly need to recognise the implications of work, but without remaining transfixed within an assumption of work centrality'. It is interesting to note, however, that within contemporary sociology leisure is increasingly assumed and subsumed under the heading of *cultural sociology*; an umbrella term that has recently come to accommodate sociological critiques of culture, leisure, sport, the arts, heritage and tourism.

It is also worthy of note that, in relation to the earlier leisure sociologies outlined above, neither Parker nor Roberts introduced gender as an influence on leisure at this stage in their writings. However, as work was a predominantly male sphere at the time of these founding leisure studies writings it is perhaps self-evident that both Parker and Roberts were primarily concerned with theorising men's leisure. As Green *et al.* (1990: 12) pointed out, 'This conceptual starting point led to a heavy concentration in both theoretical and empirical work on white male workers' class position, occupational cultures and associated leisure activities. Women, in so far as they featured at all, appeared as the partners of the men studied, and yet the findings were presented as axioms of general relevance and applicability'. The Rapoports' (1975) work *Leisure and the Family Life Cycle* was therefore significant in redirecting the academic gaze from the public sphere of paid employment to the private sphere of the home and family to account for leisure behaviour, participation and patterns.

Physical education and human movement studies were primarily concerned with active recreation and sport rather than passive leisure. However, it was within many physical education departments in colleges and universities that the study of leisure and sport theory and policy began to take place alongside the study of sport and recreation practice. Within the UK, for example, leading leisure and sport departments at Universities such as Loughborough, Edinburgh (formerly Dunfermline College of Physical Education), Leeds Metropolitan (formerly Carnegie and then Leeds Polytechnic) and Gloucestershire (formerly St Paul and St Mary's and then Cheltenham and Gloucester College of Higher Education) evolved from teacher-training institutions for physical educators. Within many of these institutions the sociology of sport has developed from the subdiscipline of the sociology of education and the subject area of physical education to form one of the fastest growing areas of research and education initially captured under the broad umbrella of leisure studies and now forming a link to the new cultural sociology outlined above.

Rural planning and countryside recreation provided an avenue for the discipline of geography to shape leisure studies. The groundbreaking work of the Tourism and Recreation Research Unit (TRRU), and later the Centre for Leisure Research, at the University of Edinburgh and the Countryside and Community Research Unit at the University of Gloucestershire were to shape research into outdoor recreation and leisure policy in the UK from the 1970s. In North America this area of research experienced a similar rate of growth with the National Recreation and Parks Association (NRPA) sponsoring research projects, conferences and an academic journal entitled the *Journal of Leisure Research* that has continued to publish research in outdoor leisure and recreation. The 1970s and 1980s also witnessed increasing recognition for the outdoor education movement which provided a bridge between many of the interests of physical educationalists and geographers. Patmore's (1972) *Land and Leisure* and *Recreation and Resources* (1983) together with the work of influential geographers such as Carlson (1980) and Coppock (1982), went on to shape the geography of leisure as another subfield of leisure studies and one that would come to provide a spatial dimension to the social and cultural analyses offered by the sociology of leisure when the new subdiscipline of social and cultural geography gathered strength in the 1990s.

The development of feminist geography and its influence on leisure and cultural research is discussed in detail in the next chapter. The focus for the remainder of this chapter is upon the sociology of leisure and leisure sociologies. Coalter and Parry (1982) posed the question *Leisure Sociology or the Sociology of Leisure?* in their work of that title. The debate concerning the relationship between disciplines such as sociology, psychology and geography and subject fields such as leisure studies, cultural studies and gender studies has preoccupied a number of academics over the years. For example, the dispute between Dann and Iso-Ahola, played out in the pages of the *Annals of Tourism Research* in the early 1980s, concerned the nature of knowledge within the field of tourism studies with Dann arguing that *tourism psychology* had developed to explain the phenomena of tourist motivation and behaviour while Iso-Ahola remained adamant that there could be no such subdiscipline as tourism psychology as we could only have the *psychology of tourism* (Dann 1981; Iso-Ahola 1982). In other words, Iso-Ahola was emphatic that we should work from underpinning disciplines to subject fields and not the other way round.

Gender and contested definitions of leisure

In spite of the preoccupation among leisure scholars with seeking an agreed definition or definitions of leisure the concept remains loosely defined and, paradoxically, is more often explained by what it is not than by what it actually is (Coalter 1989). Thus, leisure is frequently defined as not being paid work or employment or not being necessary household chores, childcare or caring. Such definitions imply rather simplistically that leisure can still be seen as merely 'free time', freely chosen time or time free from the constraints of everyday life (de Grazia 1962).

Over the last four decades leisure has been defined in a number of different ways. Haywood *et al.* (1989: 2–7), for example, examined definitions of leisure as residual time, as activities, as being functional for society, and as freedom. All of these definitions have been contested within the leisure studies literature and most have been critiqued in relation to gender. Indeed, Green *et al.* (1990) introduce their book *Women's Leisure, What Leisure?* by stating that 'The impetus for this book was our irritation and confusion about the over-defined concept of leisure' (Green *et al.* 1990: vii). Similarly, Wearing and Wearing's (1988) *Leisure Studies* article entitled ' "All in a day's leisure": gender and the concept of leisure' asked searching questions about the relevance of the developing leisure studies lexicon for the study of women's leisure. It is therefore appropriate to summarise these definitions here if only to acknowledge their influence on the development of (mis)understandings of gender and leisure relations within the subject field of leisure studies.

Of time, work and gendered leisure

The definition of leisure as *free time*, freely chosen time, or time free from constraint has been at the centre of leisure studies discourses concerning definitions of leisure (Aitchison 2000b). As outlined above, the early leisure studies literature was heavily influenced by debates concerning changing work–leisure patterns and the possibility of more leisure time in a post-industrial era. However, Thrane (2000: 109) states that 'The availability of free time remains a subject of uncertainty in social science research' and that 'scholars disagree as to whether people in Western societies, primarily as a result of reduced working hours, have gained free time during the past three decades'. Defining leisure in relation to full-time paid work has traditionally meant defining leisure in relation to men's work and therefore only offers a useful definition to a minority of women as the majority is not engaged in full-time paid employment. However, such a sweeping critique may also be problematic during a period when women's paid employment has increased dramatically in western societies. More nuanced and detailed studies of the differentiated impact of work on leisure are therefore required and Thrane (2000: 109) points to an increasing number of studies of leisure that 'have focussed on how gender, employment status, household work, and socio-demographic variables affect the amount of time spent on leisure activities'.

Thinking of leisure as free time is also problematic for women whose freedom may be relative freedom dependent on the financial support of a male partner or free time constrained by the need to provide support and care for others (Chambers 1986; Henderson and Allen 1991). The measurement and evaluation of free time availability for women has formed one of the strongest foci of the 'leisure constraints' literature. Indeed 'time' as a leisure constraint seems to have attracted more attention than discourses surrounding 'fear' and 'body image' which have both gained more prominence in feminist sociology, geography and sport studies (Choi 2000; Crawford *et al.* 1991; Henderson and Bialeschki 1991; Shaw 1994; Valentine 1989). During the 1980s a surge of research drew our attention to the gender differentiation in patterns of domestic labour and leisure in Europe, North America and Australia: Hochschild and Machung (1989) and Shaw (1988) considered the 'working woman's double shift'; Hantrais *et al.* (1984) provided comparative data of 'Time–space dimensions of work, family and leisure in France and Great Britain' (Hantrais *et al.* 1984); and increasing amounts of data were published that demonstrated the difficulties in considering free time as leisure time (Blair and Lichter 1991; Horna 1989; Kay 1998; Koopman-Boyden and Abbot 1985;

Thompson 1995). Goodale and Godbey (1988: 8–9) have also stressed that 'equating leisure with free time and limiting our notion of freedom to "freedom from" is not satisfactory ... Leisure conceptualised as a periodic quantity of a certain kind of time has entered our dictionaries and conversations but it has not, and perhaps cannot, enter our experience'. In thinking through his own conceptualisation of leisure in relation to feminist critiques, Roberts (1999) has recently acknowledged that:

> The residual concept [of leisure] ... which roughly equates leisure with time left over when other things have been done, may more or less correspond with the realities of life for most men. The concept looks far less reasonable when confronted by women with childcare and other domestic responsibilities. Do they have any genuinely free time? The titles of the books which ask questions such as *What Leisure?* (Green *et al.*, 1990) and *All Work and No Play?* (Deem, 1986) arise from the reactions of women who have been unable to recognise their researchers' concept of leisure in their own lives.
>
> (Roberts 1999: 89)

Recreating leisure as activity

The definition of leisure as *activities* is generally associated with the concept of recreation. Again, this definition sees leisure as oppositional to work or as time when people can recreate themselves after the labours of work. The concept of leisure as active recreation often prioritises physical activities, such as those associated with sport, over less physical pursuits such as relaxation, meditation and contemplation. It is this latter group of activities that may have more in common with the original Greek definition of leisure than our contemporary notions of leisure as either activity or consumption. The question of defining what activities can be classified as 'leisure' is well documented in the early leisure studies literature (de Grazia 1962; Glasser 1970; Kaplan 1960). More recently, our attention has been drawn to the multiplicity of functions that different 'leisure activities' may have for different people, or even for the same people at different times (Csikszentmihalyi 1975). For example, the major studies of women and leisure have all identified the importance of solitary relaxation to provide 'rest and recovery from the demands of everyday life' (Green *et al.* 1990: 6) in addition to sociable recreation which might provide enjoyment, fun or 'a night out for a "laugh with the girls"' (Green *et al.* 1990: x).

Although he is not a leisure studies scholar per se, Csikszentmihalyi (1990) offers a useful socio-psychological account of leisure-related enjoyment as a state of optimal experience or 'flow' which he describes, following his earlier work, as a state of being *Beyond Boredom and Anxiety* (1975). A state of flow, he claims, is achieved when one is sufficiently engaged by the experience to be wholly absorbed in it but not so taxed by the experience as to find it too difficult or demanding to accomplish. He refers to as a state of flow where the engagement in and accomplishment of the task provides enhancement to self-esteem through a sense of achievement and well-being. Rojek, on the other hand, has encouraged leisure researchers to supplement this socio-psychological perspective with a more critical sociological perspective that examines all forms of leisure, including those that may not be perceived as 'leisure' by mainstream society. Thus, Rojek has criticised leisure researchers for focusing on the 'socially approved forms of leisure ... they do not talk about deviance or deviant activities in leisure ... to my mind their work has a very impoverished view of power relations' (Rojek 1988: 14). This raises a further question that leads on to an exploration of functional definitions of leisure as there is clearly a tension between what might rather naively be defined as 'good' leisure and 'bad' leisure. Indeed, some leisure theorists have gone so far as to claim that 'anything that violates human rights cannot be called "leisure"' (Mason 1999: 237). Such a value judgement would, however, prevent leisure theorists from engaging in the critical study of activities such as sex tourism or pornography and would limit the ability of leisure scholars to contribute to the wider social science research agenda.

Gender, leisure and the functioning of the social order

The belief that leisure can be *functional* for society as well as the individual is associated with the Victorian movement of rational recreation and notions of 'muscular Christianity' (Clarke and Critcher 1985; Haywood *et al.* 1989: 211). Rojek has identified this functionalist perspective on leisure as representing the first in three phases within leisure studies 'in which different competing claims have expressed themselves strongly' (Rojek 2000: 104). The subsequent phases he identifies as 'counter-cultural criticism' where people like Stuart Hall from the Centre for Contemporary Cultural Studies at Birmingham University 'acted as a mouthpiece of left-wing radicalism' and served 'as the vital catalyst in filtering New Left thinking through to leisure studies' (Rojek 2000: 107). Although feminist critiques were only visible by their absence from these early analyses of leisure, Rojek (2000) identifies feminist perspectives as the third phase of leisure studies scholarship and it is notable that women often perform functions in support of men's leisure ranging from prostitution and pole-dancing to washing their male partner's dirty sports kit.

Stebbins (1992, 1997) has differentiated between 'serious' leisure and 'casual' leisure to illustrate the different functions that leisure can have in people's lives. In his discussions of serious leisure Stebbins has demonstrated that leisure can take on the status of work in relation to time, commitment and identity formation. In contrast, the attribution of a 'leisure function' to some activities commonly perceived as work has also been identified and may simply reflect today's diverse populations and lifestyles (Kelly 1987). But Stebbins' work goes beyond individuals' leisure and lifestyles to suggest that serious leisure can also serve to destabilise wider norms within society. For example, the coast of Cornwall in south-west England has long been popular with surfers, many of whom consider their leisure to be more significant in their lives than any form of work. For some, work is simply a means to support their leisure. Rather than associating such leisure behaviour purely with individualism, however, it is evident within environmental campaigns such as 'Surfers Against Sewage' that the seriousness of their leisure can have a wider function in bringing about social or environmental change. Similarly, many back-packers, travellers and even more conventionally defined tourists have been encouraged to join campaigning organisations such as 'Tourism Concern' in attempts to promote fair trade and environmental protection in and through tourism and leisure.

Gender and the relative freedom of leisure

Finally, de Grazia's (1962: 14) definition of leisure as 'freedom from the necessity of being occupied' may resonate with many women who long to be free of their domestic, family and employment commitments to experience leisure time or leisure activities. In tourism studies both spaces and experiences have been described as 'liminal' in that they enable the tourist to escape from the structures and strictures of both wider society and everyday life to engage in activities and behave in ways that would be neither acceptable nor normal at home. Thus the leisure space of the holiday becomes deregulated leisure space where the tourist experiences a greater sense of freedom. But there are clearly constraints to such freedom. Even where the norms of everyday life may be suspended as on an 18 to 30 Mediterranean clubbing holiday, women may be subject to sexual harassment, aggression, assault or 'date rape'. Instead of seeing freedom and constraint or the liminal and non-liminal as clearly demarcated spaces, times and activities, poststructural theory advocates the recognition of the fluid and overlapping nature of such categories. Although leisure spaces can enable participants 'to stand outside the structures of ordinary society and subject these structures to critical reflection' (Rojek, 2000: 148) such potentially subversive moments can be just moments rather than an entire leisure or tourism experience. Rojek (2000: 149) points to Turner's (1992: 57) work to advocate that 'deviant, abnormal leisure values and practices are expressed habitually as part of the ordinary relations of everyday life. They do not constitute a departure from, or break with, normality. Rather, they are a continuous part of everyday life'. Thus, the coffee break or email with friends or colleagues where gossip, jokes and banter abound, often at the expense of others in positions of authority, might offer a liminal moment in an otherwise structured and regulated day. It is these moments or *Ways of Escape* (Rojek 1993) that serve a function in *Decentring Leisure* (Rojek 1995) and add complexity to what were previously rather bounded or dualistic definitions of leisure.

Crude definitions of leisure as *freedom* present a paradox for many women. A number of leisure activities, especially family activities, may not be freely chosen as they may be part of a woman's children's, partner's or the extended family's leisure that requires facilitation by others. Deem (1999: 172), for example, has asked 'what happens to gendered power relations and domestic divisions of labour on holidays?'. Freedom, in relation to leisure, is thus 'freedom to' as well as 'freedom from' and is almost always 'relative freedom' (Goodale and Godbey, 1989: 9). Green *et al.* (1990) illustrate the complexity of constraints to women's leisure freedom by stating:

> Leisure cannot be compartmentalised and explored in isolation from other parts of life, as the character of its vital ingredients – time, resources and commitment – are indicative of the broader social structures within which they emerge; for women that generally involves a web of inequalities. A woman's right to freedom in leisure is circumscribed by her employment status and income level, her family situation and, most important, her lack of status as a woman in a patriarchal society.
>
> Green *et al.* (1990: ix)

But it is the differently constrained nature of freedom that is discussed within this book rather than the lack of freedom. By examining definitions of leisure as residual time, as activity, as functional for society and as freedom it is evident that leisure has many different meanings for different people and even for the same people at different times or in different places. There is also something rather static and naïve about many of the definitions that have been outlined above in that they seem to acknowledge only the stability of leisure and the positive benefits of leisure. Rojek (2000) has coined the term 'engaged freedom' and has attempted to direct the attention of leisure scholars to both the dynamic nature of leisure and to what he has defined as 'abnormal forms of leisure'. In exploring the differentiated and changing nature of leisure participation and provision it is essential to recognise leisure as a site of conflict, contestation, transgression and transformation. It is also important to recognise that leisure cannot be extracted from the rest of life and studied in isolation as leisure theories, policies and practice are all shaped by the wider structures and cultures of society. Rojek (1995: 1), for example, has stressed that 'one cannot separate leisure from the rest of life and claim that it has unique laws . . . the object of leisure is subsumed by the subject of culture'.

Leisure studies: from structural to cultural approaches

It has already been established above that leisure studies has a strong sociological tradition. During the 1970s and 1980s the sociology of leisure was often viewed as being polarised by two broad schools of thought: pluralism and neo-Marxism. In the UK Roberts and Parker were associated with leisure studies critiques that were described loosely as liberal, functionalist or pluralist accounts and which had become the orthodox perspective during the 1970s. In contrast, writers such as Clarke and Critcher (1985) and Rojek's earlier work (1985) were associated with neo-Marxist leisure studies that had gained ground during the 1980s. As outlined above, Rojek (2000: 104–111) identifies three broad schools of thought which, he claims, have shaped the course of leisure studies to date: functionalism, counter-culture critiques informed by a Gramscian approach, and feminism. This section seeks to address the first two of these three categories, together with a review of liberal pluralist and neo-Marxist approaches to the study of leisure. Rojek's third category, that of feminist leisure studies research, will form the focus of the next two sections of this chapter. In addition to discussing liberal pluralism, functionalism, counter-culture and neo-Marxist critiques this section will also develop Rojek's criticism that leisure studies has failed to address adequately the relationship between leisure and culture.

Rojek (2000: 104) describes functionalism very briefly as an approach which 'in leisure studies began with the concept of the free individual and attributed choice in leisure practice to individual determination'. Although Rojek (2000: 109) refers to leisure theorists such as Parker and Roberts as 'functionalists' Roberts (1988) has described himself as a 'pluralist' and has explained and defended the pluralist position as one founded on the belief that it seems:

> absolutely essential to refer to people's desires and motivations, as well as to their constraints and opportunities, in order to explain their leisure behaviour. We are also agreed that these influences did not exert their influence on leisure in splendid isolation but were interactive. The result was a whole variety of lifestyles, and hence the pluralist scenario, the conventional view of leisure.
>
> (Roberts 1988: 23)

In contrast, the counter-culture, neo-Marxist or radical position singled out the relationship between leisure and capitalism as the feature of society over all others that had a determining influence on leisure patterns, leisure consumption, leisure participation and leisure relations. Thus, Clarke and Critcher (1985) were concerned with *Leisure in Capitalist Britain* and Rojek (1985) focused simultaneously upon *Capitalism and Leisure Theory*. The emphasis of these neo-Marxist analyses was on the way in which capitalism served to shape leisure participation through both constraint and coercion or what Gramsci (1985) termed 'hegemony'. Critcher (1988: 37) offers a definition of hegemony by stating, 'I understand hegemony in part to be the way in which certain powerful definitions of us come to permeate our cultural institutions, to be inescapable and to constitute our sense of ourselves'. Wearing (1998: 61), writing in relation to gender and leisure, defined hegemony as 'the control of consciousness by cultural dominance through the institutions of society'. Although Gramsci's conceptualisation of hegemony was coined in relation to class domination feminists have adopted and adapted the term to account for the domination of women by men in the form of patriarchal hegemony and gender theorists have subsequently referred to the domination of particular forms of masculinity as hegemonic masculinity.

Although Roberts' most recent text, *Leisure in Contemporary Society*, published in 1999, does discuss the influence of sex and gender on leisure, Clarke and Critcher's (1985) book *The Devil Makes Work: Leisure in Capitalist Britain* appears to be the only male-authored leisure studies text from the 1980s that makes extensive reference to women and gender within its neo-Marxist analysis of leisure relations. Indeed, even within what is largely a materialist analysis, Clarke and Critcher (1985: 220) go as far as to state that, 'the inequality of women is produced and experienced culturally as well as materially':

> Some meanings are so entrenched that leisure cannot but give them expression. Gender we argued to be so powerful a meaning that leisure has come to be one of its principal forms of celebration. At those moments in leisure when people feel and appear most free of social roles, they are in actuality most bound to rigid expectations of gender behaviour.
>
> (Clarke and Critcher 1985: 224)

The predominantly materialist or structuralist analyses of the sociology of leisure in the UK contrasted throughout the 1980s with the largely individualist analyses of the psychology of leisure undertaken and published in North America. Coalter (1997: 255) has suggested that leisure research in the UK and North America is 'characterised by different epistemological, methodological, and theoretical perspectives'. He sees UK research as forming a collective body of knowledge termed 'leisure studies', whereas North American research has defined the field as 'leisure sciences'. Although this polarisation is clearly a generalisation, Coalter's definitions are symbolised in more than just the titles of long-established journals in the UK (*Leisure Studies*) and North America (*Leisure Sciences*):

> The predominantly sociological leisure studies has adopted a *society in leisure* approach, exploring how broader sociocultural structures

are reflected in leisure and largely ignoring issues of individual meaning. The predominantly sociopsychological leisure sciences, with its stress on positivist methodology, has often produced analyses of *leisure without society* and failed to address issues of the social and cultural meanings associated with leisure.

(Coalter 1997: 255)

Leisure sciences research appears to have been driven by methodological concerns rather than a commitment to theoretical or ideological transformation or any real concern with cultural analyses of leisure. Burton (1996: 19) has criticised this reification of methodology as producing 'an obsession with method that is divorced from substance', while Hemingway (1995: 36) has critiqued leisure science's 'tendency to reduce enquiry to technique'. Later, and reflecting the growing influence of poststructural theory within European social science research, Mommaas (1997: 251) claimed that UK and European leisure studies had witnessed a 'shift from American-based scientism and functionalism to Gramscian neo-Marxism, French poststructuralism, semiotics and psychoanalysis . . . leisure research became influenced by the ideas of Giddens, Bourdieu and Elias'. However, in his critique entitled 'European leisure studies at the crossroads? A history of leisure research in Europe', Mommaas (1997) fails to make any reference to feminist or gender research within leisure studies, in spite of the existence of both a well-developed body of feminist leisure studies research in the UK and North America at that time or the feminist research which had already emanated from French poststructuralism, semiotics and psychoanalysis. In contrast, Coalter acknowledged the contribution of feminist leisure research to both leisure studies and leisure sciences noting that:

Within leisure sciences, a major challenge to the positivist/individualistic paradigm has come from feminist researchers, with their assertion of the need to understand 'situated meaning' and the role played by structure and ideology in creating contexts and meanings . . . From a leisure studies perspective, it is interesting to note that feminist writers appear to be the most consistently international in orientation.

(Coalter 1997: 263)

However, neither the society-in-leisure approach of the UK and Western Europe, nor the leisure-in-society approach that has dominated North American leisure research have explored the complexity of the relationships between leisure and culture. Rojek (2000: 112) has claimed that all of the major schools of thought within leisure studies 'treat the concept of culture in unsatisfactory ways'. He calls for leisure studies to embrace Eco's (1994) anthropological definition of culture as comprising 'the complex of institutions, myths, rites, laws, beliefs, codified everyday behaviour, value systems and material techniques elaborated by a group of humans'. Resonating with many of the tenets of poststructural and postcolonial thinking outlined in the previous chapter, Rojek (2000: 114) claims that such an 'anthropological position is associated with a high degree of tolerance and relativism. For other cultures are not viewed as superior or inferior, but as merely involving different complexes of myths, rites, laws and so forth'. The next chapter seeks to explore ways in which recent social and cultural geographies have enabled leisure studies to break free from the constraints of functionalist, counter-culture and socialist feminist analyses to engage with the contemporary social *and* cultural critiques of poststructural analysis.

Feminist leisure studies: the first two decades

Within feminist leisure studies, the publication of *Women and Leisure: A State of the Art Review* by Talbot (1979) is viewed by a number of writers as representing the first piece of published research on women and leisure (Deem 1988: 7). Talbot's research formed one of a series of ten special reports funded by the UK Social Science Research Council (SSRC) and the Sports Council. It was accompanied by a workshop entitled 'Women and Leisure' at the 1979 Leisure Studies Association Annual Conference and was closely followed by a paper entitled 'Women's Leisure' given by Hobson at a conference Leisure and Social Control hosted by the Centre for Contemporary Cultural Studies at Birmingham University in January 1980 (Tomlinson, 1981) and then by the series of seminars 'Women, Sport, Leisure and Education' hosted by the Open University. By 1981 Talbot was writing that:

> Not only do fewer women than men participate in leisure activities but women also participate in a narrower range of activities, and watch sport, both live and on television, less than men . . . when data from surveys which include informal leisure activity are added to the knowledge gained from family and community studies, there emerges a picture of home-based, domestic leisure for women, especially for those from the lower socio-economic groups.
>
> (Talbot 1981: 35)

These events of 1979–81 can be seen as acting as a catalyst for further feminist research undertaken within the subject field over the next decade. While Stanley (1980) called for a 'radical feminist alternative' to the study of leisure, the ensuing research all tended to adopt a liberal or socialist philosophy (Deem 1986; Green *et al.* 1987; Wimbush 1986). Moreover, aspects of leisure such as pornography and prostitution, which clearly symbolise patriarchal control, received detailed scrutiny from radical feminist analyses in women's studies but escaped attention within leisure studies

(Dworkin 1981; Itzin 1992; Jeffreys 1997; MacKinnon 1995). This chapter now goes on to present a brief outline of the major feminist leisure research of the last twenty years. No claim is made, however, to review all the feminist literature within the field of leisure studies. In particular, literature relating to some specific areas of the field, such as women and sport or women and the media, is not addressed here as the intended focus of the review is on the dominant and emergent themes within *leisure* studies research.

Socialist and liberal feminism provided the dominant theoretical perspectives for a number of publications based on specific case studies produced in the UK during the 1980s. These case studies were specific to particular groups of women, particular types of leisure participation, and to clearly defined geographical areas, spaces and places. Each case study served to highlight a further aspect of the feminist leisure agenda and to clarify particular aspects of leisure and social relations. While most of the case studies were undertaken from a socialist feminist perspective, and underpinned by a concomitant and dominant interest in class relations, there seems little doubt that these studies paved the way for contemporary feminist research in leisure, much of which now adopts different theoretical perspectives, including poststructural feminist perspectives.

Dixey and Talbot's (1982) national study of women and bingo and a more detailed community study of women and bingo in the Armley district of Leeds in England served to highlight the existence of gendered leisure space, the male domination of public leisure space, and the response by women of carving out a spatial sanctuary in the form of the bingo hall. This was one of the first studies to look at women's occupation of public leisure space as previous studies had focused upon women's leisure around the home and family and the different meanings and motivations for women participating in leisure compared to men (Rapoport and Rapoport 1975).

Deem's study, undertaken between 1980 and 1982, explored the leisure of women in Milton Keynes, a designated 'new town' in central England. The study involved 497 women and the research was both multi-method and multi-phased employing 'questionnaires (postal and personally handed-out), in-depth semi-structured interviews, discussion groups with local women, meetings with leisure providers, and observation (both participant and non-participant) of local groups, clubs and activities as well as communities' (Deem 1986: 23). Deem's study involved two groups of women with the active pursuit of leisure outside the home forming the focus of the research with the first group and leisure at home forming the focus of the research with the second. Among the first group Deem identified a number of constraints on women's leisure outside the home with the most apparent being 'male attitudes towards women going out alone or with friends – many husbands or partners were only happy if the activity was approved by them (keep fit was; discos or the pub usually weren't)'

(Deem 1986: 31). Other constraints listed were 'hours of employment', 'childcare', 'housework and domestic obligations', 'access to private transport', 'lack of money and absence of close friends' (Deem 1986: 32). In relation to leisure constraints experienced by the second group Deem stressed the relationship between access to *power* and access to *leisure* by reflecting that whereas 'few women thought of themselves as having a right to leisure; many men do see themselves as having such a right' (Deem 1988: 14). She noted that the perception of having no right to leisure was felt most acutely by those women without paid employment. By means of illustration, Deem (1986: 36) quoted one research participant who stated 'I'd like to go jogging, go to the cinema, go out for the day somewhere without the others ... but I feel it's too selfish, I'd be neglecting the children ... and the house ... they come first'. Henderson and Bialeschki (1991) later synthesised and summarised these finding:

> A number of leisure researchers have indicated that women believe they have no right to leisure and this belief places a severe limitation on their construction of time for leisure and their attitudes toward leisure (e.g., Bialeschki and Henderson, 1986; Deem, 1986; Govaerts, 1985; Henderson, 1990a, 1990b; Henderson *et al.*, 1989; Wearing and Wearing, 1988; Woodward and Green, 1988).
>
> (Henderson and Bialeschki 1991: 51)

Deem's research further explored the gender differences identified in Dixey and Talbot's work by highlighting the differences *between* women in relation to their access to leisure and control of public leisure space. Her work focused on the difficulties which working-class women, or women with young children, may experience in gaining access to leisure; difficulties that middle-class women or women without children may not experience to the same degree. Moreover, Deem began to articulate the connections between the gendered construction of *leisure* and the gendered construction of *power* that creates both knowledge and the practice of leisure:

> There is, however, a more general point here, concerned with the necessity of directing feminists' attention not only to the existence of power relations but also to how and why those power relations are sustained by ideological and material factors. There is much discussion about the importance, for example, of gender ideologies but little attempt to explore how these actually work in the field of leisure.
>
> (Deem 1988: 14)

The heterogeneity among women, and of women's leisure opportunities and experiences was further identified in a study of leisure participation by women with pre-school age children undertaken by Wimbush (1986) in two distinct areas of Edinburgh. The study, funded by the Health Promotion Research Trust, attempted to 'evaluate the importance and meaning that mothers attach to their existing leisure opportunities' and 'to explore the ways in which social and recreational activities feature in their general health and well-being' (Health Promotion Research Trust 1987: 2). In meeting these objectives, the research identified and evaluated a range of factors that both constrained and facilitated women's involvement in leisure. The recommendations for leisure policy and practice outlined by Wimbush serve to summarise the emphasis and ethos of feminist intervention in leisure from the mid-1980s to the mid-1990s. The eight recommendations listed below focus on the need for structural change in the provision of public leisure services and were later adopted and adapted by other leisure providers in addition to being reiterated in future feminist leisure research:

1   play and creche facilities as an integral part of more social and recreational venues, so that children are well looked after and mothers are freed from making complicated childcare arrangements
2   places where children are welcomed and where they can participate in activities with other children or with their parents
3   settings where women feel comfortable and not threatened or out of place. Women-only sessions in sports, leisure and adult education centres taught or led by women are one way of putting women at ease and increasing their self-confidence
4   activities for women in the evening as well as during the daytime, so that participation can be fitted within the busy timetables of employed mothers as well as those working at home
5   flexible payment systems that allow participants to pay-as-you-go, so that those not able to afford block payments are not prevented from taking part, and those unable to attend regularly are not financially penalised
6   a means whereby providers and policy-makers can consult regularly with women in the community (e.g. via locally-based 'outreach' workers) and learn from the self-help arrangements that some women have developed to meet their leisure needs
7   information about leisure activities through the local media and via nurseries, clinics, health centres, playgroups and shopping centres

(Health Promotion Research Trust 1987: 2)

The largest and most frequently cited research into gender and leisure in the UK, however, was that conducted in Sheffield between 1984 and 1987 by Green *et al.* who undertook an ESRC and Sports Council-sponsored research project to investigate *Leisure and Gender: A Study of*

Women's Leisure Experiences. This research, published in 1987, later formed the basis of the last comprehensive research text on the subject of women's leisure in the UK (Green *et al.* 1990). The study consisted of interviews with 707 women aged between 18 and 59 'drawn from randomly selected areas around the city and from a range of social class backgrounds and family situations' (Green *et al.* 1990: 24). In summarising the findings of the research Green *et al.* (1990: 24) stated that:

> The findings from the survey confirmed that women's access to free time and leisure opportunities are structured by social class and income level, age and ethnic group, and their work and domestic situation. The main constraints took the form of a lack of resources such as time, money, safe transport and childcare. Limitations on their access to leisure were experienced most acutely by the women not currently in paid work, those with unemployed partners, single parents, and married women with children aged under five.
>
> (Green *et al.* 1990: 24)

The Sheffield research thus confirmed many of the findings from both the Milton Keynes project and the Edinburgh project. In all three studies there are perhaps two broad sets of findings, the importance of which cannot be overstated. First, the impact of family life and domestic commitments on women's leisure opportunities is of paramount importance. Second, all three studies revealed the significance of the social and cultural construction of leisure spaces, places and venues in which women could experience leisure. Both of these issues relate directly to constraints upon women's leisure with the first centring on constraints within the home and the second focusing upon constraints experienced outside the home but frequently constructed within the home. Thus Green *et al.* (1990) could point to tangible findings such as 'women with children under the age of five are least likely to feel satisfied with the amount of free time they have' but continually sought to contextualise these findings within 'the social processes through which women's access to leisure is constructed, defined and regulated' (Woodward *et al.* 1988: 144). This book is concerned with the social and cultural processes that construct, define and regulate women's leisure but it also seeks to explore ways in which women's leisure can be reworked. Equally, the book is less focused upon women's domestic circumstances and home-based leisure than it is with the ways in which domestic mores shape women's wider leisure experiences and the ways in which we have come to think, talk and teach about leisure.

Green *et al.* (1987) drew on both socialist and radical feminist theory to explain women's experiences of leisure. Ultimately, however, their recommendations for implementing practical change in the short-term relied on liberal feminist intervention directed at policy-makers. Drawing on socialist feminist analysis, Green *et al.* (1987) point to women's lack of disposable income as a result of their labour market position in capitalist society. Their acknowledgement of radical feminist theory can be seen in relation to the significance they attach to the patriarchal control of women's time and space, particularly in relation to private or domestic space. This focus on the dual system of capitalist and patriarchal oppression is a feature of socialist feminist analyses and is highlighted by Woodward *et al.* (1988), before emphasising that change may have to be the result of less radical and less far-reaching transformation to public leisure policy and practice:

> The best prospect for promoting women's recreational opportunities seems, in the light of this work, to be in promoting greater autonomy and power for women within relationships and in the wider society, so that these discriminatory attitudes and behaviour become anachronistic and socially unacceptable. In the meantime, policy-makers within leisure and recreation may need to 'work round' the effects of such inequalities, in relation to the pricing and time-tabling of use of their facilities, the development of women-only sessions, and the introduction of a much wider scale of transportation to and from leisure venues.
>
> (Woodward *et al.* 1988: 145)

Unfortunately, the momentum in feminist leisure studies research conducted in the UK was not maintained during the 1990s. The transformation of the polytechnics, which had been the locus for most leisure studies teaching and research, into universities in 1992 coincided with the rapid expansion of UK higher education and a shift in the curriculum from leisure studies to leisure management. The increasingly vocational agenda of the former polytechnics created an appropriate environment in which to train the next generation of leisure managers but did little to nurture the next generation of critical leisure theorists. Increasingly, the umbilical cord between the parent disciplines of sociology and geography and the newborn subject field of leisure studies was severed, leaving leisure studies to fend for itself in the rapidly changing world of social science. For a time during the mid to late 1990s it appeared as if leisure studies had lost its way or could not keep up with the new theoretical advances and methodological innovations of social science. The subject field of leisure studies had also spawned its own off-spring in the form of sport studies, tourism studies and heritage studies and, by the end of the decade, the UK's last remaining degree programme in Leisure Studies, at Leeds Metropolitan University, had become a degree in Sport and Leisure Studies.

Throughout the 1990s the subdiscipline of the sociology of sport gave rise to a new wave of critical perspectives to what, for some women, is an important aspect of leisure. With increasing links made during the

1990s between physical activity and public health, the field of sport studies expanded into physical activity and exercise forming a bridge to leisure studies. Hargreaves' (1994) groundbreaking text *Sporting Females: Critical Issues in the History and Sociology of Women's Sports* was instrumental in developing a comprehensive analysis of the structural and cultural influences shaping gender and sport relations. In the same year the first international conference on women and sport took place in Brighton in the UK. The conference developed what has become known as 'The Brighton Declaration on Women and Sport', discussed in more detail in Chapter 5, and a number of gender-related issues in sport began to be taken more seriously. Perhaps the most significant example of such an issue is that of sexual abuse in sport which has finally gained a place on the sport policy agenda (Brackenridge 2001). Throughout the 1990s, as feminist and gender studies of sport began to build a critical mass of research, it became evident that the epistemological base of the field had widened to embrace both radical feminist and poststructural feminist perspectives although not necessarily within the same research context. Radical feminist critiques attempted to make sense of women and girl's sexual exploitation in sport while poststructural feminist critiques were better equipped to make sense of the cultural nuances of the changing representation of women in sport.

Although feminist leisure studies in the UK did not grow through the 1990s the way the field had during the 1980s, the wider research arena was developed further. In the US Henderson's prolific writing on women and leisure continued to dominate the North American leisure sciences journals and, although resonant with both liberal and socialist feminist approaches, began to address issue of 'race' (Henderson and Ainsworth 2001). Bialeschki, a frequent co-author with Henderson, was also making in-roads into new territory by the end of the decade in research that began to acknowledge the significance of what Valentine (1989) had described previously as 'the geography of fear' as an influence on women's outdoor activity. The development of research focusing on women's leisure outside the home was mirrored by research of women's leisure inside the home where Samuel's (1996) collection *Women, Leisure and the Family* provided new insights on the interpretations provided by the Rapoports' research of leisure and the family.

Leisure spaces outside the home are discussed in more detail in the next chapter in relation to leisure places. This is not to either deny or denigrate the importance of domestic and family relations in informing women's leisure as such a denial would be anathema to a feminist or gender analysis. Instead, the explanation of the focus of this book is, in large part, a recognition that the original theoretical and empirical research underpinning each chapter is primarily concerned with the more abstract construction of leisure theory, policy and practice than with detailed analyses of leisure and the family. Other writers currently working in the area of leisure and the family are far better placed to provide empirical and theoretical insights into the interrelationships of gender, leisure and the home (Kay 1996, 1998, 2000; Samuel 1996; Schor 1991; Shaw 1985, 1992, 1997; Shaw and Dawson 2001; Zuzanek *et al.* 1998). These analyses of gender, leisure and the family have served to revisit and redefine many of the earlier analyses of leisure time and leisure relations through their research of work–leisure relationships, gendered definitions of leisure and socialist feminist critiques of gender and employment.

Gender and leisure studies: the influence of poststructuralism

The influence of socialist feminism is evident throughout the major case studies of women's leisure undertaken in the UK in the 1980s and outlined in the section above. There seems little doubt that the majority of previous feminist leisure studies has viewed class relations as a major determinant of leisure relations. For example, Woodward *et al.* (1988: 99) list six determinants of women's leisure with the first three emphasising the influence of social class: 'the most significant influences on women's leisure were their social class, level of household and personal income, employment status, age group, marital status and stage in the family life cycle'. Thus, while the major feminist studies of leisure conducted in the 1980s undoubtedly disrupted the discourse of leisure studies, they can also be viewed as part of leisure studies' own structuralist sociological tradition where 'from the very beginning, leisure research in Europe was a topic oriented field of research dominated by sociological perspectives but strongly leaning toward public policy interest' (Mommaas 1997: 241).

Wearing (1996: 186), drawing on poststructural feminist theory, offered a critique of these previous feminist leisure studies when she stated that, 'Feminist theorists have challenged the male bias in such theories, but still have concentrated on the labour aspects of the family as explanation'. Wearing's work has been instrumental in introducing poststructural analyses of gender to the subject field of leisure studies. In contrast to the frequently levelled criticism that poststructuralism and postmodernism are theoretical projects devoid of real life application or meaning for women outside academia, Wearing points to the lives of ordinary women as giving sense to poststructural critique:

> one of the dangers of the socialist feminist position in the late 1980s was that such thorough documentation of women's oppression, theoretically linked to structural causes, implied that nothing that individual women could do would make any significant change in their lives. A pessimistic position, to say the least. And one which breeds a victim mentality. There was a shift from the 'victim blaming', 'bootstraps' approach of liberalism to the 'poor victim' approach of

socialism. Yet in the everyday lives of the women I knew, and those I came to know through my research, women were continually constructing survival strategies, struggling, negotiating, contesting and sometimes transforming power relationships at an individual and group level.

(Wearing 1998: 37)

Writers including Wearing, Mommaas and Rojek have all questioned leisure studies' reticence to engage with poststructural analysis (Aitchison 1999a, 2000a, 2001a; Wearing 1998; Mommaas 1997; Rojek 2000). At a time when gender research in cultural studies, gender studies and social and cultural geography was struggling to come to terms with the disruption of theories of deconstruction, diversity, and the arrival of postmodernism in the 1980s, leisure studies still seemed to be engaged in liberal and socialist feminist analyses of a kind that was increasingly viewed as out-moded in the former disciplines (Aitchison 2001a, 2002a). Mommaas (1997: 251) captured the essence of this increasing divide between the structuralism of leisure studies and the growing interest in poststructural-ism that seemed to be sweeping the academy: 'leisure research has related itself rather ambivalently to postmodern thinking' and postmodernist inter-jections have been 'made by people from outside the conventional domain of leisure research and remain on a rather general level of analysis' (Mommaas 1997: 251). Indeed, in an appraisal of Rojek's (1993) work Coalter acknowledges that 'postmodernism has produced a crisis in leisure studies' collectivist theorising and has undermined the ability of most leisure studies scholars to sustain their commitment to emancipatory politics (Coalter 1997: 259). This feeling of crisis can be identified in femi-nist leisure research as the theoretical developments made in the 1980s, and measured in the form of tangible outputs such as feminist leisure texts (Deem 1986; Wimbush and Talbot 1988; Green *et al.* 1990), do not appear to have been matched by similar progress in the UK during the 1990s. Scraton attributed part of this crisis to 'the new malestream world of theory that is engaging with postmodernity debates':

Leisure research in the postmodern world appears to focus on conspic-uous consumption – the public world, the tourist gaze, hyperrealities of Disney World, theme parks, heritage, etc. There is a need to put the personal and political back on the research agenda. Feminist research has always rejected the political separation of the public and the private. It has highlighted the significance of the private world for women, a world that is highly gendered. Leisure research has begun to open this silenced, private world by recognising the importance of the private sphere in the control of women's leisure (Deem 1986; Green *et al.* 1987). Issues of time, space, sexuality, regulation, control, and power remain important in the 1990s and need to be further explored. By turning our leisure gaze onto the public arena the gendered reality of the hidden private world becomes once more invisible and ignored.

(Scraton 1994: 259)

More recently, and in rather less constructive terms than other calls for the need to explore poststructural feminist theories of leisure, Rojek (2000) has critiqued the way in which socialist feminist leisure studies have failed to consider the potential contribution of poststructural and postmodern analyses of gender and leisure or to consider culture and the relationships between leisure and culture (Aitchison 2000a, 2001a; Rojek 2000). By arguing that 'patriarchy precedes culture in the feminist scheme of things' Rojek (2000: 113) accuses feminist leisure researchers of a mode of theorising where 'being stuck in a 1970s problematic of "liberating the collective subject" has generated a "siege mentality"' where 'debates tend to get bogged down in defensive counter-reactions rather than productive exchange' (Rojek, 2000: 111–112). He goes on to claim that this lack of receptivity to contemporary cultural analysis 'is evident in the work and political interventions of Talbot, Deem, Scraton, Brackenridge, Green, Hebron, Woodward, Bialeschki and Henderson' and that it 'produces a high degree of repetition of argument, as is perhaps most evident in the recent writing of Henderson *et al.* (1989, 1996)' (Rojek 2000: 112). Such scathing attacks fail to acknowledge the relationship between feminist leisure studies and women and gender studies more broadly or to appreciate the nuances in the developmental journey of feminist leisure studies where there is now a growing body of gender research across leisure, sport and tourism that engages with poststructural feminist critiques of cultural forms and processes (Aitchison 1999a, 2000a, 2001a; Aitchison *et al.* 2000; Fullagar 2002; Green 1998; Hargreaves 1994, 2000; Pritchard *et al.* 2002; Wearing 1998).

In spite of Scraton's critique of postmodernism referred to earlier, her later work does acknowledge that Foucault's 'notion of power as ubiquitous and fluid rather than harnessed has some value' to feminist leisure studies (Watson and Scraton 1998: 126). Further, it is argued here that poststructuralist studies of gender and leisure conducted within gender studies, cultural studies, cultural sociology and social and cultural geography have offered alternative ways of seeing and theorising 'time, space, sexuality, regulation, control and power' within gendered leisure relations (Aitchison 1999a). In stark contrast to the concern expressed by Watson and Scraton (1998: 125) that poststructuralism has offered 'a predominantly male gaze onto the public arena', and refuting Rojek's critique of contemporary feminist leisure studies, Green (1998: 173) states that 'the postmodern concern with diversity and difference has opened up areas of 'private' life previously neglected by key social theorists in the 1970s and 1980s'. In addition, two significant advances during the 1990s, which have contributed to feminist and gender leisure research, can be seen as symbolic of a wider restructuring of feminist and gender analysis. First, within the UK, feminist leisure studies have been adopted and adapted by other disciplines and subject fields in a move that is representative of the increasing breakdown of disciplinary boundaries within the academy. Second, advances in feminist and gender research in other countries with an established record of leisure research, such as the US, Canada, Australia and New Zealand, have had an impact upon UK feminist and gender leisure research. As Henderson (1994: 129) has emphasised 'new understandings of power may help to present a framework that transcends the dualism of sex differences by presenting the complexity of powerlessness which some women and other "disenleisured" groups confront in their daily lives'. Both of the developments outlined above have engaged with poststructural theory in ways that leisure studies in the UK has been reluctant to encourage to date. Wearing (1996) comments that:

> In most poststructuralist feminist analysis there is a shift from thinking about 'patriarchy', with its emphasis on male control of the structures of society, to the notion of 'phallocentrism' which denotes male control of language, symbols, definitions, discourses, sexuality, theory and logocentric thinking.
>
> (Wearing 1996: 39)

Butler (1990) sees poststructural feminism as providing a challenge not just to *phallocentrism* but also to *compulsory heterosexuality* which, when combined with phallocentrism, enable the continuation of male domination through both structures *and* cultures. Increasingly, leisure analyses undertaken within other subject fields and disciplines in the UK, such as social and cultural geography, cultural sociology, gender studies, and cultural studies, have drawn extensively on Butler's work, on poststructuralist theory in general, and have been instrumental in developing critiques of binary divides and dualistic thinking in social theory (Aitchison 1999a, 2000b, 2001b, 2003a; Wearing 1996, 1998). Moreover, research from the US and Australia has been influential in bringing poststructural analyses of power and resistance, and of the intersections between gender, 'race' and class, to studies of leisure and gender (Arnold and Shinew 1998; Samdhal and Jekubovich 1997; Shinew *et al.* 1995; Swain and Momsen 2002; Wearing 1996, 1998).

Overview

This chapter has sought to chart the rise of leisure studies as a recognised subject field within the academy and to contextualise feminist leisure studies and the study of gender within the subject field. The chapter introduced the relationship between subject fields and their underpinning disciplines through a discussion of leisure sociologies and sociologies of leisure. Two major schools of thought were introduced and discussed under the headings of pluralist/functionalist and neo-Marxist/counter-culture with the influential work of Roberts (1978), Parker (1983), Clarke and Critcher (1985) and Rojek (1985) introduced. The discussion then moved on to consider competing definitions of leisure, an area that has preoccupied the subject field since its inception in the 1970s. Definitions of leisure as time, activity, function and freedom were evaluated in relation to women's leisure and feminist critiques of leisure. The origins of leisure studies were then identified and discussed in relation to three academic areas: the sociology of work; physical education and human movement studies; and rural planning and countryside recreation. The chapter then considered what Coalter (1998) defined as the competing approaches of the UK-dominated 'society in leisure' approach and the US-dominated 'leisure in society' approach before considering ways in which post-structural theory offers opportunities to integrate studies of leisure and culture (Rojek 2000).

The influence of feminist research in leisure studies was then evaluated through a review of a series of major case studies of women's leisure that were researched in the UK during the 1980s. These case studies, developed by Deem (1986), Wimbush (1986) and Green *et al.* (1988) were critiqued as structuralist accounts of women's leisure informed by a socialist feminist perspective before the chapter moved on to explore the recent impact of poststructural critiques of gender and leisure. Here, the work of Wearing (2000) was identified as instrumental in re-focusing the gaze of feminist leisure scholars from material structures to cultural relations. This discussion of the shift from structural to post-structural theory within sociological accounts of leisure mirrors the pattern developed in the next chapter where geographical analyses of gender and leisure are explored and the shift from structural to cultural critiques is discussed.

4   Gender and leisure places

Introduction: placing gender and leisure

The previous chapter demonstrated the significance of sociological analyses of gender and leisure to the development of the subject field of leisure studies in general and studies of gender and leisure in particular. This chapter seeks to *place* gender and leisure within a similar discussion of geographical theories. Recent links between geography and leisure have, arguably, been witnessed most closely in relation to studies of gender relations, gender identities and sexualities. Together with the theoretical perspectives offered by recent social and cultural geographies, analyses of the social and cultural construction of gender, sexuality and leisure space have combined to forge new alliances between gender studies, leisure studies and geography as a result of the theorisation of spatialised feminism, gendered space and the sexuality of space. Central to such theorisation has been the conceptualisation of the gaze, dualistic thinking and the representation of Others.

The chapter introduces these concepts through an evaluation of a series of geographical discourses that have informed research into gender and leisure. Each discourse is reflective of wider contemporaneous perspectives within social science and, as such, each is indicative of leisure theorising of the time. The review seeks to provide a historical overview of geographical analyses of gender and leisure relations and an evaluation of how such relations shape the production and consumption of leisure and tourism spaces and places as both gendered sites and sights. This chronology progresses from accounts that stress the physical, material and absolute nature of space to more recent analyses that emphasise the socio-cultural, symbolic and relative nature of space (Aitchison 1998a, 1999a, 2000c). As such, the early accounts reflect the positivist paradigm within the social sciences where research of women and gender was largely invisible. Later research reflects the dominance of structuralism and socialist feminism, and more recent critiques are testimony to the increasing purchase of poststructural theory within the academy and the attendant rise of poststructural feminist analyses within gender studies.

Alvesson and Billing (1997: 24) alert us to the dangers of such unilinear chronologies as descriptive frameworks when they state that 'all distinctions and ways of dividing up a complex, heterogeneous and rapidly expanding research area are problematic. They inscribe order and obscure disorder, ambiguity and variety'. There is, however, a purpose to such classifications as they seek to clarify the main focus and guiding principles of a body of knowledge or research while simultaneously attempting to situate the research area within a historical context. For example, McDowell (1993a: 162), writing about feminist geography, has commented that 'Contemporary feminism is a diverse and pluralist project. Despite this warning, a chronological classificatory framework helps in understanding the changing emphases and context of feminist scholarship'.

The first discourse outlined in this chronology is that of *geographies of leisure and leisure geographies.* Just as the previous chapter attempted to ascertain the balance between the discipline of sociology and the subject field of leisure studies so this chapter evaluates the relationships between geography and leisure studies. The second phase of the chronological account, *structuralist theories and spatialised feminism*, explores the rise of structuralist interpretations of space and place within geography and the subsequent development of spatialised feminism as an explanatory framework developed by socialist feminist geographers. The next phase, *social and cultural geographies and gendered leisure space*, explores the impact of geography's so-called 'cultural turn', the development of 'the new cultural geography' and the incorporation of studies of leisure, including gendered leisure space, into recent social and cultural geography. The next section then examines *the place of 'the gaze'* within these more recent geographies of gender and leisure. The chronological journey then addresses *poststructural theories of sex and gender* and draws on the particularly influential work of Judith Butler (1990, 1993). *The place of the 'dualism'* is introduced and explored as pivotal in the production and reproduction of gendered power relations and, hence, gender–leisure relations. This section acknowledges the sexuality of space in a discussion of poststructural geographies and what have been termed 'queer theories' of sexuality and leisure spaces defined as 'gay space'. The penultimate phase in the chronology of geography, gender and leisure then explores the development *from colonial to postcolonial geographies.* In relation to these discussions, *the place of 'the Other'* is introduced and ways of representing Others are explored in relation to gender and leisure. It is worth noting here that this final phase of the chronology also incorporates material from tourism studies that has served to illuminate postcolonial geographies of gender.

Geographies of leisure and leisure geographies

The relationship between geography and leisure research is well established (Barbier 1984; Carlson 1980; Mowl and Turner 1995). Indeed, the first issue of *Leisure Studies*, published in 1982, included an article by Coppock entitled 'Geographical contributions to the study of leisure' in which he chronicled the increasing involvement of geographers in the field of recreation and tourism since the 1930s (Coppock 1982). The article paid particular attention to methodological developments in the spatial analysis of recreation and tourism during the 1970s, the decade preceding publication. Since Coppock's article was written, however, the discipline of geography has undergone radical and transformative developments both resulting from and contributing to a number of new and competing philosophies within the social sciences.

Following the First World War, the large-scale redrawing of the world map illustrated that human actions were as much responsible for defining national boundaries as any physical landforms. The resultant shift towards human or cultural geography was simultaneously mirrored by a move from regional to systematic geography. This shift resulted in a number of regions being studied in relation to a particular phenomenon or topic rather than studying a number of topics or phenomena in relation to a single region. Topics or phenomena that became established within the systematic approach included agriculture, urbanisation and, more recently, tourism and recreation. Such a development meant that, for example, instead of studying the geography of South-East Asia, the focus shifted to studying topics such as tourism where the topic would be studied in a global context rather than simply in relation to one region.

Within human geography, academics tend to define themselves as being interested in, or belonging to, a particular subdiscipline. Social, political, economic and historical geography all combine geography with another academic discipline to provide a multidisciplinary analysis of the relationships between people, places and the environment. Urban, environmental and cultural geographies offer a more interdisciplinary analysis of the social construction of space and place. More recently, feminist geography has provided a systematic analysis of the spatial nature of patriarchal relationships within particular fields of human geography, while geography's 'cultural turn' has emphasised the importance of social and cultural constructs such as gender, sexuality, 'race' and disability in constructing spatiality. What unites all of these geographical analyses, however, is their investigation of the relationships between people, places and the environment and the consequent interaction of society, space and nature.

Until the emergence of critical geographies in the late 1960s, there was a heavy reliance on mathematical and statistical modelling within geographical research and theory (Coppock 1982: 4). Initially, these theoretical approaches were not concerned with leisure, culture, recreation, sport or tourism. Driven by the demands of maturing industrialised nations, geography's 'founding fathers' had little interest in developing leisure theory in the first half of the twentieth century (Weber 1909; Losch 1940; Alonso 1960). Barnes and Gregory (1997: 1) referred to 'the hegemony of spatial science' when discussing the development of positivist geography in the post-1945 period. They claimed that theoretical developments comprised the 'three C's': *certainty*, *coherence* and *cumulation* in relation to the development of geographical knowledge. For half-a-century between the 1930s and the early 1980s the positivist paradigm of geography was thus evident in all areas of the discipline. From the landscape evaluation and mapping of scenic amenity in leisure and recreation to the formulation of typologies of land use in tourism, geographers attempted to employ the epistemology and methodology of the natural sciences to the study of social, cultural and spatial phenomena with no consideration of gender (Brown 1935; Stamp 1948; Gilbert 1939; Butler 1980). This early concentration on locational analysis and spatial science resulted in spatial determinism or a kind of geographical essentialism. Descriptive and predictive models were devised to explain the development of cultural geographical phenomena within a physical geographical context. Many of these models were to shape geographical thinking and research for decades to come and were strongly embedded within early recreation and tourism research within geography.

Whereas the previous chapter illustrated that leisure studies was embracing sociological concepts from Marxist, structuralist and humanist theory in the 1960s and 1970s, tourism studies and recreation research appeared to hold on to their more positivist paradigm. Analyses of recreation and tourism continued to rely on quantitative methods to devise theories which mapped, modelled, coded and classified recreation and tourism development, provision, participation and impacts (Coppock 1982; Duffield and Owen 1970; Glyptis 1991; Patmore 1972, 1983). Glyptis (1991: 96) pointed to the difficulties of measuring demand for countryside recreation compared with that of leisure use at built facilities that have clearly defined entrance points. Consequently, many of the models developed to explain countryside recreation provision and participation are now seen as providing a rather narrowly defined analysis of recreation and tourism. This criticism echoes that levelled at the early sociology of leisure research, and outlined in the previous chapter, with its similarly narrow definition of leisure as the corollary of paid (male) employment.

Structuralist theories and spatialised feminism

By the 1960s, the focus of geographical research had begun to shift and a more critical approach was becoming evident. Gregory *et al.* (1994: 3) assert that this transitional period signalled a move 'away from a preoccupation with the statistical laws of spatial distribution to the historical and material processes of uneven urban and regional development inherent in the "laws of motion" and "crisis tendencies" of capitalism'.

During the 1960s and 1970s Marxist analyses had re-emerged in other disciplines through the works of Thompson (1968) in social history,

Althusser (1971) in social theory and Williams (1961, 1965, 1977) in literary criticism and cultural studies. Geography followed this trend with Harvey producing some of the most notable work in the form of *Explanation in Geography* (1969) and *Social Justice and the City* (1973). Harvey attempted to explain the spatial structure of the urban landscape by applying a Marxist analysis to production and consumption patterns. Production and capital accumulation, according to structuralist perspectives, were intrinsically linked to the labour market process and the design and function of urban areas. As capitalism has developed, and cities have grown in size and complexity, there has been a shift from manufacturing to service industries as the major urban economic activity. This, in turn, has transformed the urban landscape from being one of production to one of near-simultaneous production and consumption or what de Certeau and others have referred to a 'productive consumption' (Aitchison and Evans 2003). It is in these urban locales that the combined forces of leisure, culture and commerce appear to have most impact in shaping personal and social identities and these sites, processes and performances will be evaluated further in this chapter. The Marxist analyses outlined above were not, however, extended to leisure and tourism geography as this field remained dominated by the positivist paradigm. Moreover, although the late 1970s and early 1980s were to be identified as a period of common reorientation as a result of the impact of Marxist and structuralist theory within many of geography's subdisciplines, any continuity was short-lived. A series of new approaches, labelled variously as post-Marxist, poststructuralist, critical–realist, structurationist, feminist and postmodernist, were soon to pose challenges to the newly established structuralist orthodoxy.

Within social and cultural geography there is an established literature of *spatialised feminism* spanning over two decades (McDowell 1993a). Spatialised feminism refers to feminist analyses that identify and explain the spatial dimensions of power relations between the sexes. These spatial dimensions include the differential use, control, power and domination of space and place and can often be seen in the representation and consumption of leisure-related spaces and places.

The term spatialised feminism serves to encapsulate a wide range of research, undertaken between the mid-1970s and the early 1990s, which drew on structuralist analysis, and particularly socialist feminist analysis. McDowell (1993a) identifies Burnett (1973) as producing the first paper to discuss gender issues in geography. Burnett and other contemporary researchers were largely concerned with issues related to gender and urban space or gender and 'third world' development (Garcia-Ramon *et al.* 1988; Peake 1989; McDowell 1993a, 1993b; McDowell and Sharp 1997; Women and Geography Study Group 1984, 1997). In relation to these research themes, McDowell (1993a) has stated that:

a considerable body of knowledge was built up throughout the 1980s documenting the extent to which women were unequal and subordinate to men. Mapping the forms of this subordination and the extent of geographical variation in their (our) status in the contemporary world is perhaps the most clearly geographical project that has been undertaken by feminists in the discipline.

(McDowell 1993a: 163)

It is only retrospectively, however, that the connections between these previous areas of research and research in gender and leisure have been recognised and articulated. For example, Horst (1981) edited the first book by geographers on 'third world' women, making explicit the gender relations of global capitalism that had been recognised only implicitly by previous research. Horst and others therefore provided, unwittingly, a series of foundations for later feminist analyses of the gender relations of tourism as a significant component of global capitalism. Similarly, Massey (1984) added a feminist perspective to previous work that had analysed the spatial and social divisions of work and urban labour. The interrelationships between the sexual and spatial division of labour and similar divisions visible in leisure and tourism are now apparent and are discussed more fully in Chapter 7 (Adkins 1994; Aitchison 2000d; Jordan 1997; Kinnaird and Hall 1994; Sinclair 1997).

The spatialised feminism of the 1970s conveyed a certainty about the category woman as a key social division. This homogenous vision of women has since been criticised as failing to problematise fully the complex interrelations between gender, sexuality, spatiality and power. One source of this alleged failure was the emphasis on structural rather than cultural determinants of spatial relations and this chapter will go on to illustrate the importance of cultural and symbolic representations of gender and leisure. The spatialised feminist research within geography thus relied upon distributive data to demonstrate that society's gender relations were replicated and/or mirrored in the spatial relations of housing, transport and the workplace.

As the previous chapter indicated, the feminist studies of leisure undertaken in the 1980s contributed most visibly to the sociology of leisure. However, these sociological critiques also contained a significant amount of geographical data. Deem's study of women and leisure in Milton Keynes, for example, found that 'women do not usually feel free to move around town or city centres alone, especially after dark. In Milton Keynes, because of the combined cycle/footpaths and associated underpasses/heavy shrub undergrowth this is a major problem even in daylight hours' (Deem 1986: 46). Deem's research played an important role in beginning to establish the spatial inequity of perceived leisure opportunities for women and men. Whereas men's leisure choices were often determined by 'location, social class, money and interest', women's leisure choices were dominated by fear of violence where the desire for 'safe' leisure meant 'going where there are other women, good transport, and few or no men' (Deem 1986: 7). Similarly, Green *et al.*, reporting on initial findings from their research, stated that:

> women do not feel comfortable or safe on the streets if they are alone there after dark. They cannot therefore come and go as they please, but have to make careful choices about where they spend their leisure time, and about who they spend it with ... not only was travelling to leisure venues a problem for women ... many women did not feel comfortable inside such venues. The majority of women said they would not feel comfortable going by themselves to pubs, clubs, wine bars or cinemas.
>
> (Green, Hebron and Woodward 1985a: 37)

The Sheffield researchers went on to identify that women's policing of their own behaviour was a result of a complex mix of their attitudes to men both as strangers and familiar partners. For example, not only did women often need 'permission' from male partners to frequent certain types of leisure space but women also policed their leisure behaviour in response to male occupation of these leisure spaces and in response to the potential occupation of leisure space for predatory purposes as a result of 'stranger danger'. Thus, women's desires to visit public leisure spaces 'without male partners are often seen as signals of dissatisfaction with current relationships, and may signify the search for a new partner' (Green *et al.* 1990: 121). It is this complexity of interlinking constraining and enabling factors that poststructural feminist theory seeks to untangle to make sense of gender relations.

Social and cultural geographies and gendered leisure space

The first section of this chapter provided evidence to illustrate that the contribution of geography to leisure research is well established. The next section then demonstrated the ways in which the relationship between geography and feminism developed as a result of the theorisation of spatialised feminism. In spite of sociological research of gender and leisure, the relationship between spatiality, gender and leisure remains less clearly articulated. Moreover, while the concepts of spatialised feminism and, more recently, gendered space have been well-documented in geography this is less true in relation to leisure studies. Only recently have leisure and tourism scholars begun to acknowledge that the synergy between gender relations and spatial relations is a major contributor to leisure relations (Aitchison 1999a; Aitchison *et al.* 2000; Watson and Scraton 1998; Wearing 1998). This recent shift can be attributed, in part, to geography's 'cultural turn' and the development of a new kind of social and cultural geography that has included leisure, culture and tourism in its spatial analyses of the last decade (Skelton and Valentine 1997). This section reviews a range of research from social and cultural geography that has impacted upon the development of leisure studies and, more specifically, on the study of gendered leisure space. Much of this research adopts a poststructuralist perspective and integrates social geography with cultural sociology to provide accounts of the spatiality of social and cultural relations in everyday life (Bennett and Watson 2002). In discussing these accounts, the concept of the gaze is also introduced and developed as a means of illustrating the complexity and interrelated nature of social and cultural power in defining leisure relations.

The development of a focus on gendered space rather than spatialised feminism can be seen as an attempt to accommodate many of the criticisms levelled at the structuralist feminist approaches outlined previously. Acknowledgement of the role of gender–power relations in shaping spatial relations has turned our attention from the recognition of *sex inequality* to the recognition of *gender difference*. This perspective can be identified as another of the post-positivist discourses identified by Barnes and Gregory (1997: 2) and introduced above. Together, the perspectives of poststructuralism, postcolonialism, postmodernism and poststructural feminism can be seen as providing a challenge to the homogenising and totalising category *woman*. Indeed, Haraway has stated:

> There is nothing about being 'female' that naturally binds women. There is not even such a state as 'being' female, itself a highly complex category constructed in contested sexual scientific discourses and other social practices. Gender, race or class consciousness is an achievement forced on us by the terrible historical experience of the contradictory social realities of patriarchy, colonialism, racism and capitalism.
> (Haraway 1985: 191)

Theorising gendered space thus offers acknowledgement that gender–spatial relations, which manifest themselves in the productive consumption of spaces and places, are contextually, temporally and locally specific. As outlined in the Introduction, Elshtain (1981) has described structuralist or socio-structural theories as 'narratives of closure' in reference to their totalising explanations of social phenomena as products of material relations. These theories, emphasising the social and material nature of power, often explain power relations in terms of their repression and domination of social groups. In contrast, socio-cultural theories stress that power is 'productive, relational and everywhere' (Cooper 1994). Socio-cultural analyses that focus on the cultural and symbolic nature of power are thus more receptive to the concepts of resistance, transgression and disruption, particularly in relation to the renegotiation of power relations by marginal groups. The remainder of this chapter therefore examines some of these forms of disruption in relation to gender and leisure.

Soja (1985) introduced the concept of *spatiality* to emphasise the socially produced and interpreted nature of space. Contemporary social and cultural geographies demonstrate that space, place and landscape act as *sites* and *sights* of social and cultural inclusion/exclusion and are not fixed but are in a constant state of transition (Urry 1995). These spatial trans-formations result from continuous, dialectical struggles of power and resistance among and between the diversity of providers, users and medi-ators of leisure space (Wearing 1998: 63–70). As such, recent social and cultural geographies place emphasis upon both agency and structure but are simultaneously critical of the work of previous human geographers who 'celebrated' place and failed to problematise space and place in rela-tion to socio-cultural constructs such as gender, sexuality, 'race', class and (dis)ability (Gleeson 1999; Shurmer-Smith and Hannam 1994).

Giddens' (1984) theory of structuration, and the interplay or dialectic between structure and agency, can certainly be identified as influential in these social and cultural geographies. In this recent geographical work, however, structuration theory is widened to embrace the diversity and plurality of agencies, to include the role of agencies previously defined as marginal or peripheral, and to recognise the significance of micro-social and cultural phenomena and subcultures in shaping complex spatial rela-tions. Theorisation of the relationship between society and culture by social and cultural geographers has also drawn on the humanist Marxist tradition of Gramsci (1985), Williams (1977), Thompson (1968) and Berger (1963), all of whom saw the material and symbolic dimensions of the production and reproduction of society as inextricably intertwined.

Current social and cultural geographies therefore provide a meeting ground for the anti-foundationalist movements of postmodernism, post-structuralism and postcolonialism. Their analyses attempt to embrace the complexity of spatiality rather than engaging in the spatial determinism or essentialism of the early twentieth century or the grand narratives of structuralism from two decades or so ago. As Gregory *et al.* (1994: 5) emphasise, 'geography's task is now seen to involve dialogue with other disciplines rather than instruction of them, to produce complication as much as simplification, and to issue admissions of doubt as often as decla-rations of certainty'. This task is in stark contrast to that emphasised by Barnes and Gregory (1997) and outlined at the start of this chapter where *certainty* of empirical observations, *coherence* of patterns, forms and pro-cesses, and *cumulation* of knowledge and discovery were seen as central tenets of a systematic science. This emphasis is not shared by contempo-rary social and cultural geographies where difference and diversity between and within genders and sexualities are frequently revealed in the nuances of marginal social and cultural phenomena and spatial transformations.

Theories emphasising the social *and* cultural construction of space and place have played a central role in establishing the discourse of contemporary social and cultural geographies. Over the last fifteen years a number of prominent geographers have illustrated that, rather than being a physical or objective reality, 'landscape is a cultural image, a pictorial way of representing, structuring and symbolising surroundings' (Daniels and Cosgrove 1988: 1). Spaces and places are seen to represent a social and cultural *geography of the imagination* (Gregory *et al.* 1994) and this point is illustrated aptly by Rose who states, 'Whether written or painted, grown or built, a landscape's meanings draw on the cultural codes of the society for which it was made' (1993: 89). These codes are embedded in social relations and frequently reflected in cultural symbols.

A number of feminist theorists have cautioned against the wholesale adoption of a poststructuralist perspective, as such contextually specific analyses negate theories of power as systemic phenomena. As Chapter 2 highlighted, with no systemic power relations there can be no overall system of domination and oppression, only specific contexts of subordination, resistance and transformation. One of the questions raised in this chapter, then, is the extent to which systemic male power – that is, patriarchy – exists in relation to the production and consumption of leisure space and/or the extent to which localised, contextualised and pluralised power relations exert their influence on the spatiality of leisure and gender. This cautionary note has been signalled by social and cultural geographers too. Bondi (1992a: 166), for example, has urged against prioritising the cultural over the social or the 'unharnessing of the symbolic and the sociological'. As the previous chapter suggested, shifts from structural to cultural analyses within many of the social sciences have led some commentators to view poststructuralism, with its emphasis on the symbolic, as having unharnessed itself from any theoretical perspective that provides a sufficiently rigorous analysis of social, material and systemic power (Gregory *et al.* 1994: 10).

The challenge for social and cultural geographies of gender and leisure is therefore to provide a broad analysis of the cultural 'fragments and differences' in the interrelationships between these social and cultural phenomena while simultaneously attending to broader structural relations of power and place. A number of social scientists have recently attempted to achieve just such synergy between structural and cultural analyses of gender, leisure and place although this research has rarely been framed explicitly as *leisure geographies* or *geographies of leisure*. A brief summary of a sample of recent research and writing serves to demonstrate the centrality of leisure to contemporary social, cultural and gender analyses of space and place. Here it is worth distinguishing between place as an objective and locational reality and space as the social and cultural manifestation of such locations. In this way, place can be conceived of as fixed while space is fluid and subject to transformation as a result of social and cultural change. For example, recent research has contributed to our under-standing of leisure and tourism spaces ranging in scale from the proximity of body space to the intangibility of cyber space (Duncan 1996; Crang *et al.* 1999). In addition to their focus on urban space, social and cultural geographies of leisure have also addressed issues of performance space, transitory space and liminal space: definitions of space that are central to leisure and tourism studies' discourse. Clearly defined leisure and tourism sites that have formed the basis of geographical research have included the gym, the pub, the club, the holiday, the theme park, the monument, the festival, and the parade, among others (Aitchison 1999b, 2000e; Aitchison and Jordan 1998; Aitchison *et al.* 2000; Bell and Binnie 1998; Nast and Pile 1998; Pritchard *et al.* 2002; Shurmar-Smith and Hannam 1994; Skelton and Valentine 1997).

Gender, leisure and the place of 'the gaze'

Implicit within many of the analyses referred to above, and central to the discussions throughout the remainder of this chapter, is the concept of the gaze. References to *the tourist gaze* entered the discourse of tourism studies following the publication of Urry's book of that title in 1990. Previously, the concept of 'the gaze' was more commonly discussed by poststructuralist writers such as Foucault (1976: 89). Central to the concept of the 'gaze' is the belief that knowledge is both socially constructed and socially constructing. The power of the gaze is unequally distributed and the object of the gaze is constructed according to the locus of power and control. Theories accentuating the social–cultural nexus emphasise that, through the act of the gaze, people, 'differently engaged and differ-ently empowered, appropriate and contest their landscapes' in different ways (Bender 1993: 17). Bender goes on to claim:

> Landscapes are thus polysemic, and not so much artefact as in process of construction and reconstruction ... The landscape is never inert, people engage with it, re-work it, appropriate and contest it. It is part of the way in which identities are created and disputed, whether as individual, group, or nation-state.
>
> (Bender 1993: 3)

One of the most significant sites and sights of leisure represented in this recent literature is that of the street. Geographies of the street have shifted from viewing the street as a place of residence or business to a place of leisure, productive consumption, identity formation, fashion, spec-tacle and performativity. Poststructural analyses, embraced by contem-porary social and cultural geographies, offer an insight into the contested, negotiated and renegotiated nature of the street as a site of leisure. In the introduction to *Images of the Street*, Fyfe (1998: 1) describes streets as 'the terrain of social encounters and political protest, sites of domination and resistance, places of pleasure and anxiety'. Rendell (1998: 75) demonstrates how, even in the early nineteenth century, the street became a site for the 'spatial representation of gendered identities'. Wearing (1998: 64) points out that more recently, 'In our own time we have the use of public spaces such as streets and parks in leisure time for demonstrations focussed on the Vietnam War, Aboriginal land rights, gay rights, women's rights, environmental and peace issues'. In addition to organised protest, however, the street is a site of everyday ritual and resistance where formally planned places can become culturally contested spaces. In analyses that acknowledge the continuing influence of the structural constraints of class and gender while simultaneously engaging with the poststructural possibilities of cultural contestation, Skeggs (1999) and Pritchard *et al.* (2002) reveal the difficulties that women experience in appropriating space in Manchester's gay village as a result of what Pritchard *et al.* (2002) refer to as the 'homo-patriarchic power dialectics characterising its socio-cultural construction'. This theorisation builds on previous research that has contended that gender is critical to the construction of leisure and tourism space and that the interrelationship between gender and space can be conceptualised as a 'gender–space dialectic' (Aitchison 2004; Aitchison and Reeves 1998).

Foucault introduced us to the concept of social and cultural surveillance. The introduction of closed-circuit television (CCTV) has increased the surveillance capacity of modern cities (Rule 1973). Surveillance of the street has, according to Fyfe and Bannister (1998: 263), contributed to the privatisation, purification and homogenisation of public space. This perspective views the proliferation of activities deemed counter to the interests of business, civic pride or city residents as arrested, both metaphorically and literally, as a result of the gaze of the camera. The prohibition of certain types of leisure-related behaviour, such as consuming alcohol in the street in certain towns and cities, is given greater enforcement under the watchful eye of CCTV. Miles (1997: 197) refers to the 'spread of surveillance culture' within urban streets and Foucault, invoking a central tenet of poststructural theory, suggested that this regulation of public space was also a regulator of bodies and body space (Grosz 1995a). We are perhaps more familiar with the presence of surveillance cameras in our indoor streets or shopping malls and Davis (1990: 240) refers to the contemporary shopping centre as 'the mall-as-panoptican-prison' which presents an interesting interplay between the concepts of the gaze and surveillance theorised in *Discipline and Punish* (Foucault 1977). There is a counter-discourse, however, that views CCTV as a protector of diversity. The presence of the cameras can be used for protective as well as punitive policing. Proponents of the use of CCTV point to its central role in policing racist attacks and harassment of women in our city centres. Indeed, the use of CCTV has almost become a marketing feature in place promotion. The English town of Cirencester, for example, informs visitors arriving by road that they are entering 'Cirencester: now a safer town with CCTV'.

Grosz (1995b) points to the male domination of public leisure spaces such as the street by the *flâneur*. Wilson (1995: 65) describes the conceptualisation of the nineteenth-century *flâneur* as 'a man of pleasure, a man who takes visual possession of the city, who has emerged in postmodern feminist discourse as the embodiment of the 'male gaze' through his use of public space to display and perform his hegemonic social and cultural identity.' Poststructural critiques of the *flâneur* draw on de Certeau's notion of 'space as practiced place' where, 'the street defined by urban planning is the place which becomes transformed into space by the people who use it' (de Certeau 1988: 117). Grosz (1995b) and Wearing and Wearing (1996) develop the concept of the chora to articulate a space with the potential for women to belong, to be and to become rather than to be gazed upon. Wearing (1998: 133) sees *flâneurs* as 'involved in fleeting observations rather than interacting people with possibilities for expansion of the self through leisure experiences'. She advocates the use of the term 'Choraster' 'as a feminised conceptualisation of those who interact in a constructive or creative way with others in city leisure spaces' (Wearing 1998: 133). Thus, both the *flâneur* and the choraster are involved in 'performing' gender although the performances themselves serve to construct the very genders they appear to express (Butler 1990, 1993; Grosz 1994). Butler (1990: 33) explains the performative nature of gender as 'a set of repeated acts within a highly rigid regulatory frame that congeals over time to produce the appearance of substance'. This conceptualisation of performativity, developed from Lyotard's theorisation of the way in which particular actions become legitimised within society, has been important in recent theorisations of leisure within both everyday and embodied contexts and has thus addressed a significant gap in the previous leisure studies literature (Lyotard 1984).

Poststructural theories of sex and gender

The previous chapter discussed ways in which the binary divide of work–leisure has served to marginalise many informal leisure activities, including women's leisure, from the leisure research agenda. Consequently, the attention of leisure researchers was initially directed away from everyday leisure spaces and towards the leisure environments associated with paid leisure-related employment and formal leisure participation as recreation from paid employment. 'Hidden' forms of leisure associated with the home, with children, or related to household work, shopping, or everyday consumption have frequently been omitted from empirical research within mainstream leisure studies. In contrast, informal leisure has begun to be researched and theorised within social and cultural geography, cultural sociology, cultural studies and gender studies. These subject areas have also been receptive to studying the leisure participation of individuals and groups such as gay men and 'lesbians' who were previously hidden or marginalised from mainstream research that either ignored women or homogenised women by treating them as one group.

In 1991, the publication of David Bell's article, 'Insignificant others: lesbian and gay geographies', together with an Economic and Social Research Council project undertaken by Gill Valentine to research 'The geography of a lesbian community', drew geographers' attention to the role of spatiality as an important factor in shaping sexual identity, particularly in relation to leisure spaces and places. Valentine's research resulted in a series of articles in mainstream geography journals that were to confirm the place of gender and sexuality on the newly mapped agenda of poststructural social and cultural geographical research (Valentine 1993a, 1993b, 1993c). The following year saw the introduction of *Gender, Place and Culture, A Journal of Feminist* Geography which published 'All hyped up and no place to go', an article that embraced poststructural theory to address the spatiality of sexuality and leisure and which stimulated considerable critical debate within the next issue (Bell *et al.* 1994):

> Work on what we might call lesbian and gay spaces has made equally apparent this notion of a mutual relationship between space and identity. It has been shown that sexual identity impacts on the use and reading of space, and that the socially and culturally encoded character of space has bearing on the assuming and acting out of sexual identities.
>
> (Bell *et al.* 1994: 32)

The relationship between male sexualities and leisure had already received critical attention a few years earlier when Shields combined sociology and cultural geography to give his account of the role of spatiality, sexuality and leisure in transforming both the material and symbolic landscape of Brighton. Chronicling the place of Brighton's mods, rockers, 'the dirty weekend', and gay sex, in a chapter in *Places on the Margin: Alternative Geographies of Modernity*, Shields was to generate further interest in leisure phenomena within other areas of the social sciences. Similarly, Mort's (1996) *Cultures of Consumption: Masculinities and Social Space* linked cultural sociology with cultural geography to provide an analysis of the interactions between gender, consumerism, fashion and leisure space.

In 1995 Routledge published Bell and Valentine's co-edited collection *Mapping Desire: Geographies of Sexualities* that brought work on previously marginal topics further into the mainstream of geographical discourse. Each chapter focused upon the geography of sexuality and examined the construction of sexual identities through a variety of leisure forms, activities and locations including literature and film, street culture and body fashion. In economic geography, traditionally the preserve of positivist research, the impact of poststructural geography together with gender studies and queer studies, began to be felt as leisure providers acknowledged the value of the 'pink pound' and 'lavender leisure' (Aitchison and Reeves 1998; Aitchison, Macleod and Shaw 2000; Bell and Binnie 1998; Gluckman and Reed 1997; Knopp 1995, 1997; Lauria and Knopp 1985; Munt 1995; Pritchard *et al.* 1998). Gluckman and Reed (1997: xvii) stated that 'whatever its implications for the gay community as a whole – the recognition of gay men and lesbians as an important economic constituency in the early nineties was a long time in the making'. Duncan's (1996) edited collection, *BodySpace: Destabilising Geographies of Gender and Sexuality*, then brought together a collection of research identifying 'knowledge as embodied, engendered and embedded in the material context of place and space'. By the end of the 1990s, research papers addressing the sexuality of leisure and tourism space had been published in many of the major leisure and tourism journals. Many of these geographies demonstrated the 'normalisation' of heterosexuality or heterosexual performativity within leisure spaces. Here, dominant and reiterated performances of sexuality were seen to inscribe and repeat particular forms of spatial identity from a corporeal scale through to the scale of the city itself. But, the contestation, subversion and transgression of such dominant spatial identities and patterns has become an increasing focus of contemporary social and cultural geographies (Aitchison 1999a; Pritchard and Morgan 2000; Skeggs 1999).

Gender, leisure and the place of 'the dualism'

In addition to interrogating the work–leisure dichotomy, recent post-structural research has identified the need to appraise such dichotomies or binaries as 'dualisms' or couplings where one part of the couple is dependent on the other for its definition and identity. The distinguishing feature between a dichotomy and a dualism is that of an identifiable power relationship. Whereas a dichotomy is constructed of two equal parts, a dualistic construct is formed where one part of the dichotomy is attributed or imbued with more power than the other. Paradoxically, however, the dominant part of the dualism is dependent upon the existence of the subordinate part to create the appearance of power that then serves to sustain such a power relationship. Thus, 'binary oppositions always support a hierarchy or an economy of value that operates by subordinating one term to another' (Peters 1999: 13). Within feminist geography, the gendered construction of dualisms has been revealed in relation to the dichotomies of nature–culture, urban–rural, masculine–feminine (Rose 1993). The post-Enlightenment valorisation of such dualisms within western society is founded on, and subsequently reproduces, constructions of the subordinate, the subaltern and 'the Other'. Such dualistic power relations are the outcome of the zero-sum-game that has constructed both capitalist and patriarchal relations. But poststructural theory goes further than the critiques offered by spatialised feminism in that it extends the critique of such couplings to the relationship between sex and gender.

Previous liberal, socialist and radical feminist theories have asserted that sex is the fixed biological nature of the body in contrast to gender as the mutable character of the body (Brooks 1997). In other words, sex has been assumed to be a pre-given biological category to which bodies are *ascribed* and gender is seen to be the socially constructed character with which bodies are *inscribed*. Thus sex is seen to form the site upon which gender is then constructed (Nicholson 1995: 41). The feminist project has focused on the construction of gender and has attempted to seek equality between genders without questioning the categories of sex. This has resulted in calls from liberal, socialist and radical feminists for the deconstruction of the gender categories of masculine and feminine rather than questioning the existence of the sexes of male and female per se. This splitting of body and mind is attributed to the Cartesian dualism of mind–body where the mind is associated with male rationality, mastery, culture and superiority and the body is associated with female irrationality, subordination, nature and inferiority. As Wearing (1996: 47) points out: 'It is, however, a reflection of the present day male-defined dichotomy of mind/male, female/body that sociological studies to date, even those with a feminist emphasis, have generally concentrated on women's bodies and men's minds'. Thus many social sciences, including leisure studies and tourism studies, have been 'disembodied' in their study of the subject field and the subject itself (Aitchison 2001b, 2001c, 2003b).

In contrast, poststructural feminist theorists have revealed the interdependent and dualistic character of the categories of sex and gender. The distinction between sex and gender has, therefore, been criticised as yet another dualism that has served to elevate the male sex at the expense of the female gender. Writing from a poststructural feminist perspective, Butler (1990, 1993), Grosz (1994, 1995a) and Gatens (1992, 1996) contend that sex is not an objective reality but that the two ideal types of male and female are constructed hierarchically through cultural and discursive practices and performances including the practice of gender. Such theorists then talk about 'performing' our genders or 'doing gender'. Such a perspective views the reworking of the category of gender as only a partial reworking of the regulatory power of sex and gender that defines women and therefore femininity. Moreover, Butler's (1990) work has been instrumental in destabilising the authority of sex in the sex–gender dualism by arguing that it is through regulatory practices that gender reproduces sex as the embodiment of cultural practice:

If the immutable character of sex is contested, perhaps the construct of 'sex' is as culturally constructed as gender, with the consequence that the distinction between sex and gender turns out to be no distinction at all ... Indeed, sex, by definition, will be shown to have been gender all along.

(Butler 1990: 7–8)

Wearing (1998: 108–109), in reviewing the poststructural position, states that 'gender subsumes sex' because 'sex is not a pre-given object, but an ideal construct reified through cultural discourses'. Thus feminist analysis has identified the dualism of male–female as illustrative of patriarchal power relationships and poststructural gender analyses have extended this analysis to the sex–gender dualism. The body of theoretical work labelled 'queer theory' has taken such analyses to another level by pointing to the heterosexual–homosexual dualism as an essential foundation for the maintenance of compulsory heterosexuality:

The institution of a compulsory and naturalised heterosexuality requires and regulates gender as a binary relation in which the masculine term is differentiated from a feminine term, and this differentiation is accomplished through the practices of heterosexual desire. The act of differentiating the two oppositional moments of the binary results in a consolidation of each term, the respective internal coherence of sex, gender, and desire.

(Butler 1990: 23)

From colonial to postcolonial and 'Other' geographies

The early emphasis on physical geographical analysis was often developed in relation to specific regions of the world and coincided with the maturing of the nation state, colonial expansion, and imperialist interest in defining, mapping and characterising areas of the globe according to identified regional characteristics or differences. Indeed, Barnes and Gregory (1997: 16) point out that it can be argued that geography 'helped to provide a logistical basis for modern warfare, to foster a sense of national and imperial identity, to administer colonies, and to compile resource inventories for commercial exploitation'. In other words, geography did not develop as an impartial, detached, neutral set of perspectives through which 'objective knowledge' and 'truth' could be established. Instead, geography's *modus operandum* was inherently related to the legitimisation and reproduction of existing and emerging power structures.

These uncritical approaches, however, serve to construct place identities imbued with cultural meanings. Places may be represented differently across time and space and even between different people at the same time and in the same place. Shurmer-Smith and Hannam (1994: 13) alert us to this view by emphasising that 'place is a deceptively simple concept in geographical thought'. From a distance, places can be seen as foreign and exotic, while they may be familiar or even 'home' when viewed from close proximity. Dualistic notions of near and far, home and away, local and distant, familiar and foreign then serve to construct that which is perceived to be known and unknown. The known places and people are those that we view as being similar to, alike, or the same as us, whereas those places and people with which we are unfamiliar often take on the image of the Other.

Postcolonial geographies are concerned with identifying, explaining and invoking notions of the Other and can be viewed as part of a wider series of *post-positivist geographies* including postmodernism and poststructuralism (Barnes and Gregory 1997: 2). Although the focus of each post-positivist geography is different, they embrace a commonality in their rejection of the grand narratives and totalising visions of truth and objectivity that were portrayed by the previous positivist geography. Indeed, Sibley (1995: 137) asserts that this emphasis on difference and devolution of power has posed a problem for 'a subject whose history is so much bound up with colonialism'.

Rose (1995: 116) explains this process of constructing the Other or Othering as 'defining where you belong through a contrast with other places, or who you are through a contrast with other people'. Later, drawing on the work of Irigary, Rose (1996) illustrated that the binary distinctions between self and other, and real and imagined space, are part of what Butler (1990: 13) has referred to as 'the epistemological, ontological and logical structures of a masculinist signifying economy'. Thus, the construction of dualisms or binary opposites is inherently related to the construction of the Other. Developing work by Cixous (1983/92), it is possible to identify three fundamental relationships within this process. First, the construction of the Other is dependent upon a simultaneous construction of 'the Same', or something from which to be Other to. Second, this relationship is one of power whereby that which is defined as 'Same' is accorded greater power and status than that which is defined as Other. Third, that which is defined as Other is attributed a gender and this gender is usually feminised: 'the concept of women as Other ... involves the central claim that Otherness is projected on to women by, and in the interests of, men, such that we are constructed as inferior and abnormal' (Wilkinson and Kitzinger 1996: 3–4).

Both feminist and anthropological analyses have informed the theoretical conceptualisation of Othering (de Beauvoir 1949; Wilkinson and Kitzinger 1996; Clifford and Marcus 1986; Fowler and Hardesty 1994; Said 1978, 1993). Leisure studies has, until very recently, given little attention to the subject of Othering (Aitchison 2000a). Tourism studies literature, however, has addressed the issue but has drawn almost exclusively upon anthropology rather than, or in addition to, feminism to inform its analysis of the Other (Aitchison 2001a). Most writers in tourism anthropology and tourism sociology cite Said (1978) as the originator of the concept of the Other, in reference to the western social construction of 'Orientalism' (Selwyn 1996). The existing literature within the fields of tourism anthropology and tourism sociology can thus be seen to have contributed to a tension with feminist and gender studies. Discussions of the concept of the Other in relation to anthropological representations of 'race' and ethnicity have thus formed part of a male-dominated discourse that ignores the wealth of feminist writing on the Other underpinned by the much earlier references to woman as the Other by de Beauvoir (1949: 18) in which she described how 'Humanity is male and man defines woman not in herself but as relative to him ... He is the Subject, he is the Absolute – she is the Other'.

Developing de Beauvoir's critique, poststructural feminists have challenged the totalising theories propounded by radical feminism's grand narratives. Radical feminists such as Jeffreys (1999), who has attempted to provide a feminist analysis of sex tourism, have been criticised for what appears to be a willingness to speak for and on behalf of others. Addressing Rojek's criticism that feminist leisure studies had failed to address deviant leisure, Russell offers a radical feminist critique of pornography and prostitution as 'leisure' (Rojek 2000). In contrast to Rojek, however, Russell defends the totalising perspective of radical feminism by arguing that if she is not to represent the Other then she would have to restrict her research to 'upper-class, white South African-born ex-Anglican women in their 50s, who now live in America. If we do not continue to "take on the whole world", many of us could not do research or publish material that contributes to furthering radical feminist goals' (Russell 1996: 92).

Wilkinson and Kitzinger (1996: 5) draw our attention to different ways of theorising Otherness, including *Other Others* as a way of revealing marginalised groups within an already marginalised group. Stanley (1997: 13–14) asks in relation to feelings of not belonging: 'is this because lesbian women are among the other Others? Because feminist women are among Other others? And when I feel an alien among lesbians and a stranger among feminists, is that just my personal oddity?' hooks (1990), writing from a postcolonial and black feminist perspective has stressed poignantly:

> I am waiting for them to stop talking about the 'Other', to stop describing how important it is to be able to speak about difference. It is not just important what we speak about, but how and why we speak ... Often this speech about the 'Other' annihilates, erases: 'no need to hear your voice when I can talk about you better than you can speak about yourself. No need to hear your voice. Only tell me about your pain. I want to know your story. And then I will tell it back to you in a new way. Tell it back to you in such a way that

it has become mine, my own. Re-writing you, I write myself anew.
I am still author, authority. I am still the colonizer, the speaking
subject, and you are now at the center of my talk.

(hooks 1990: 151–152)

In relation to tourism, the 'speaking subject' is frequently the western
tour operator and the 'centre of the talk' the former colony and colonised
people. In this respect, both postcolonial and poststructural feminist
analyses of tourism might find it difficult to argue that power is located
in anything other than white capitalist/imperialist hands. In spite of theoretical progress in gender studies and cultural theory more widely, tourism
studies has afforded few critiques of the colonial legacy or gendered
construction of Othering that forms such a central component of the
tourism industry. Tourist destinations as *sites* for tourists, and the people
within them as *sights* for the tourist as *flâneur*, are frequently rendered
Other by a tourist industry that has developed an unsigned colonialist
and gendered hegemony in the form of a set of descriptors for constructing
and representing *tropical paradise*. These descriptors signify a colonial
legacy where places are viewed as mystical or treasured landscapes
preserved by time to be explored, and often exploited, in their natural
state. The people within these landscapes are frequently portrayed as
passive but grateful recipients of white explorers from urbanised and industrialised countries searching for their authentic origins. For example, in
promoting Antigua and Barbuda, a Thompson holiday brochure (1999:
261) emphasised whiteness and equated whiteness with purity and
femininity: 'The sand is so soft, white and so fine you could almost use
it for baking. On Barbuda, tinted by coral, it is faintly pink – like a very
pale face powder'.

The construction of the Other is thus pivotal to the (post)colonial culture and global capitalism of leisure and tourism. Characterised by
dualisms, the process of representing Others inevitably defines norms and
deviants, centres and margins, cores and peripheries, the powerful and the
powerless. For example, the ethnographic postcard or the tourist brochure
purports to illustrate that which is both indigenous and authentic. These
images (re)construct and (re)present both people and places out of context,
while simultaneously projecting a particular symbolism in the way in which
artefacts and events are pictorialised. Invariably, such images, whether they
are of people (usually women) or places, convey impressions of exotic,
unspoilt, natural, virginal and desirable spaces. These spaces and places,
including corporeal landscapes, are frequently represented in tourist brochures as 'hidden treasures' or as canvases upon which the explorer or the
tourist can make his (sic) mark without any local resistance.

While critiques of Othering appear to have escaped the tourism industry,
they are beginning to be made more visible within tourism studies. Edwards
(1996), for example, has undertaken extensive anthropological analysis of

the ethnographic postcard reiterating Enloe's (1989: 19) assertion that, 'selecting postcards is one of those seemingly innocent acts that has become fraught with ideological risks'. Edwards (1996: 200) argues that 'The metaphorical or semiotic framework in which postcard imagery operates is . . . clearly articulated if it is related to two influential theories of tourism: first, MacCannell's analysis of the quest for the authentic (1976) and, second, Graburn's hypothesis (1977) that tourism is akin to a sacred experience'. She goes on to critique MacCannell's theory as 'deeply structuralist and totalising' but the search for authenticity is still clearly represented in the tourist media. Similarly, Dann (1993) has provided extensive sociological and gender critiques of tourist brochures. Building on Bourdieu's (1984) concept of cultural capital, Urry (1990) has also acknowledged that the medium through which the tourist destination is consumed contributes to our cultural capital of travel-related knowledge. These cultural representations are clearly gendered and are communicated through the structures and practices of the tourism industry.

MacCannell (1976) initially explained the desire for images of exotic and virginal *tropical paradises* as the tourist's search for authenticity. The tourism industry, in its appeal to the *Robinson Crusoe* or *Castaway* in what Plog (1974) termed the 'allocentric tourist', panders to such imaginings by brand-marketing destinations such as Mauritius as *Maurice: Ile Paradis*. This desire to discover and consume our own Xanadu or Eldorado has come to typify the human condition and our insatiable desire for what is perceived to be the authentic Other:

> The guide begins to paddle back to shore. As they round the spit into the lagoon, they see the pristine stretch of sand, the thicket of jungle with its chaste sprinkling of thatched roofs, and, beyond, them, boldly silhouetted against the golden sunset, the black tracery of a gigantic crane. He feels cheated. He had come a long way to get here, and he would have to go even further to get nowhere.
>
> (Lencek and Bosker 1999: 269)

Acknowledging the futility of this search for authenticity, and building on the work of Boorstin (1964), Turner and Ash (1975) have reflected on the possibility that tourists seek out, not authenticity, but the pseudo-event. In other words, there is an awareness among some tourists that they are engaged in consuming and (re)producing the Other. For many tourists, however, the destination can never live up to the paradise and gendered image of the air-brushed brochure. Thus an irony of global capitalism, and its mainstay of enforced homogeneity, is that the world's largest industry relies upon the marketing of *difference*, and the (re)production of both places and people as the desirable Other, to sustain itself: 'Exotic, indigenous beaches were painstakingly and self-consciously re-decorated to appear "authentic", as though they had not in fact been expressly constructed, in the manner of stage props, for an ethnographically accurate experience of the beach' (Lencek and Bosker 1999: 275).

In developing such critiques both poststructural feminism and post-colonial feminism have placed emphasis on the textual, discursive and performative construction of the Other in the reinscription of gender–power relations. Together, these post-positivist perspectives have laid bare tourism's inherent paradox: although associated with a globalised melting pot where postmodern deconstruction and reconstruction have induced the breakdown of previous national, cultural and geographical bound-aries, the mechanisms employed in contemporary tourism development have simultaneously served to strengthen, rather than destabilise, gendered representations of space and place alongside notions of nationalism and bounded cultural identities. In other words, while crossing national boundaries, the global tourism industry simultaneously serves to reinscribe the Otherness of culture and, particularly, the Otherness of women and black people: 'Host societies differentiated by race/ethnicity, colonial past, or social position from the consumer societies are sold with feminised images. The tourism product – as a combination of services, culture, and geographic location – is consumed in situ, in various transactions from tourist gazing to the selling of otherness' (Swain 1995: 249).

The increasing ease of travel to what, until only recently, were defined as long-haul destinations provides both stimulation and demand for these images of Others. This invitation to recreate colonial consumption is rein-forced through the language, images and discourse of tourist brochures produced by tour operators and displayed on the shelves of high street travel agents from where they are consumed by potential tourists. Central to this process of productive consumption is the construction of places and people as foreign, exotic and Other. Tourist destinations and tourism hosts are represented as pure and authentic rather than being viewed as constantly evolving places and people with changing characteristics resulting from the mutually informing processes of production and consumption derived from that in-betweenness of global and local, tourist and host. Feminised, sexualised and racialised imagery can be seen to inform a symbiotic relationship between colonialism and sexism that constantly reinvents itself within the globalised tourism industry. While there are tensions between poststructural and postcolonial feminisms, the contribution of both to feminist analyses of tourism should therefore be acknowledged.

Rojek and Urry (1997: 11) have stressed that cultural tourism disrupts the dichotomies of home–abroad and host–guest by producing 'spaces of in-betweenness inhabited by various types of traveller and tourist'. Edensor (2000) has also argued that distinctions can be drawn between tourist performances conducted in *enclavic* tourism spaces and those conducted in *heterogeneous* tourism spaces. Heterogeneous tourist spaces he describes as 'usually located in non-Western destinations where tourism has often emerged in an unplanned and contingent process' (Edensor 2000: 331). Although neither Rojek and Urry (1997) nor Edensor (2000) develop a gender analysis, a fusion of their theories does suggests the potential contribution that poststructural analyses can make to our understanding of these heterogeneous spaces of in-betweenness, while postcolonial analyses offer insights into power relations between colonial powers and many nonwestern destinations. Wearing (1998: 179) has suggested that the tourist metaphor of intermixing of different ethnic cultures through hybridity 'may be applied to male and female cultures as well as to racial and ethnic cultures based on geographical location. Leisure then becomes a space for both men and women to move beyond gendered stereotypes'. Thus, instead of seeing relations between people, places and power as immutable, these cultural webs and networks, including their spaces of in-betweenness, offer connections and conduits to processes of cultural transformation and hybridity:

> These [tourist] cultures are impure and are being continuously re-invented ... if this is the case it poses a major challenge for the traditional understanding of travel within the sociology of tourism. The dominant position is that tourism should be interpreted as a quest for authenticity.
>
> (Rojek and Urry 1997: 1)

Overview

This chapter has sought to place gender and leisure within a discussion of geographical theories that complements the critical appraisal of gender and leisure from sociological perspectives presented in the previous chapter. The chapter offered a chronological account of the development of geographical theories that have engaged with studies of gender and leisure. Within this chronology, the gaze, dualistic thinking and the representation of Others were introduced as key concepts in social and cultural geographies of gender and leisure. The chronological review provided a historical overview of geographical analyses of gender and leisure relations together with an evaluation of how such relations shape the production and consumption of leisure and tourism spaces and places as both gendered sites and sights. Commencing with accounts that stressed the physical, material and absolute nature of space, the chronology progressed to a discussion of recent analyses that emphasise the socio-cultural, symbolic and relative nature of space.

Geographies of leisure and leisure geographies formed the first phase of the chronology and this phase was characterised by positivist approaches and the absence of feminist or gender analyses. The second phase of the chronological account charted the rise of structuralist interpretations of space and place within geography and the development of spatialised feminism as an explanatory framework developed by socialist feminist geographers. The chronology then took a 'cultural turn' by exploring the gaze of social and cultural geographers and the inclusion of leisure and cultural analyses within the new cultural geography. This then informed a critique of poststructural theories of sex and gender following which the concept of the dualism was explained as a central axis in the production and reproduction of gender-leisure relations. The final phase in the chronology of geography, gender and leisure then explored developments from colonial to postcolonial and 'Other' geographies where the concept of 'the Other' was introduced and ways of representing Others were explored in relation to gender, leisure and tourism. The concept of the Other is revisited in Chapter 6 when the place of women and gender research in higher education is evaluated in relation to leisure studies. First, however, the book shifts its attention from gender, leisure and geographical theory to leisure policy as the mechanism by which theory is translated into practice.

5 Gender and leisure policy

Introduction: the politics of equity

Policy is the mechanism by which theory is translated into practice in a coherent and accountable way. The development, implementation, monitoring and evaluation of policy enable values and principles espoused in social and cultural theory to become enshrined within leisure provision and management. Feminist input into leisure policy is therefore crucial in ensuring progress towards gender equity. With a few exceptions, there has been limited research of leisure policy undertaken from a feminist perspective (Aitchison 1995, 1997b, 2002b; Aitchison *et al.* 1999; Henderson and Bialeschki 1993; Kay 2000; Parratt, 2002). However, as Chapter 3 discussed, there is a strong tradition of research within leisure studies that explores issues of social inclusion more generally and this is particularly the case within leisure studies in the UK. Since the 1980s and 1990s, the leisure studies literature has expanded to include evaluations of the role of the arts, leisure, sport and tourism in a range of policy initiatives designed to promote social inclusion, community development, urban regeneration, neighbourhood renewal and healthy living (Aitchison 2003c, 2003d; Aitchison and Evans 2003; Appleton 2002; Bianchini and Parkinson 1993; Bramham 1989; Coalter 2001; Coalter *et al.* 1988; Hardy *et al.* 1996; Haywood 1994; Henry 1997; Long *et al.* 2002; McCarthy and Lloyd 1999; McDonald and Tungatt 1992; Richards 1995; Veal 2002; Voase 1997; Wynne 1992). It is within this body of academic literature, alongside wider critiques of social and public policy, that we must read between the lines to form accounts of leisure policy as it serves to construct and contest the dominant leisure policy agendas and the inclusion and exclusion of marginalised groups, including women and girls, within these agendas (Bauman 1998; Byrne 1999; Sibley 1995). Insights into the ways in which social policy shapes leisure relations can also be gleaned from studying the influence of social policy on the family and the way in which family structures and relations then shape gender relations. However, a discussion of this area is beyond the scope of this chapter and has been articulated clearly in research by Kay (2000). The chapter does, however, explore how we can discern valuable information about the ways in which gender is included and excluded in leisure-related policy by evaluating the extensive literature on sport policy that has evolved over the last two decades.

In spite of leisure being a predominantly market-led sector, it is clear that the UK's public-policy-driven leisure in society approach, as outlined in Chapter 3, has been highly influential in determining leisure policies that have sought to reduce inequality in leisure provision and participation. Rojek (2000), however, is critical of the policy responses of the three major leisure studies' schools of thought and the way in which each has sought to shape leisure policy:

> Inequality is part of every known society. As such, issues of inequality are central to leisure. The bankruptcy of the functionalist approach to leisure lies precisely in its failure to deal with questions of inequality in a convincing way (Parker 1983, Roberts 1978, 1981). But the critical analysis of Marxist writers on leisure (Clarke and Critcher 1985) or feminist commentators (Bialeschki and Henderson 1986; Scraton and Talbot 1989), hardly suggests more tenable responses. Each emphasises the looming presence of respectively, class and gender in leisure relations, so that the genuine autonomy achieved in leisure practice is obscured.
>
> (Rojek 2000: 206–207)

There are now some very detailed historical accounts of the ways in which leisure and sport policy has influenced the development of women's leisure and sport participation. These accounts serve to chronicle the many ways in which women's 'autonomy in leisure practice has been obscured' (Bailey 1978, 1989; Bland 1995; Clarke and Critcher 1985; Cunningham 1980; Davies 1992; Guttman 1991; Hargreaves 1994; Henry 1993; Holt 1989; McCrone 1988, 1991; Walvin 1978). This chapter begins with an overview of the ways in which public policy shaped the leisure experiences of English working-class women from the eighteenth to the early twentieth centuries (Parratt 2002). The chapter then moves on to examine the development of contemporary leisure policies designed to address social exclusion. This section highlights the influence of socialist feminism and structuralist critiques more generally in the creation of policies that have sought to adopt leisure-related strategies as a means of addressing social exclusion. The UK's central government department responsible for leisure policy development is then introduced in a section that outlines the structure and organisation of leisure and sport policy in the UK. This section reveals the significance of Sport England (formerly the Sports Council) in implementing policies designed to promote gender equity in sport. Although it is possible to point to a range of policy successes this section also highlights some of the failings of gender-related sport policy, the role of the media and commerce in sustaining gender inequity in sport, and the need for other mechanisms for bringing about change. One such change agent has been the UK Women's Sports Foundation (WSF) and the work and policies of the WSF are examined in detail.

The chapter then redirects attention from national policy debates to the implementation of leisure-related policy at a local level. Here, the changing nature of local authorities and their impact on leisure provision and participation is examined in a discussion of UK local authority leisure policy spanning the last two decades. The introduction of the market to public sector leisure provision is critiqued in an account of the implementation, in the late 1980s, of Compulsory Competitive Tendering (CCT) in UK leisure services and the subsequent impact of CCT on women's leisure participation. The role of leisure plans and strategies in the delivery of gender equity is then explored and the recent development of Local Cultural Strategies, with their frequent focus on social inclusion, is discussed.

A historical context to gender and leisure policy

Although leisure scholars have been able to draw on texts illuminating sport history (for example, Vamplew (1988) *Pay Up and Play the Game: Professional Sport in Britain 1875–1914*) and women's sporting history (Hargreaves (1994) *Sporting Females: Critical Issues in the History and Sociology of Women's Sports*), our knowledge of leisure history has been less well supported by academic literature. In the UK, for example, Clarke and Critcher's (1985) *The Devil Makes Work: Leisure in Capitalist Britain* and Cunningham's (1980) even earlier *Leisure in the Industrial Revolution: 1780–1880* still provide the mainstay of teaching related to leisure history. In contrast, Parratt's (2002) *More Than Mere Amusement: Working-Class Women's Leisure in England, 1750–1914* provides a chronological critique of gender and leisure from the beginnings of industrialisation in England to the outbreak, in Europe, of the First World War. The scale of the revolutionary changes that took place during this 165-year period in both work and leisure and, more importantly, in the relationships between work and leisure, cannot be overstated. Parratt's history of leisure or a leisure history therefore provides a useful addition to the leisure studies literature by incorporating 'women and their leisure experiences into the existing scholarship on the history of English working-class culture and thus begin to fill a significant gap in what is otherwise an extensive body of work' (Parratt 2002: 2). Parratt's tripartite analysis of gender, leisure and history is therefore an important addition to the better-established body of knowledge integrating gender, leisure and sociology and outlined in Chapter 3 or the emerging body of work in gender, leisure and geography introduced in Chapter 4.

Parratt (2002: 3) acknowledges that she found the established 'socio-logical studies of contemporary women's leisure, especially feminist leisure studies' helpful in framing her research. Throughout the book she high-lights historical evidence in support of the earlier structuralist or socialist feminist leisure studies that viewed gender as 'a crucial, constitutive force on women's leisure ... leisure reciprocally builds and reinforces gender hierarchies, inequities and identities' (Parratt 2002: 4). However, drawing on more recent poststructural gender studies of leisure, culture and consumption, Parratt (2002: 5) also engages with the view 'that leisure is an arena in which gender can be confounded, interrogated, even resisted' and subsequent chapters elicit the ways in which leisure 'has been a source of and a site for cultural and social tensions' (Parratt 2002: 6).

Similar to the work of Clarke and Critcher (1985), Parratt offers a chronological account of women's leisure that focuses upon three distinct periods of time and the policy developments associated with each of these eras: 1750–1850, 1850–1880 and 1880–1914. The earliest period is char-acterised by the decline of 'hearty physical activities and games' (Parratt 2002: 13) in favour of functional, managed, licensed, educational and rational recreations promoted by the combined forces of industrialisation, urbanisation and evangelicalism. The account of the second era explores 'two of the most basic of leisure resources, free time and money, and their availability to working-class women' (Parratt 2002: 82). This account expands existing histories of leisure by exploring women's waged and unwaged work including work within the home and the detrimental impact of such working hours on women's ability to claim a share of the increased leisure time that was beginning to be experienced by men. Parratt then demonstrates that by the end of the nineteenth century both philanthropic and industrial interventions in leisure policy and provision resulted from a wider view of leisure 'as a sphere in which to shape working-class girls and women into good wives and mothers, and as a tool with which to do that shaping'. However, Parratt (2002: 147) concluded that 'both groups found that the girls and women upon whom they worked were not always tractable, that, whether as a tool or a sphere of gender construc-tion and social reformism, leisure could be somewhat less than perfect'.

Thus leisure-related policy, whether developed for purposes of main-taining or challenging hegemonic structures and cultures within society, does not always result in the desired effect. This is not only true in rela-tion to the 1750–1914 period that Parratt was concerned with but can also be evidenced more recently, as outlined in the sections below.

Gender, leisure and policies of social inclusion

Equity, access and inclusion have formed enduring themes within central and local government leisure and cultural policy and provision for over three decades. Previous research has demonstrated, however, that the main beneficiaries of public sector leisure, recreation, sport and art subsidies have tended to be those groups already overrepresented in leisure-related participation statistics (Aitchison 2003d; Coalter 2001; Jowell 2002; Long *et al.* 2002). Following the creation by the UK Government of the Social Exclusion Unit after the 1997 Labour Party general election win, eighteen Policy Action Teams (PATs) were established to inform policy that would contribute to social inclusion by developing regeneration, lifelong learning and healthier and safer communities. The Policy Action Team for Sport and the Arts (PAT 10) explored a central aim of the Department for Culture, Media and Sport (DCMS) by evaluating ways in which access could be widened to cultural and recreational resources. The findings and case studies outlined in the report from PAT 10, *Sport and the Arts: A Report to the Social Exclusion Unit* (Department for Culture, Media and Sport 1999), emphasised the potential of locally determined cultural solutions in contributing to a 'joined up' approach to social and economic problems.

The potential of cultural investment to stimulate economic and social development was therefore highlighted in the PAT 10's report to the Social Exclusion Unit on the role of sport and the arts in tackling social exclusion (DCMS 1999). The Policy Action Team for Sport and the Arts (PAT 10) was one of eighteen teams established following the publication of *Bringing Britain Together: A National Strategy for Neighbourhood Renewal* (Cabinet Office 1998). *Arts and Sport: A Report to the Social Exclusion Unit* was intended to report on 'best practice in using arts, sport and leisure to engage people in poor neighbourhoods, particularly those who may feel most excluded such as disaffected young people and people from ethnic minorities' (DCMS 1999: 5).

Such integration of social and economic policies has become a hallmark of the 'Third Way' politics practised by the two successive New Labour UK Governments since 1997. Through the creation of the Regional Development Agencies and Regional Cultural Consortia, together with the remit given to local authorities for the development of Local Cultural Strategies, public policy related to culture and leisure has sought to illustrate the government's 'joined-up thinking' approach to urban regeneration, neighbourhood renewal, social inclusion, healthy living and lifelong learning. Thus a series of policies and practices have been designed to stimulate interrelationships between the extrinsic and intrinsic benefits of economic capital, cultural capital and social capital. Within these recent national policy developments, however, the place of leisure in the lives of women, and the need to provide equality of opportunity for men and women to participate in leisure, remains unclear. Although there has been an increasing focus on 'culture', 'community' and the role of cultural relations in developing leisure within communities, the policies are underpinned by structuralist ideologies focused on issues of social class and socio-economic capital.

The policy rhetoric of equality and social inclusion, based upon a dualism of inclusion–exclusion, has served to construct notions of a single dominant culture or community to which those excluded are presumed to aspire. These constructions emphasise hierarchies of difference and can serve to militate against notions of cultural diversity and heterogeneity. The inclusion–exclusion dualism thus appears to imply that to move from being excluded to being included requires excluded individuals and groups to adopt and conform to a predetermined set of roles, behaviours and values already in place. This hegemonic discourse, frequently and inadvertently imposed from national to local levels, reflects the dominant discourses of both leisure policy and leisure studies outlined in Chapter 3 but is contested by social and cultural geographies emphasising difference and diversity and underpinned by poststructural theory as outlined in Chapter 4 (Aitchison *et al.* 2000).

Gender, leisure and sport policy: the role of Sport England

Recognising the significance of sport to the social and economic well-being of the country, the Labour Government elected in 1997 renamed the Department for National Heritage the Department for Culture, Media and Sport (DCMS) and responsibility for sport moved from the Department for Education to this new department. The Secretary of State for Culture, Media and Sport is supported by a Minister for Sport. In 1999, Kate Hoey, MP became the first woman to be Minister for Sport in the UK and in 2001 Tessa Jowell became the first Minister in charge of the Department for Culture, Media and Sport.

The DCMS is the major department within the UK Government responsible for promoting the arts, culture, leisure, tourism, media and sport both within the UK and internationally. The department is structured in three divisions: the Sport and Recreation Division, the Arts Division and the Tourism Division with each area having its own Minister and agency or agencies responsible for policy delivery. Sport England and UK Sport both receive policy direction and funding from the Sport and Recreation Division of the DCMS and are directly accountable to Parliament through the DCMS. Sport England is responsible for the development of sport within England whereas UK Sport oversees sports development at a UK level and also has a remit for international sport.

Sport England (formerly known as the Sports Council) was established by Royal Charter in 1972. Today, Sport England aims to see more people involved in sport, more places to play sport and more medals gained in sport through higher standards of performance. These three aims are often referred to as *more people, more places, more medals*. To realise these aims Sport England has concentrated on three major policy areas: young people, development of excellence and the National Lottery.

The National Lottery has provided an unprecedented level of funding for the development of sport in the UK. From its launch in January 1995 until January 2000 the Fund distributed over £600 million in grants to improve and develop sport throughout England (Sport England 2000). Sport England has distributed grants from the Sport England Lottery Fund and provided advice to applicants seeking funding for projects relating to sports facility planning, development and management. Prior to March 1997, lottery funds were only available for capital grants and facilities and not for individuals. This meant that funding could be obtained to build new sports venues or for sports equipment but was not available to assist individuals with the inevitable personal financial costs involved in developing individual excellence in sport. Today, however, grants can be awarded to capital projects and individuals. The introduction of Lottery funding has made a positive contribution towards increasing gender equity as organisations applying for funding must provide evidence that they are an equal opportunities organisations or are at least striving towards the full implementation of equal opportunities policies and practices for men and women. However, as Chapter 7 clearly demonstrates, the existence of an equal opportunities policy does not always ensure the presence of equal opportunities practice.

Sport England has a twenty-year history of policy initiatives designed to increase opportunities for women in sport (Aitchison 2001d). These developments in policy are embraced by the ideal of 'sport for all', a principle enshrined in the former Sports Council's Royal Charter. Women's sport emerged as a particular focus for development in the policy document titled *Sport in the Community: The Next Ten Years*, published in 1982. It was here that women were first recognised as a 'target group' for increased participation in sport and recreation and the document set targets for increasing women's participation in indoor sport by 70 per cent, and in outdoor sport by 35 per cent, both by 1993. In 1987, and half-way through the period for which these targets had been set, the then Sports Council undertook a review of progress and published its findings and recommendations in a second policy document titled *Sport in the Community: Which Ways Forward*. The document concluded that the gap between men and women's participation rates had declined. This was especially true of indoor sport where the health and fitness industry was beginning to have a positive impact on women's participation in sport with the advent of activities such as aerobics. However, the Sports Council acknowledged that progress towards achieving 'sport for all' was slower overall than had been hoped and was hampered by a range of additional social, cultural and economic factors including social class, age, ethnic origin and disability.

Sport in the Community: Into the Nineties – A Strategy for Sport 1988–1993 represented the next Sports Council policy document to address the 'sport for all' theme (Sports Council 1988). The document presented the findings of the 1982 initiative to achieve increased participation levels in sport by 1993. The report concluded that 'Nearly one million extra women have been attracted into indoor sport in the past five years – marginally short of the target, but nevertheless a major social phenomenon. However, the number of women participating in outdoor sport has fallen' (Sports Council 1988: 1). Over the same time period, 1983–1988, participation by men had increased in both indoor and outdoor sport. Finding that the gap between women and men's participation in outdoor sport had actually increased during the period when women were being targeted as a priority group was extremely disappointing. The Sports Council was forced to conclude that 'Sporting participation has grown in popularity and facilities have increased, but resources have been inadequate and progress insufficient to meet all the Council's targets' (Sports Council 1988: 1). The report recommended that the Sports Council's strategy for the next five years should be 'organised around two broad themes which reflect the Council's principal objectives – promoting mass participation, and promoting performance and excellence' (Sports Council 1988: 58). Within this strategy the Sports Council stated that 'In promoting mass participation the Council's strategy for the next five years has two principal targets – young people and women' (Sports Council 1988: 58). The identification of women as a target group for policy and action therefore continued into the 1990s.

Simultaneously, however, it was recognised that many of the sports promotion campaigns operated by the Sports Council and local authorities were simply increasing participation levels among women who already participated in sport rather than attracting those women who did not take any form of active leisure (Aitchison 1997a: 99). Another criticism centred on the provision of sports on a 'come and try' basis. These schemes provided one-off opportunities for women to take part in sports they had not participated in before but were not developed sufficiently after the taster session to maintain women's interest and sustain their participation. Moreover, the policy of targeting women as potential participants has been criticised for ignoring women as equally potential sports performers, leaders, developers, coaches and managers.

Gender equity and national policy frameworks for sport

Recognising some of the limitations highlighted above, the Sports Council's next policy document *Sport in the Nineties: New Horizons* (Sports Council 1993a) identified a vision for the future of sport where sports equity, including gender equity, would form a key element. In the same year the Sports Council published *Women and Sport: Policy and Frameworks for Action* (Sports Council 1993b). This policy document formed one of a series aimed at increasing participation levels among priority groups such as young people and people over the age of 50. The series of documents recognised that 'Sports equity is about fairness in sport, equality of access, recognising inequalities and taking steps to redress them. It is about changing the culture and structure of sport to ensure that it becomes equally accessible to everyone in society, whatever their age, race, gender or level of ability' (Sports Council 1993b: 4). As such, these policy documents can be seen as continuing the *Sport for All* objective set out twenty years earlier. Acknowledging the need for women to be more involved in sport coaching and leadership positions, *Women and Sport: Policy and Frameworks for Action* emphasised that the Sports Council's aim was to 'increase the involvement of women in sport at all levels and in all roles' (Sports Council 1993b: 6). The document identified six objectives designed to achieve this aim: first, to encourage equality of opportunity for girls to acquire basic movement skills and to develop positive attitudes towards an active lifestyle; second, to increase opportunities and reduce constraints to enable all women to participate in sport; third, to increase opportunities and reduce constraints to enable women to improve their levels of performance and reach publicly recognised levels of excellence; fourth, to increase the number of women involved in the organisation of sport and encourage them to reach senior positions; fifth, to encourage all appropriate organisations to adopt gender equity policies and practices; and, finally, to improve communication about women and sport and establish appropriate communication networks.

In addition, *Women and Sport: Policy and Frameworks for Action* provided clearer guidance for translating policy into action than the previous documents. This document mapped out a framework for change that addressed the significant elements in the organisational network influencing women and sport. These were identified as education, local authorities, the media, voluntary sector organisations for sport, women and young people, in addition to the major public sector sports providers. The recognition of the wider social and cultural environment in which sport development took place represented a significant advance in translating leisure-related theory into policy and practice. In conclusion, and signalling an area that was to become increasingly important over the next decade, the report emphasised that 'Partnerships are the key to the provision of improved opportunities for all women to become involved in sport and physical recreation and to realise their potential' (Sports Council 1993b: 24).

Developing the principles of the 1993 *Women and Sport: Policy and Frameworks for Action* document, a major international conference entitled 'Women and Sport and the Challenge of Change' was hosted in Brighton, England by the Sports Council in 1994. The conference represented the first world conference on women in sport and 280 policy and decision-makers from sport attended from 83 different countries. The two major outcomes from the conference were a set of principles referred to as the Brighton Declaration on Women and Sport and an International Women and Sport

Strategy for developing sport for women. The International Women and Sport Strategy sought to develop a co-ordinated approach to women and sport in all countries in an attempt to share good practice around the world. The Brighton Declaration on Women and Sport's overriding aim was 'to develop a sporting culture that enables and values the full involvement of women in every aspect of sport' (Sports Council 1998: 3). The declaration addressed ten key areas designed to cover the entire organisational network of women and sport: equity and equality issues in society and sport; sports facilities; school and junior sport; developing participation; high performance sport; leadership in sport; education, training and development; sports information and research; resources; and domestic and international co-operation. In 1998, the second world conference on Women and Sport took place at Windhoek in Namibia, Southern Africa and brought together around 400 delegates from 74 countries. The conference highlighted the role of sport in developing human rights for women around the world and in empowering women who were disenfranchised or oppressed. At the 1998 conference delegates endorsed the Windhoek Call for Action 'which builds on the Brighton Declaration to bring about more positive action to enhance the overall quality of women's lives using sport and physical activity as a vehicle' (Women's Sports Foundation/Sport England 1999: 1). The two Women and Sport conferences then resulted in the publication of *Women and Sport: From Brighton to Windhoek – Facing the Challenge* (Sports Council 1998).

In 2000 Sport England launched its new strategy entitled 'A Sporting Future for All' aimed at increasing sports participation and enhancing performance. The strategy focused on schools and young people and continued to develop the tripartite theme of *more people, more places, more medals* embraced in the 1995 policy document *Sport: Raising the Game* which focused on schools, sporting culture, higher education and excellence. In 1997 this strategy had been developed in *England, the Sporting Nation: A Strategy. A Sporting Future for All* (2000) then embraced a series of programmes designed to encourage more people to take part in sport and to sustain their commitment to sport. These programmes were identified as *Active Schools, Active Sports* and *Active Communities*. Within each programme a further series of measures was designed to fulfil the aims of the specific programme. For example, *Active Schools* introduced an initiative called 'sporting ambassadors' aimed at introducing sports stars to primary and secondary pupils. Within this initiative, sportswomen can be important role models in encouraging younger women and girls to participate and excel at sport. *Active Communities* developed a series of measures for encouraging sports provision and participation through the designation of 'sport action zones' in areas experiencing social and economic exclusion. In these areas Sport England's existing training programme for sports administrators entitled *Running Sport* was targeted at community groups to develop *Sport for All*, thus

Table 1 Thirty years of policy for women and sport: a summary of key dates and policy developments

Year	Events and policy documents
1970	Sport England (Sports Council) formed
1982	*Sport in the Community: The Next Ten Years*
1987	*Sport in the Community: Which Ways Forward*
1988	*Sport in the Community: Into the Nineties*
1993	*Sport in the Nineties: New Horizons*
1993	*Women and Sport: Policy and Frameworks for Action*
1993	Brighton Women and Sport Conference
1995	*Sport: Raising the Game*
1997	*England, the Sporting Nation: A Strategy*
1998	Windhoek, Namibia Women and Sport Conference
2000	*A Sporting Future for All*

echoing the original Sports Council ethos formed two decades earlier. Table 1 summarises three decades of UK policy for women and sport.

The Women's Sports Foundation: tackling inequitable structures and cultures

Although many organisations and policies outlined above have attempted to include women and girls within their remit, sport is still dominated by men and boys. For this reason, national organisations such as the UK Women's Sports Foundation have been created to support women and girls in sport. The Women's Sports Foundation (WSF) is a non-governmental national organisation solely committed to improving and promoting opportunities for women in sport in all roles and at all levels. The WSF is a non-profit membership-based organisation dedicated to increasing opportunities for women and girls in sport, fitness and physical activity through advocacy, information, education, research and training. The organisation was founded in 1984 by women working in sport who were concerned about the lack of sport and recreation opportunities for women and girls and the low representation of women in sport coaching, sport management and the sports media including sports photography. Since the foundation of the WSF many similar organisations have been established in other countries reflecting a global concern about gender equity in sport Hargreaves 2000: 217)

The WSF has been involved in a variety of projects to promote women's sport. These have included the Tampax-sponsored Women's Sports Foundation Awards for Girls and Young Women which provided £100,000 in grants to young sportswomen during 1992 and 1993. The WSF has also initiated the production of a variety of women and sport resources including posters, information packs, photographic exhibition and fact sheets. Training and education have been prioritised by the WSF since its inception in 1984 and the organisation has offered training to Britain's top sportswomen on working with the media, attracting sports sponsorship, employment opportunities in sport and recreation, and receiving benefits from sports science support. Thus, the WSF has recognised the wider social, cultural, economic and political constraints facing the development of women's sport. The increasing role of the media and commerce in sport has meant that such cultural, economic and political objectives need to be seen in relation to the social objective of 'sport for all'. The WSF has been instrumental in drawing attention to the cultural inequity in media coverage of women's sport and the economic inequity in sport-related earnings and sponsorship.

The underrepresentation of sportswomen in all forms of media, together with the underrepresentation of women involved in the production of sport-related media, has long been of concern to those trying to increase the visibility of women's sport. The role of the media in contributing to the conditions in which women's sport operates cannot be overestimated. The media plays a crucial role in raising the public profile of women's sport, in publicising positive role models for other sportswomen, in contesting stereotypes of women in sport, and in enabling women's sport to become more visible, more acceptable and more likely to attract commercial sponsorship. Writing about televised sport, Jennifer Hargreaves (1994) reported that:

> The forms of discrimination in the printed media's coverage of women's sports are paralleled by discrimination on television. Men's boxing, cricket, football, horse-racing, motor-racing, rugby, snooker and 'imported' men's sports such as American wrestling, American football, baseball, rally cross and sumo wrestling fill most viewing hours. Magazine programmes such as *Grandstand*, *Match of the Day*, *Saint and Greavesy*, *Sportsnight* and *World of Sport* concentrate on men's sport, and at times when the men's Cricket, Football, Rugby or Snooker World Cups are on, television is saturated with these events.
>
> (Hargreaves, 1994: 195)

Hargreaves (1994: 196) went on to cite sports quiz shows such as the UK's *A Question of Sport* as providing further male bias. Almost ten years later, and in spite of the addition of Sue Barker, a former tennis player, as the show's host it is rarely the case that more than one out of six of the panellists are women. This reflects the situation within the major terrestrial and satellite television channels where men's sport is prioritised over women's sport. When particular sports such as football or cricket are televised they invariably refer to men's football and men's cricket. On satellite television the top sport shown by Sky and Eurosport is men's football while on terrestrial television men's football and men's cricket are dominant. It is therefore hardly surprising that more men than women watch sport on television, making televised sport the only form of television programme type that attracts more male viewers than female viewers (Cooper-Chen 1994: 266). The Sports Council (1993b) concluded that television coverage of women's sport made up only between 0.5 to 0.6 per cent of all sports coverage. Hargreaves (1994: 196) summarised the impact of televised sport on women by stating 'The construction and marginalisation of female sports provide a hidden, but very powerful, message that they are less important than men's sports and that men are keener to participate and naturally better suited to do so'.

The UK's BBC Sports Personality of the Year award provides a telling example of male domination in televised sport. The award is made on the basis of votes from the general public who usually make their selection informed by the sports coverage provided by television. In the award's forty-eight-year history women have won it eleven times. Five of these awards were during the ten-year period from 1963 to 1972 illustrating that women won exactly half of the awards during that particular decade (Anita Lonsborough 1962 – swimming; Dorothy Hyman 1963 – athletics; Mary Rand 1964 – athletics; Ann Jones 1969 – tennis; Princess Anne 1971 – three-day-event; Mary Peters 1972 – athletics). But only five of the ten wins have been in the last twenty-five years and one of those was awarded jointly with a sportsman when Jayne Torvill and Christopher Dean won the award for ice dance (Virginia Wade 1977 – tennis; Jayne Torvill and Christopher Dean 1984 – ice dance; Fatima Whitbread 1987 – athletics; Liz McColgan 1991 – athletics; Paula Radcliffe 2002 – athletics). In other words, the number of women winning the award of BBC Sports Personality of the Year has decreased significantly since the 1960s. In the early years of the award it was dominated by athletics and tennis but in the last two decades it has been dominated by sports participated in exclusively by men or by sports where only the men's competitions are televised. During the 1990s, for example, motor-racing drivers were awarded the prize on three occasions. It is not possible to provide evidence of a direct correlation between media and sponsorship support and public acclaim but it is interesting to note that motor racing receives more sponsorship than any other sport with many of the sponsors using the opportunity to advertise products aimed at a predominantly male market.

In the twenty-first century it is still quite usual to open the sports pages of national newspapers and find no coverage of any women's sport in sports sections that often extend up to fourteen pages in length. This assessment reiterates the findings of a small study by Matheson and Flatten (1996) that demonstrated a decrease in the amount of newspaper coverage of women athletes over a ten-year period between 1984 and 1994. In their study of six national UK and Sunday newspapers (*Telegraph, Guardian, Independent, Express, Mail* and *Mirror*) Matheson and Flatten found that between 1984 and 1994 there was actually a 5.2 per cent decrease in the number of articles on women's sport, a 5.2 per cent decrease in the actual space taken up by newspaper coverage of women's sport, and a 7.1 per cent reduction in the number of photographs of women's sport. Paradoxically, these reductions in the coverage of women's sport took place at a time when participation in sport by women was increasing, making the disparity between levels of participation and levels of newspaper representation even more marked.

As sport has become more commercialised, so spending on sports sponsorship has increased. With large television viewing figures sport sponsorship provides a cost-effective advertising medium aimed at mass audiences. In 1997 the sports sponsorship sector occupied 56 per cent of total sponsorship spending by commercial and non-commercial companies and organisations and the sponsorship spending directed towards sport was over three times that received by the arts (Mintel, 1998). During the 1990s there was a steady increase in spending on sports sponsorship from £265 million in 1994 to £347 million in 1998 (Sport England 2000). Like media coverage, however, sponsorship deals were made almost entirely with sports*men*.

The reasons why commercial sponsors are not attracted to women's sport reflect the status of women's sport and women in society more generally: women's sport receives less television coverage, women's sport receives less newspaper coverage, sportswomen are less likely than men to be treated as celebrities outside sport, sport is seen as desirable for men while for women many sports are still seen as undesirable, fewer women than men watch sport and therefore form a smaller audience for sponsorship-related advertising, and women have less spending power than men and are not seen as such a profitable target market for sponsorship-related advertising. In spite of such disadvantages, many sports, including women's tennis and women's golf, have campaigned to secure lucrative sponsorship deals and prize money for top competitors. Even in these sports, however, the corporate investments and prize money have been significantly less for women compared with men. However, there have also been some more encouraging signs for sports sponsorship. The rapid rise of mobile phone and Internet-related companies during the 1990s increased the level of sponsorship from the communications and technology field. Fulham Ladies, for example, as the first English women's football team to turn professional, were sponsored by Demon Internet and the English Women's Cricket team received sponsorship from Vodaphone who also sponsored the men's team. British Telecom has also been active in sponsoring sports participation through the BT TOP Sport programme aimed at young people.

It seems no coincidence that in tennis, where women have received a relatively high level of media coverage, a number of women players have been commercially successful. However, their sponsorship and prize money is considerably lower than that received by their male counterparts. This has caused ongoing controversy particularly in relation to the Wimbledon Championship where male players such as Tim Henman have spoken out, arguing that women should receive less in prize money because their game, with only three sets, is less demanding than the men's game. For international tennis players there have, however, been notable successes in relation to sponsorship and prize money. Chris Evert became the first woman to win $1 million and was soon overtaken in the early 1990s by Martina Navratalova and then by Monica Seles who, by 1992, had become the highest paid female athlete in the world and the twelfth highest paid athlete in the world among men and women (Hargreaves 1994: 205). It has been observed, however, that unlike men's sponsorship, where sponsors are often attracted by newsworthy personalities, sponsors of sportswomen are often attracted by women perceived to be 'feminine' and representing 'feminine' sports. These sports would include tennis but would exclude rugby and football which are still seen by many as unsuitable sports for women. For example, although the England women's rugby, cricket and football teams have been highly successful in international competitions they have all found it difficult to secure sponsorship. One explanation is that sponsors are unsure about allying themselves with women's sports that challenge traditional notions of appropriate sporting behaviour for women. Allied to the gender differential in sponsorship is the significant difference in male and female earnings from sport, the domination of predominantly male sports such as boxing and motor racing as the sports of the top three sports earners in the UK and the absence of women from this list of Britain's highest earners in sport (Rojek 2000)

Concerned with the continuing underrepresentation and underfunding of women's sport, the WSF published its *National Action Plan for Women's and Girls' Sport and Physical Activity* in 1999 in partnership with Sport England's Women and Sport Advisory Group. The WSF *National Action Plan* advocated a multi-agency approach to promoting sport and physical activity for women and girls and was designed to encourage sport-related organisations to identify targets and actions that would help to achieve sporting gender equity. The plan identified eight interrelated areas where change was required to enhance opportunities for women and girls. A list of aims was highlighted within each target area together with a series of stated commitments to implementing the plan by sport-related organisations. The areas identified and their associated aims were as follows:

Equality
- With state and governmental organisations, to work towards the elimination of discrimination against women and girls, raising awareness of the contribution that physical activity and sport has made and makes to society, and to the health and quality of life of women, girls and their families.

- To ensure that the issues surrounding women's and girls' sport are known, understood and supported, particularly by key influencers and decision makers.
- To challenge instances of inequality and discrimination that women from different cultural, social and religious backgrounds experience in sport and physical activity, and to seek to bring about change.

Leadership

- To increase the number of women leaders at all levels of sport and physical activity.
- To seek at least equal representation by women on decision-making bodies and in decision-making positions.
- To support the personal and career development of women in physical activity and sports administration and management, whilst providing more opportunities for women to access these areas of sport and physical activity.
- To support the personal and career development of women at all levels in coaching, officiating, sports administration and management and to raise their profile.

Education, training and research

- To provide a continuum of personal development and training and research and education opportunities for women and girls in physical activity and sport.
- To ensure that those responsible for providing sport, recreation and physical education in schools and colleges deliver an equitable range of opportunities and learning experiences.
- To increase the knowledge and understanding of women's and girls' sport and physical activity through positive action focusing on women's experiences and increase opportunities for women to engage in sports and physical activity research.

Young people

- To increase opportunities for participation by girls and women in a wide variety of sport, physical activity and recreation, and to generate more positive attitudes to sport and physical activity by girls and young women.
- To promote positive images of girls' and women's sporting and physical activities in order to generate more positive attitudes to girls' and women's sports participation.

Facilities and participation

- To increase participation by women and girls in a wide variety of sports, recreation and leisure opportunities.
- To ensure that the planning, design and management of facilities meets the needs of women in relation to childcare provision, accessibility, membership and participation.

High performance sport
- To enable women and girls with sporting ability to achieve sporting excellence in all areas of sport.
- To maximise the support, profile and opportunities available to elite British sportswomen.

Information and resources
- To increase and maximise the resources available for women's and girls' physical activity and sport.
- To provide valued and current information and resources on women's and girls' sport and physical activity.
- To encourage positive images of women in all publicity, information and marketing materials and to ensure that the diversity of women from different backgrounds and with different abilities is appropriately portrayed.
- To ensure that resources are allocated equitably and a monitoring process is in place to ensure that the needs of women and girls are adequately addressed.

National and international co-operation
- To raise the awareness, support and understanding of the key issues relating to women's and girls' sport and physical activity.
- To adopt a multi-agency approach when working on strategies and actions that influence women's sporting and physical opportunities.
- To provide, distribute, share and promote positive solutions and examples of good practice relating to the promotion of opportunities, achievements and successes of women and girls' sport nationally and internationally.

(Women's Sports Foundation/Sport England 1999)

Local authorities and leisure provision

In addition to policy formulated at a national level by both central government departments and agencies and non-governmental organisations such as the WSF, leisure policy is also developed at a local level by a variety of agencies and organisations. One of the most important local providers of leisure is local authorities and each local authority employs personnel such as leisure services officers, leisure centre managers and sports development workers to improve policies, services and facilities with the aim of enhancing leisure opportunities. In 1998/99 it was estimated that UK local authorities spent £1,704 million on cultural services (Department for Culture, Media and Sport 2002). Local schools also have a large responsibilities for providing sport and physical education through the national curriculum and many schools are also active in providing and encouraging competitive sport through extra-curricula activities. Local sports clubs affiliated to the National Governing Bodies of sport are also major providers of sport at a local level and these clubs may make use of local authority sports facilities and/or school sports facilities. The links between these different local providers have enabled working partnerships to be formed to bring about multi-agency sports provision of the type called for in the WSF's *National Action Plan* outlined above.

Local authorities have a long history of providing recreational opportunities and facilities to the UK public with the first public baths and libraries having been opened in most major towns and cities towards the end of the nineteenth century. Today, however, there is a much wider range of facilities and services with a diverse group of sports-related personnel employed to operate facilities and manage services. For example, in 1998 there were 1,300 public indoor swimming pools in the UK, in 1995 there were 1,450 leisure centres in the UK, and in 1994 there were 77,946 playing pitches in England alone (Sport England 2000). Provision by local authorities and local authority-maintained schools forms part of public sector provision whereas the local sports clubs affiliated to the National Governing Bodies are from the non-profit or voluntary sector. In addition to provision by the public and non-profit sectors, however, the commercial or private sector is a major provider of sport and physical activity at a local level. The 1990s saw enormous growth in the number of commercially owned and managed gyms, health and fitness clubs and leisure centres and there were more than 2,500 commercial health and fitness clubs by 1998 (Sport England 2000). These clubs have been instrumental in developing links between health and fitness and increasing awareness of the health-related benefits of exercise following the publication of the government reports *The Health of the Nation* (Department of Health 1992) and *Saving Lives: Our Healthier Nation* (Department of Health 1999). Both of these reports demonstrated particular concerns about low levels of physical activity among young women and local providers of sport and physical activity have attempted to address these concerns.

One way to assist the management of *Sport for All* is to develop more opportunities for women to participate in sport and physical activity. In 1999, Sport England conducted a public opinion survey to find out why people did not participate in sport and what would encourage them to take up sport or physical activity. The survey reported that 57 per cent of women did not currently take part in sport and that 52 per cent of these non-participants said there was nothing that would encourage them to take part. In other words, half of those who do not take part in sport had no desire to be persuaded to take up sport or to be encouraged into taking regular physical activity. For this group of the population (30 per cent of all women) there are clearly health-related issues that need to be addressed through long-term education and cultural change. For the remaining 48 per cent of non-participants there may be strategies that those involved in sport-related policy and provision can employ to encourage women to take up sport. Of those non-participants who said they could be encouraged to take part, having more leisure time was cited by 21 per cent as the most important factor. Nineteen per cent of women said that having more money or lower prices was the most important factor that would encourage them to take part, whereas only 12 per cent of men felt this was a significant factor. Having friends to take part with was cited by 15 per cent of women but only 7 per cent of men ranked this as an important incentive to take part in sport or physical activity. Having better childcare provision was listed by 12 per cent of women compared with only 3 per cent of men, and overcoming embarrassment and lack of confidence was given as the most important factor by 9 per cent of women compared with 4 per cent of men. The Sport England (1999: 4) survey concluded that: 'Generally speaking, men are more likely to refer to improvements in facility provision in their locality as important in encouraging them to take part than women. The emphasis amongst women is more on personal and broader lifestyle/social circumstances'.

During the 1980s a number of local authorities appointed women to act as Women and Sport Development Officers, sometimes in designated Women and Sport Development Units. According to Collins (1995) the number of sports development officers (SDOs) employed by local authorities in the UK rose from 180 in 1988 to 1,400 in 1994. Today, however, SDOs are more likely to combine the promotion of sport to women and girls with the promotion of sport for particular age groups or local populations or through the development of specific sports. These new SDO posts are frequently initiated by National Governing Bodies of sport in addition to being created by local authorities and commercial sector sports contractors.

The privatisation of leisure services

The focus on women as a 'target group' for UK leisure policy was undoubtedly disrupted in the late 1980s by the introduction of Compulsory Competitive Tendering (CCT) to local authority leisure services (Aitchison 1995, 1997a). Exemplifying the wider socio-economic principles embodied in Conservative public policy, CCT was charged with bringing the disciplines of the market to the public sector as a means of increasing efficiency, economy and effectiveness whilst simultaneously increasing the power and choice of the individual consumer. Services and functions that had previously been regarded in a social or political context were, by the late 1980s, viewed in an economic context following a decade of Conservative rule. Within local authorities this shift in public policy represented a transition from local government as provider to facilitator or enabler.

Privatisation of public services can take a number of forms and the UK's four consecutive Conservative governments spanning the period

1979–97 were in favour of all forms. It should be noted, however, that Conservative policy did not define 'contracting out' as privatisation because it only privatises *production* and not *ownership* of facilities. *Contracting out* or compulsory competitive tendering involves the privatisation of production such that private contractors are invited to tender and compete for the contract of managing and operating public services and facilities. In contrast, *charging* is defined as the privatisation of financing and, although this method has existed within local government services almost since the inception of local government itself, its significance was greatly increased following the introduction of the local council tax to individual households in the late 1980s. *Denationalisation* involves the sale of public enterprises such as telecommunications, gas, water, electricity and rail, and *Deregulation* liberalises state monopolies to allow private competition. Denationalisation and contracting out are capable of providing privatisation on a wider scale than charging and deregulation and, consequently, have been subject to the greatest opposition and criticism.

The Local Government Planning and Land Act (1980) introduced CCT to the areas of building and highway construction and maintenance. Five years later, the Department of the Environment published a consultation paper entitled *Competition in the Provision of Local Authority Services* (1985) which set out the Government's proposals to introduce CCT to local authority refuse collection, street cleaning, cleaning of buildings, school and welfare catering, other catering, grounds maintenance and vehicle maintenance. The Local Government Bill, addressing the above areas, was introduced to Parliament in June 1987. In September 1987 the Government circulated a consultation paper entitled *Competition in the Management of Local Authority Sport and Leisure Facilities* (1987) which outlined their proposals to add the management of local authority leisure and sport facilities to the previous list of local government functions to be subject to CCT. The management implications of CCT in leisure and sport centred round the client–contractor relationship which, unlike the other service areas included in the act, involved a substantial number of professional and management positions. The Local Government Bill received Royal Assent in March 1988 and the consultation period continued throughout 1988 with sport and leisure added to the Act in 1989.

The New Right embraced CCT in leisure and sport as it added further to their efforts to 'roll back the welfare state' within the UK and to redefine democratic freedom in terms of individualism and consumption based on free market choice. Within the left, however, there was also some support for the new policy development as it was argued that CCT had the potential to offer a redistribution of resources from recreationally advantaged groups to recreationally disadvantaged and minority participant groups by targeting specific groups more directly. This chapter has already provided evidence to demonstrate that blanket subsidies to local authority sport and leisure benefit young, white, middle-class men disproportionately as they are already higher users of sport and leisure services than the rest of the population. The Audit Commission (1989), in its report entitled *Sport for Whom*, argued that CCT would allow local authorities to target minority users and disadvantaged groups more specifically while simultaneously reducing costs by abolishing blanket subsidies.

Research concerning the impact of CCT on leisure services has been limited. Three types of research were published either just before or immediately following the implementation of the legislation. However, with the exception of Aitchison (1997a) the published research provided limited insight into the impact of CCT on women's leisure or, indeed, the leisure participation of other underrepresented groups. The first type of research consisted of large-scale surveys conducted to compile quantitative databases about largely economic and procedural matters related to CCT in leisure and sport. Second, there was limited academic research with most focusing on evaluating CCT in relation to management standards such as Total Quality Management. Third, the leisure and sport industry itself undertook a limited amount of research to inform a series of short papers and guidance notes designed to advise leisure practitioners on procedural matters related to implementing the legislation rather than providing any critique of the legislation per se. There was, therefore, a lack of critical or qualitative research and it is notable that more research was undertaken prior to full implementation of the legislation into the possible impacts of CCT than there has been research into the actual impacts of CCT since the legislation was fully implemented in 1993.

Five large-scale surveys of CCT in leisure and sport services were conducted between 1989 and 1992. The Institute of Sport and Recreation Management (ISRM 1989) questionnaire survey of the impact of CCT was largely concerned with obtaining views of the future of local government leisure services under CCT. As the survey was conducted prior to the implementation of the legislation it was inevitably impressionistic. Moreover, a quantitative survey was not the ideal research method to employ as it was perceptions and impressions that were being sought rather than quantitative data. Although the survey only achieved a 25 per cent response rate, which is about average for a postal questionnaire, some of the findings are worthy of note. When asked if local authorities were optimistic, pessimistic or uncertain about the future of leisure services under CCT, 56 per cent of respondents stated that they felt optimistic, 13 per cent stated that they felt pessimistic and 13 per cent remained unsure. Local authorities did seem to have a fairly accurate perception of the outcome of the tendering process as 86 per cent of responding authorities believed that the outcome of CCT would result in leisure being retained by the local authority's own service providers, to become known as the Direct Service Organisation (DSO). Only 12 per cent thought that CCT would result in private contractors taking over the management of their leisure facilities. However, in spite of the optimistic outlook, a number of areas were identified as vulnerable to potential decline and the changes identified would certainly have a negative impact on women both as leisure providers and participants. Overall, decreases in net revenue, the capital programme, employee costs and employee numbers were thought to be between three and four times more likely than increases in these areas.

The second ISRM survey (1992) achieved a higher response rate than the initial ISRM survey and revealed that 91 per cent of contracts awarded in 1992 had gone to DSOs. Only 31 per cent of contracts had received competition from outside contractors and the results confirmed the earlier predictions of local authorities that only a very small proportion of contracts would be won by the commercial sector. Notwithstanding these results, later research went on to demonstrate that, even where a contract had been awarded in-house, there were significant changes to organisational policy, culture and operation.

The third research project was undertaken by the Institute of Public Finance (1992) which found that 81.1 per cent of contracts awarded had been won by DSOs. The commercial sector had won most of its contracts in London and South-East England and none in Scotland, Wales, the North of England or Yorkshire and Humberside where the ethos of public sector service provision remained much stronger than in the south. By 1992 'sixteen private companies had won a total of 42 local authority sports and leisure management contracts' (Institute of Public Finance 1992: 58). However, the main five contractors had secured 62 per cent of private contracts demonstrating concentration of management among very few providers within the commercial sector.

A fourth study, conducted by Richards (1992) confirmed the findings of the ISRM and IPF research by demonstrating that a high proportion of contracts were being won in-house. The findings revealed similar geographical disparities in the awarding of contracts when compared to those identified in the IPF research. Richards (1992) revealed that only 39 per cent of authorities felt they had maintained full control of programming of leisure activities. This finding was of particular concern as it appeared to indicate that contract specifications were not sufficiently tight to ensure the implementation of local authority leisure policy by the leisure contractor. The loss of programming control would have implications for target group provision and it was this finding that suggested the need for more detailed research of the impact of CCT on women's leisure within local-authority-provided services.

The fifth and final national survey, conducted by Coalter for the Sports Council, represented the most comprehensive study of CCT in leisure and sport services. The survey confirmed many of the findings of the previous research but located these findings within a clearer analysis of public policy (Sports Council 1993c). With the exception of a few references to women as a target group in Coalter's research, none of the academic research relating to contracting out of local authority leisure services had analysed the impact of CCT on women either as leisure participants or providers and there had been no mention of the effect of employment restructuring upon women in management positions or upon the career prospects of women aspiring to management positions within leisure services. (See Chapter 7 for a more detailed discussion of women's career patterns in leisure management.)

Research by leisure's professional associations had been equally uncritical with an emphasis on advising the leisure management sector on general procedural matters related to a speedy and efficient transition to CCT rather than any questioning of the more structural or cultural implications of the changes. The two main professional associations in leisure services (the Institute of Sport and Recreation Management and the Institute of Leisure and Amenity Management (ILAM)), together with the Sports Council, were keen to provide advice to their members who were now tasked with drawing up tender specifications for the implementation of CCT at very short notice. The Sports Council in particular was keen to ensure that local authorities used CCT as an 'opportunity to shape the future development of their leisure services' advising that strategies to promote participation by minority and under-represented groups should be strengthened and incorporated specifically into tender specifications (Sports Council, *Competitive Tendering and Sport for All*, undated). Unlike the Sports Council, neither ISRM nor ILAM provided guidance on target group programming and both seemed to embrace CCT at an early stage. Following the publication of the Parliamentary Order on Sport and Leisure on 25 October 1989 *Leisure Manager*, ILAM's monthly journal, stated:

> While the disruption and costs to departments cannot be underestimated it cannot be denied that CCT is already achieving its desired aim. Leisure Services are becoming leaner, keener and more efficient and that can only be good for managers, the profession and customers alike.
>
> (*Leisure Manager* November/December 1989)

There is evidence to support the view that CCT's introduction to other service areas, in addition to imposing the disciplines of the market on local government, was implemented to undermine or at least contain the position of a heavily unionised and growing sector of blue-collar workers (Dunleavy 1986). Le Grand and Bartlett (1993) argued that this dual motivation of service efficiency and depoliticisation resulted in the creation of 'quasi-markets'. Their assertion is supported in the case of leisure services where local authorities were allowed to maintain control over three crucial aspects of target group provision: opening hours, admissions policy and pricing, and programming. However, Richards (1992) revealed concerns by local authority leisure providers that there had been an informal erosion of control over opening hours, admissions and pricing. Richards (1992) also highlighted the possibility that target group provision could deteriorate when passed into the hands of commercial sector contractors and this scenario seemed more likely in London than elsewhere as a result of the comparatively large number of contracts won by the commercial sector in London. Primary research was therefore required to investigate the impact of CCT on women's leisure provision and participation in the thirty-three London boroughs (Aitchison 1995, 1997a).

The research was designed to provide a theoretical analysis of the impact of CCT on women's leisure supplemented by new empirical research in the form of policy analysis, a regional questionnaire survey and in-depth interviews with leisure providers and participants. The regional survey took place in Greater London with the thirty-three London boroughs forming the sampling frame. Across the authorities surveyed, sport and leisure provision was located in a variety of departments with a number of specific Sport and Leisure Services Departments created in the 1980s having since been amalgamated or subsumed within departments such as Education or Environment. The research was intended to examine the impact of CCT on active leisure and sport for women and, as such, did not address other aspects of local authority leisure provision such as libraries, arts, culture and play.

The questionnaire was designed to elicit information relating to the following five areas: the awarding of contracts including timing and names of successful bidders; contract specifications including reference to women as a specific target group and the monitoring of participation levels among this group; the employment of sports development officers with responsibility for women's leisure before and after CCT; changes to levels of women's participation, opening hours, pricing and programming since CCT and increases and reductions in 'women only' sessions since CCT. The questionnaire also invited more qualitative responses and the results of the qualitative section provided input to the schedule of questions for the follow-up in-depth interviews that were carried out with client services officers, sports development officers and leisure centre managers. Discussions were also held with the Women's Sport Foundation based in London and with the WINNERS Forum (Women's Information Network, News and Education in Recreation and Sport) with the questionnaire and interview results informing focus groups with women leisure participants. The following section provides a brief summary of the main findings in relation to: the awarding of contracts; contract specifications; sports development officers; and women's participation and women only sessions.

Two authorities, Westminster in central London and Barnet on the northern edge of Greater London, had awarded their first contracts in 1988 and two other authorities, Wandsworth and Kensington and Chelsea, both in the relatively affluent south-west of the capital, had awarded their first contracts in 1989. All authorities entering into CCT before the necessary initial deadline were Conservative controlled and throughout the first round of CCT Conservative-controlled authorities received many more bids from commercial contractors than did their Labour counterparts. Of the 18 responding authorities, eight (44.4 per cent) had awarded contracts to commercial sector contractors demonstrating that the commercial sector had become more involved in the management of local authority sport and leisure facilities in London than in any other part of the country. While the Institute of Public Finance Survey (1992) had emphasised the concentration of contracts within the hands of relatively few private contractors, the situation in London was even more pronounced with only five commercial contractors cited by the respondents.

Of the 18 responding authorities, 13 (72 per cent) stated that their authority's contract specification had made reference to women as a specific target or priority group. This figure was higher than the national average of 64 per cent identified by Coalter but could be explained by the higher proportion of Greater London authorities with a leisure strategy (Sports Council 1993a). Coalter's research revealed that references to specified user groups were more frequently made to disabled people (85 per cent), young people (80 per cent), unemployed people (74 per cent) and people over the age of 50 (74 per cent) than to women (Sports Council 1993b). It was of concern to note that two authorities that employed officers with specific responsibility for women's sport and leisure had not even mentioned women as a target group in their specification thus indicating a lack of co-ordination between those writing the policies and those charged with their delivery. Only five of thirteen authorities that had referred to women as a priority group employed officers with designated responsibility for this area. Two authorities did not refer to women in the specification and did not employ anyone with specific responsibility for women's leisure and eight authorities had referred to women in the contract specification but did not employ anyone to take responsibility for the development of women's leisure.

At the time of the research 87.5 per cent of directors of London local authority leisure services were men, 89 per cent of senior managers were men and 78 per cent of the newly created posts of client managers had been awarded to men following the introduction of CCT (Aitchison 1995). Although women were better represented in sport development there was increasing concern that this new career pathway was developing to be a cul-de-sac for many Sport Development Officers (SDOs). The role is often perceived as 'outreach' work rather than management and gender stereotyping has resulted in women being seen as better suited for this kind of work than the new CCT-related posts of contract and client manager. Following the introduction of CCT, the number of authorities employing SDOs in the form of Women and Sport Development Officers with specific responsibility for women's participation decreased by 45.5 per cent among the responding authorities. The reduction in the number of posts was even more pronounced with a 73 per cent fall in the number of SDOs. Following the introduction of CCT, responsibility for the development of sport and leisure among women and girls moved into more generic sport and leisure development rather than being concentrated in specific development work for women. The critique of women as a homogenous group, and outlined in Chapter 2, offers some support for such a change as it is difficult to locate identity within just one category, particularly when black women, disabled women or older women will fall into more than one sports development 'category'. In relation to sport, many authorities have also now appointed SDOs with responsibility for particular sports rather than specific participant groups with this policy shift echoing Sport England's prioritisation of particular sports. However, the research also revealed that some local authorities had shifted responsibility for the development of women and girl's sport to Youth and Community Services Departments, many of which went on to suffer large funding cuts during the 1990s.

The research in Greater London demonstrated that, in some authorities, there had been an increase in leisure provision for women but this was usually in the form of mass participant and therefore revenue generating activities such as aerobics, step aerobics and general fitness classes. Although most of these classes attracted many more women than men very few of the classes were women only. Where women-only sessions had been programmed, they were by no means sacrosanct. One contract manager stated that, 'there is a tendency on the contractor's part to minimise publicity and encourage general (mixed) use of times allocated to women to improve income levels'. Such practices corroborated the findings of the Equal Opportunities Commission study that reported that interviews with managers revealed a poor understanding of equal opportunities policies and 'little commitment to implement equal opportunities policies' (Equal Opportunities Commission 1995: 21). For example, the research in Greater London revealed that one commercial contractor timetabled fifty fitness classes each week at their leisure centre with only four of these classes aimed at beginners and only two classes designated as 'women only'. Moreover, only one class from the available fifty was aimed specifically at the 40-plus age group and only one class at the 60-plus age group. One Inner London authority stated that their contractor had been persuaded to organise women-only sessions only if it was proved that such a session could attract more users than a mixed session, meaning it is virtually impossible to move away from mass-participant activities like aerobics. Another Inner London authority stated that their contractor would provide women-only sessions only if the local authority paid for crèche provision. Thus, contractors were primarily concerned with increasing numbers of visits of existing users rather than widening the range of users or providing facilities for all sections of the community. These findings pointed to the weakness of some specifications which had not addressed adequately the needs of different groups of women. Coalter's research also found that 'the widespread failure to accompany service objectives with methods of implementation or non-financial performance measures may act as obstacles to sports development policies and the achievement of sporting equity' (Sports Council 1993: 67).

The research outlined above revealed that feminist and gender critiques are not only lacking in service sector research related to sport and leisure provision but are also lacking in research into local government and public policy more generally. Whereas there has been extensive research analysing the changing nature of local government in the UK, there has been little analysis of the impacts of change on women as 'clients' or as employees of local authorities or contractors (Cochrane 1993; Farnham and Horton 1993; Le Grand and Bartlett 1993; Self 1993; Gamble 1994; Leach *et al.* 1994). The emphasis on management standards as gender-neutral mechanisms for improved service delivery is but one example of a discourse that has frequently served to marginalise feminist debate by focusing on the functional and operational aspects of policy implementation rather than the structural and cultural determinants and consequences of policy, employment patterns and organisational cultures. Women's experience of leisure within a local authority context therefore needs to be understood within a political framework which acknowledges the implications for equality of opportunity when boundaries between the public and commercial sectors are renegotiated. Leach *et al.* (1994: 8) identified four key dimensions of any analysis of the conceptual framework of local authority strategies: structures, cultures, processes and systems, and staff management. As Chapter 6 will go on to discuss, each of these aspects of a local authority's strategy contributes to the sexuality of organisation and the way in which gender issues are perceived and addressed.

The replacement in 2000 of CCT with a duty of 'best value', together with the requirement that all local authorities were to produce a Cultural Strategy that includes leisure and sport by the end of 2001, went some way towards this wider acknowledgement of the structures and cultures that inform and are informed by leisure policy. These new measures were developed as a result of the Local Government Act 1999 which sought to replace the drive for economy and efficiency at the centre of CCT with a new focus on 'continuous improvement' in the delivery of services. In a further blurring of public and private provision, the Government gave its backing to the development of public–private partnerships (PPP) in 2000 when it was deemed that the Private Finance Initiative (PFI) could be used to fund capital development where such financial arrangements represent 'best value' in the delivery of public services. In emphasising the economic benefits of leisure and sport to local communities, the task for local authorities has therefore been how to ensure that the social and cultural needs and demands of communities are built into these strategies.

Leisure plans and Local Cultural Strategies

The development of Local Cultural Strategies is intended to provide a 'joined up' approach to leisure, sport and cultural provision and to redress some of the shortcomings and inequitable outcomes of previous local leisure plans and leisure strategies:

> These strategies will help local authorities to express their own cultural visions and priorities in response to the needs and aspirations of local communities. They will provide a strategic overview, recognising the role of cultural services in tackling the wider objectives of social inclusion, regeneration, lifelong learning and healthier and safer communities.
>
> (Department for Culture, Media and Sport 2002)

Moreover, the existence of a cultural strategy is one of seven Cultural Service Best Value Performance Indicators against which local authorities need to demonstrate continuous improvement in cost and efficiency in the development and delivery of services (Appleton 2002; Department for Culture, Media and Sport 2002). DCMS guidelines on the production of Local Cultural Strategies have advocated what is termed 'a thematic approach' to the new strategies. Such an approach has encouraged local authorities to select a combination of themes designed to address local needs and aspirations within a national policy context. These themes are intended to link different areas of service provision such as sport and the arts, to incorporate different user groups such as women and girls, young people and disabled people, and to cut across geographical divides within local authority areas. In response to both local needs and national policy agendas many local authority leisure services departments have attempted to prioritise social inclusion and equal opportunities as themes within their Local Cultural Strategies (Aitchison 2003c).

The creation of the Department for Culture, Media and Sport, and its subsequent advocacy of Cultural Strategies at national, regional and local levels, has resulted in a reappraisal of the meaning of the word 'culture' within UK public policy. No longer associated solely with the high arts, 'culture' has begun to be seen, in public policy circles at least, as an all-embracing term. This inclusive definition of 'culture' embraces everything previously encompassed by the terms leisure, recreation, performing and visual arts, creative industries, sport, tourism, museums and heritage, countryside visits and activities in addition to various forms of commercial consumption such as eating out, drinking, night clubs, entertainment and events, fashion and the media. The shifting semantics of the cultural and leisure-related sectors have posed a challenge for policy-makers and practitioners. Just as the general public has caught up with the replacement of the term 'recreation' by 'leisure', so public policy has acted as a catalyst in replacing the term 'leisure' with 'culture'. This evolving language has yet to be embraced fully by the general public among whom the term 'culture' is still associated with the arts and particularly with the high arts. The development of a cultural strategy therefore requires clarity concerning both the definition of culture and the role of cultural development within the community. Bone and Mitchell (2000: 8) state that 'culture represents many important parts of our daily lives, not just what we choose to do in our spare time. Culture is about values; leisure is more about purposeful (or otherwise) activities we carry out for our recreation'. They go on to emphasise that:

> At the heart of any cultural strategy there must be a real understanding of culture's characteristics, role and functions. The popular misconception of culture only being what is commonly referred to as 'high art' must be dispelled at the outset. All stakeholders need to share an unambiguous definition so they can recognise what culture can achieve for the area ... It is shaped by, and responsive to, the external environment. It is affected by language, geography, history, faith and religious beliefs, ecology, demography, customs and social norms. It can and does:
>
> - improve the quality of life
> - bring stimulation and purpose to existence
> - enable people to give full rein to self-expression
> - bring people together and underpin communities
> - enhance communication and understanding
> - unlock creativity and problem-solving
>
> Other valuable by-products of culture include:
>
> - developing self-confidence and capacity in individuals and communities
> - improving local identity and pride
> - promoting interest in the environment
> - providing positive solutions to problems presented by social exclusion
> - enabling people to imagine the future in positive and creative ways.
>
> (Bone and Mitchell, 2000: 7)

DCMS guidelines on developing Local Cultural Strategies intimate that culture is not just *what* we do in our spare time but *how* we do it and *why* such activities might have a useful purpose for the communities we live in. A definition of culture as more than just things to do in one's spare time is essential to communicate the overarching role of culture in acting as a vehicle for enhancing community development and social and cultural change. Such a view recognises the catalytic or supportive role that leisure and culture can play in enhancing the development and delivery of other areas of public policy and service provision such as education, employment, health, housing, transport and welfare; all of which will have a positive impact on women's lives. Thus, instead of focusing simply on the development of cultural services within the community there has been a shift towards the development of communities through cultural services (Coalter 2002).

The extent to which the Local Cultural Strategy reflects the aspirations of the community or challenges the norms and values of the community is central in determining the acceptance and success of the strategy. If a strategy is to be implemented successfully as a vehicle for social and cultural development then there has to be an element of challenge to the maintenance of the status quo combined with a recognisable degree of reflection of existing norms and values. Such a delicate balancing act requires careful consideration and is crucial in the shift in emphasis from the development of cultural services to the development of social capital (rather than just cultural capital) to aid community development (Baron *et al.* 2000; Putnam 2000; Lin 2001; Lin *et al.* 2001). Whereas Bourdieu (1984) identified cultural capital as individuals' acquired knowledge and familiarity with the arts and education and the ways in which such insights shaped their tastes and lifestyles, social capital relates more closely to the acquisition of the means by which individuals work together to enhance cultural and corporate capital within their communities.

The Department for Culture, Media and Sport, concerned to encourage such self-help within communities, issued guidance suggesting that local authorities should adopt a thematic approach to the development of their Cultural Strategy. In describing such an approach, Bone and Mitchell, (2000) state that a thematic approach,

> means that the strategy is focussed on delivery across a number of inter-connected topic areas, enabling high-level links to be made ... This is the philosophy behind the current emphasis on joined-up thinking – set against a traditional governmental background of all-too-often isolated initiatives tackling the same problems. The thematic approach also reflects the interests of partners and the needs and aspirations of local communities, which will inevitably be wider than those of the local authority acting in isolation.
>
> (Bone and Mitchell 2000: 26)

Local Cultural Strategies and their associated Community Strategies, within which Local Cultural Strategies are beginning to be subsumed, require that a balance between national policies and local priorities be achieved through the conciliatory management of consensus and conflict. Such an approach requires careful consideration of the needs of women and girls as one local group but also requires appreciation of the differentiated needs of women and girls who cannot be seen as one homogeneous group devoid of differences inscribed and reinscribed by social class, age, 'race', disability and wider social, cultural, economic, political and environmental circumstances.

Overview

This chapter started by stressing the importance of policy as a vehicle for implementing theory in practice. The need to contextualise leisure policy within wider social and public policy was also highlighted and the ensuing discussions demonstrated the relationship between leisure policy and social or public policy at both national and local levels and in relation to both leisure and sport. These discussions were informed by the structuralist theories of gender inequality outlined in Chapter 2 and by the theoretical underpinnings of the 'society in leisure' approach outlined in Chapter 3. The origins of contemporary leisure policy were placed in a historical context of public sector intervention in leisure from the eighteenth century. The chapter then moved on to examine the development of contemporary leisure policies designed to address social exclusion, including women's marginalisation in leisure. Both historical analysis and contemporary social critique illustrate the influence of socialist feminism and structuralist perspectives more generally in the development of policies that have sought to adopt leisure-related strategies as a means of addressing social exclusion.

The focus of the chapter then moved from these wider contextual discussions to an illustration of policy development in the area of sport and the role of national bodies such as Sport England (formerly the Sports Council) and the Women's Sport Foundation in implementing policies designed to promote gender equity in sport. This illustrative case study highlighted the relationship between gender and culture in relation to the role of the media and gender and structure in relation to the economics of sport sponsorship and funding for women in sport. The discussion pointed to both successes and failures in the delivery of gender equity-related sport policy and demonstrated the need to explore the structural provision of sport within a wider cultural context.

The chapter then turned the reader's gaze from national policy debates to the implementation of leisure-related policy at a local level. Here, the changing nature of local authorities and their impact on leisure provision and participation was examined in a discussion of UK local authority leisure policy spanning the last two decades. The role of strategic approaches in the delivery of gender equity through leisure and sport policy was then explored and the recent development of Local Cultural Strategies, with their frequent thematic focus on social inclusion, was discussed. The chapter concluded that, while such structural approaches to gender equity are still relevant, there needs to be a recognition by policy-makers of the wider cultural context within which gender relations are constructed, normalised and reproduced within society. Such a conclusion emphasises the role of both structural and cultural perspectives, in addition to the inter-relationship between the structural and the cultural, in developing our understanding of gender and leisure.

6 Gender and leisure education

Introduction: sociologies of gender and education

Leisure studies education provides a series of sites that are significant in the production, legitimation, reproduction and reworking of gender–power relations. These sites take the form of the school, the university and the professional institute where leisure education is organised in formal programmes and courses in leisure studies and leisure management and in the many leisure-related fields of study such as culture, media, heritage, tourism, sport, physical activity, exercise and physical education. In addition, sites of leisure participation associated with educational institutions offer further arenas in which the gender order within leisure, education and leisure education is played out. This is particularly the case in relation to active leisure participation in North America where the college network has traditionally provided a focus for the development of sport. Within the UK, where there is growing concern about the implications of decreasing levels of participation by young people in physical activity, the arts and classical music, it is the education system that has been singled out as failing to make use of leisure provision to promote health and well-being in a population educated for leisure through the acquisition of appropriate levels of cultural capital. This chapter, however, is not so much concerned with leisure provision and participation offered by the education system as with the study of leisure that takes place within education and specifically within higher education.

Within higher education in the UK there are now more women entrants to degree courses than men. The growth in women undergraduates is reflected in leisure studies/management but is not experienced evenly across leisure-related subject fields where men still comprise the majority of entrants to sport studies and sport science courses and women continue to outnumber men in tourism studies and tourism management programmes. However, the overall increase in women undergraduates is not reflected at postgraduate level where men continue to outnumber women. This is particularly significant as men continue to outnumber women in the upper levels of higher education. The increasing number of undergraduates means that postgraduate qualifications are often required to secure more senior employment positions or posts that would previously have been filled by someone with an undergraduate degree. Clearly, if male postgraduates outnumber female postgraduates it is almost inevitable that men will continue to be advantaged in seeking employment simply by dint of their higher level of qualification.

Similarly, increasing gender equity in the composition of the body of staff that teach undergraduate or postgraduate students is not advancing at the rate seen in relation to undergraduate student numbers. In contrast to those being educated, the educators are predominantly men and this imbalance increases with each increasing grade of staff. In the UK this means that the proportion of women staff decreases through the grades of lecturer, senior lecturer, principal lecturer, reader, professor and head of department. In North America a similar decrease in the representation of women is experienced with progression from assistant professor, to associate professor to full professor and chair of department. Moreover, these gender disparities are exacerbated by differentials between full and part-time employment in the UK and tenured and untenured employment in North America. This chapter seeks to review these gender relations and to explore their impact upon leisure studies education and the continued development of leisure studies as a subject field within the academy.

There is now an established body of feminist scholarship within the sociology of education that points to the complex nature of gender relations within the education system and its related sites, processes and practices (Acker 1989, 1990, 1992, 1994; Acker and Warren Piper 1984; Arnot and Weiner 1987; Barton and Walker 1983; Currie *et al.* 2000; David 1989; Gillborn and Youdell 2000; Mavin and Bryans 2002; Morley and Walsh 1995; Myers 2000; Salisbury and Riddell 2000; Walker and Barton 1983; Weiner 1985; Weiner and Arnot 1987; Whyte *et al.* 1985; Wyn *et al.* 2000). Just as the seats of learning in the form of sites of educational institutions have not been equally receptive to male and female staff, Acker (1994: 19) has emphasised that educational processes have not been uniformly or consistently receptive to feminist analysis: 'for some areas, like child development, women had always played a visible role, and "sex differences" had long been a respectable subject of study. For others, such as the study of higher education, women were scarce and feminist influence minimal'. Thus higher education has received less feminist attention than pre-school, primary, secondary or further education. Moreover, as Chapters 3 and 4 have illustrated, this disparity is emphasised further in relation to leisure, sport and tourism education where feminist and gender scholarship developed later than in other disciplines and subject fields.

Acker has been described by David (1994: 1) as 'one of the foremost feminist writers in the field of the sociology of education'. This chapter draws on Acker's work, and what David (1994: 1) has termed Acker's 'engendering of education'. The concept of engendered education is contextualised within the wider bodies of literature emanating from the sociology of education and more recent feminist sociologies of education. This literature then provides the necessary theoretical context against which to introduce and evaluate two models of gender scholarship in curriculum development (Schuster and Van Dyne 1984; Packer 1995). A review of the feminist and gender scholarship in leisure, sport and tourism education and research over the last three decades, and previously discussed in Chapter 3, affords an opportunity to assess the applicability of these models to leisure studies. Three similar models of research and curriculum development in leisure, sport and tourism are discussed and their unilinear approach to the development of gender scholarship evaluated. This discussion and evaluation subsequently informs the development of a composite model of stages of research and curriculum development in leisure, sport and tourism in higher education. Although the chapter acknowledges that trends towards gender scholarship are discernable in leisure, sport and tourism education, a cautionary note warns against the wholesale acceptance of uniform and unilinear developments towards gender scholarship in all subject areas at all times. In this respect, a poststructural analytical framework serves to render visible some of the more complex cultural relations that might militate against the development of more progressive gender scholarship. Through rendering visible the sites and processes of knowledge construction, legitimation, reproduction and reworking the aim of gender scholarship is then revealed as challenging existing inequalities and contributing to more inclusive higher education curricula. A further intended outcome of such a discussion is the development of more sophisticated research in the field of gender and leisure research so that the criticisms made by Rojek (2000: 112), and outlined in Chapter 3, might be addressed explicitly in future research. These aims are reflected in a number of research 'tasks' that Acker identified in responding to her own question of 'How might a feminist approach contribute to the sociology of education?:

> Filling gaps in our knowledge about the education of girls and women; Reassessing and reinterpreting data and findings from past studies that contain some information on women and sex differences; Asking questions through making problematic those commonsense assumptions about women and women's education that have so far passed as fact; Uncovering and replacing what I have called elsewhere 'deficit models of women' – essentially, approaches that blame the victim for her lack of some quality that is defined as desirable because it is normally associated with men; Discovering exactly why and how schooling shapes the lives of women in particular ways.
>
> (Acker 1994: 37)

Theorising 'engendered education'

Within higher education, Acker (1994: 125) points to three areas of challenge to women: 'the conflicting demands of family and career', examined under the heading *greedy institutions*; 'the relative powerlessness of minorities', examined under the heading *negotiating from weakness*; and 'the male domination of knowledge and practice', examined under the heading of *consciousness of women*. Acker stresses that her purpose is not to add to the burgeoning distributive research literature on employment status, pay and promotions, but to undertake relational research that examines 'engendered education'.

This chapter, together with the book as a whole, has a similar emphasis upon *relational*, rather than *distributive*, data. Although the major sources of empirical research demonstrating discrimination and segregation within higher education are acknowledged, the chapter's focus is upon the sites and processes related to the production, legitimisation, reproduction and reworking of knowledge and power within academia. (See Higher Education Statistics Agency Limited 2002 and Wilson 1997 for distributive data relating to male and female employees in higher education). So, while it is fully recognised that only ten years ago men held over 95 per cent of all professorial positions in the UK (Acker 1994), this chapter attempts to go beyond these statistical data on inequality within organisations to examine the processes involved in the production and reproduction of gender–power relations within higher education. In other words, this chapter seeks to explore the cultural relations that inform and are informed by the structural inequalities evident in higher education in general and reproduced within leisure studies education.

Theory on gender in higher education has emanated both from the sub-discipline of the sociology of education and, later, from feminist sociology and then the feminist sociology of education. According to Acker:

> A discipline, or even a sub-discipline, has certain identifying symbols: a textbook, a journal, a professional association or other means of constructing an intellectual community. Lacking a comfortable home in either the professional associations of sociology or of education, British sociology of education needed a new network. Mainly through the efforts of Len Barton, then at Westhill College of Education and now at Sheffield University, the subdiscipline was given such a base, first in the annual International Sociology of Education Conference, which began in 1978 and continues still, and second in the creation in 1980 of a new flagship journal in the field, the *British Journal of the Sociology of Education* (BJSE).
>
> (Acker 1994: 15–16)

The sociology of education developed through the 1960s and 1970s to a point where the field could be characterised by two competing paradigms, loosely described as 'neo-Marxist' and 'ethnographic'. The early neo-Marxist research concerned itself with the effects of social class and economic background on educational participation and performance. Like neo-Marxist research within leisure studies, and outlined in Chapter 2, the neo-Marxist work in education can be criticised for its neglect of other social variables such as gender and race, and for its failure to examine the role of process, interaction and discourse in the production and reproduction of education, knowledge and power. Much of the neo-Marxist work was influenced by research from the US, or what was termed the 'new sociology', and Acker has (1994: 15) identified *Schooling in Capitalist America* (Bowles and Gintis 1976) as a key publication from this paradigm and this era. Bowles and Gintis echoed the earlier work of Althusser (1971) who contended that education, as 'a state apparatus', mirrored the relations of capitalist production by serving the interests of the ruling class. In contrast, ethnographic research within the sociology of education drew upon symbolic interactionism and its emphasis on process, interaction and discourse in the construction of knowledge and the production and reproduction of education. Young's *Knowledge and Control*, published in 1975, provided a key text for future discussion on the nature of the production and legitimisation of knowledge and the relationship between power and knowledge. Similarly, Bourdieu (1973) argued that education reproduced the social relations of power and knowledge by defining both materialities and discourses that constituted 'cultural capital'.

These two approaches, sometimes overlapping and sometimes polarised, were joined by a third approach in the late 1970s with the development of the feminist sociology of education. In 1978 Deem's book *Women and Schooling* was published before she went on to be a key figure in the development of feminist leisure studies in the 1980s. Together with Byrne's *Women and Education*, also published in 1978, Deem helped set the agenda for the creation of a sub-field of the subdiscipline of the sociology of education. In other words, a specialist area of research on gender and education was created within the already established subdiscipline of the sociology of education. Between the late 1970s and late 1980s, the area of gender and education then developed its own signifiers of academic status just as its parent subdiscipline, the sociology of education, had done a decade before:

> By the mid 1980s, the visibility of what Arnot (1985) has called the sociology of women's education had increased still further. One of the sociology of education conferences was devoted to questions of race and gender and its papers were published (Barton and Walker 1983; Walker and Barton 1983). Other collections with sociological content included Acker *et al.* (1984), Weiner (1985), Whyte *et al.* (1985), Arnot and Weiner (1987) and Weiner and Arnot (1987). The

culmination of many of these efforts to carve out a new scholarly field was the founding of the journal *Gender and Education* by June Purvis in 1989.

(Acker 1994: 19)

More recently, and again mirroring developments in other disciplines, subdisciplines and fields of study, the subdiscipline of the feminist sociology of education has encountered, though not fully embraced, poststructuralist theory so that at least some of the research now talks about gender and genders rather than the single homogenising category 'women'. This recognition of diversity within the category 'women' has increased calls for 'gender scholarship' in preference to 'feminist scholarship' which is sometimes deemed to be homogenising and essentialist of women and invisibilising of men and the interrelationships between women and men. Such poststructuralist acknowledgement of the importance of complex interrelationships, webs and networks of power has given further emphasis to the interconnections or interdependence of material and symbolic power, structures and cultures of power or, what is defined within this book as 'the social–cultural nexus' of power.

The developments outlined above serve to recognise the increasing complexity with which gender relations are viewed. Thus Wallace and Hall (1994), in their research into secondary school management, identified a dual perspective or 'power–culture metaphor' as a means of exploring 'the expression of both the shared values of a culture and the differential use of power to realise particular interests' (Wallace and Hall, 1994: 27). Their work combined Ball's (1987) theory of political power within organisations and Nias's (1989) theory of cultural power to demonstrate what Giddens (1984) had referred to previously as the 'transformative capacity' of power. In developing a transformative model of curriculum and research development, and drawing of poststructural analyses, integrated social and cultural perspectives acknowledge the complexity and fluidity of education and research as both sites and processes of structural and cultural power. Instead of viewing power relations and inequality as immutable, such an approach offers scope for transformation by change agents that seek to enhance gender equity and inclusion in education and research and in the areas addressed by such education and research.

Curriculum development and engendered education

Engendered education can be seen quite visibly in the structures of higher education where teaching, administration, research and management reflect structures of sex-segregation with men and women occupying different positions. Sex-role stereotyping and sex-role spill-over maintain cultures rather than structures of engendered education with women and men concentrated in roles that are deemed to be feminised and masculinised respectively. There is ample distributive research pointing to the concentration of women in the lower grade posts in higher education, supplemented by relational data which demonstrate that women perform a disproportionate share of the unacknowledged administrative support work, even when employed on the same grade as men:

> In a recent diary-keeping exercise, it was shown that academics already work an average 53.5 hours per week, that administrative duties take up as much as 17–18 hours of this, and that the bulk of personal research, nearly 40 per cent, was being squeezed into evenings and weekends. It was also clear that women carried a greater administrative load than men. Furthermore, women at every level actually worked longer hours than men. The average working week of a woman professor was 64.5 hours compared with an average for male professors of 58.6 hours.
>
> (Davies and Holloway 1995: 16)

This culture of the 'greedy university' is sustained, according to Currie *et al.* (2000: 269), by the 'masculinist discourse ... in these institutions, which acts to disenfranchise all those who do not operate within its restricted and restrictive boundaries'. Within such institutional cultures Bagilhole (1993) defines women academics as 'good campus citizens' in that they are more inclined to undertake pastoral duties which can be seen as a form of sex-role stereotyping, sex-role spill-over or what Parson and Bales' (1955) functionalist theory would have identified as 'expressive' rather than 'instrumental' roles. The works of both Acker (1994) and Bagilhole (1993) contain numerous references, both explicit and implicit, to the social construction of gender roles and the influence of such constructions upon women as teachers and academics. Acker's and Bagilhole's work echoes that of many other feminist writers who have commented on the construction of women as outsiders and Others within 'malestream' environments. In chapters with titles that refer to 'no-woman's land' and 'Women, the Other academics', Acker points to the marginalisation and isolation of women within academia with such Otherness explained, in part, as a product of the replication of the gender–power relations of society within the education system (see Chapter 4 for a fuller discussion of Othering).

McDowell (1990: 328) has drawn on both structural and poststructural feminist analyses to identify the gender division of labour in academia as both a material and cultural factor in contributing to women's lower status in higher education. She has commented on the ways in which women actually support the advancement of men's careers to the detriment of their own by focusing on teaching and administration while their male colleagues engage in research activities which she describes as the 'paramount criterion for promotion'. While McDowell was writing from

Stages	Questions	Incentives	Means	Outcome
Invisibility (The closed door)	Who are the great thinkers?	Maintaining standards of excellence	Back to basics	Fixed products Students as vessels
Search for missing women (Door still closed)	Who are the great female Darwins, Shakespeares?	Affirmative action/compensatory	Add data within existing paradigms	'Exceptional' women and role models added to syllabus
Women as subordinate and oppressed (The revolving door)	Why is women's work marginal and devalued?	Anger/social justice	Protest existing paradigms but within perspective of dominant group	'Images of Women' courses
Women studied on own terms (Door continues to revolve)	What was/is women's experience?	Intellectual	Outside existing paradigms	Interdisciplinary courses
New scholarship challenges disciplines (The door ajar)	How valid are current definitions of norms for behaviour	Epistemology	Testing the paradigms Gender as category of analysis	Beginnings of transformation Theory courses Students as collaborator
Visibility; transformed curriculum experience (The open door)	How can we account more fully for the diversity of human experience	Inclusive vision of human experience based on differences and diversity not sameness and generalisation	Transform the paradigms	Reconceptualised and inclusive core; dynamic process

Figure 1 Stages of gender scholarship in curriculum development
[Source: adapted from Schuster and Van Dyne (1984) and Packer (1995).]

the perspective of the 'old universities' in the UK, the majority of teaching and research in leisure, tourism and sport studies is undertaken in the UK's 'new universities' and this situation is mirrored in many of the Australian universities where leisure and recreation studies have developed in what were often institutes of technology. However, over the last decade, new universities in the UK and Australia have placed greater emphasis upon research as a promotion criterion and many research professors in new universities are now more highly paid than heads of school or department who have secured promotion through their focus on administration. The male domination of research and the production of knowledge have led a number of feminist sociologists of education to highlight the difficulties inherent in the gender transformation of the curriculum and research and in women's success in securing promotion.

Progressive developments towards a more inclusive gender scholarship have been noted, however. Schuster and Van Dyne (1984), for example, have illustrated a possible transformative process within education and have identified six stages of curriculum development with each advancing stage demonstrating an increasing feminist commitment. Figure 1 (see p. 125) combines Schuster and Van Dyne's model with that of Packer (1995) who, in a similar critique, used the analogy of the closed, revolving, ajar and open door to signify the increasing degree of receptiveness towards feminist scholarship afforded by a subject field or discipline. By combining these models, feminist research can be seen as moving from the study of what Acker (1994: 13) termed a 'deficit model of women' to a model where knowledge is viewed as social power. This model is revisited towards the end of this chapter where similar chronologies of 'gender scholarship' are presented from leisure studies, tourism studies and sport studies.

Research and engendered education

> Most of the knowledge produced in our society has been produced by men: they have usually generated the explanations and the schemata and have then checked with each other and vouched for the accuracy and adequacy of their view of the world. They have created *men's studies* (the academic curriculum), for, by not acknowledging that they are presenting only the explanations of *men*, they have 'passed off' this knowledge as human knowledge. Women have been excluded as the producers of knowledge and as the subjects of knowledge, for men have often made their own knowledge and their own sex, representative of humanity; they have, in Mary Daly's terms, presented false knowledge by insisting that their *partial* view be accepted as the whole.
>
> (Spender 1981: 2)

The social science literature reveals that research continues to be a male-dominated arena measurable in quantitative terms but also identifiable in terms of research values, prestige, reward and promotion (Acker 1994;

Weiner 1986). Morley (1995: 118), drawing on the work of Cole (1979), states that even 'when productivity is equal, rewards for women are smaller'. She goes on to say that this has been explained 'by suggesting that women's work is judged less favourably than men's, particularly if it is from a feminist perspective as this is diminished as minor or self-serving by mainstream academics (Morley 1995: 118). Roberts (1981) emphasises the difficulty of developing feminist research within a male-dominated academy:

> Feminists, in stressing the need for a reflexive sociology in which the sociologist takes her own experiences seriously and incorporates them into her work, expose themselves to the challenges of lack of objectivity from those of their male colleagues whose sociological insight does not enable them to see that their own work is affected in a similar way by their experience and views of the world as men.
>
> (Roberts 1981: 16)

A number of authors have also pointed out that feminist researchers investigating the position of women within higher education, or the nature of feminist research itself, are open to even greater accusations of self-interest and subjective research. Acker (1994: 137), for example, has stated that 'the literature on academic women in Britain is rather sparse, probably reflecting a tendency to consider them members of an elite rather than a disadvantaged group worthy of feminist research'. Chapter 3 demonstrated that within feminist leisure studies the preoccupation has been with research identifying gender inequity in leisure participation and recommending revised policies and practices to bring about greater levels of gender equity. The gender inequity within the sites of such knowledge production has rarely been called into question.

The intended outcome of the majority of research activity is publications and, as Spender (1981: 188) notes: 'when it is mostly men who are in the position to decide what gets published and what does not, there is a problem of male dominance, which demands feminist attention'. The 'publish or perish' mantra cannot be overstated in the current global academic climate. In North America, Australia and New Zealand a track record of publications in international-refereed journals is often required to secure tenure and receive promotion. In the UK, the Research Assessment Exercise demands that individuals publish to achieve or maintain respectable research 'ratings' for their institution which, in turn, influence research funding and graduate student recruitment (Higher Education Funding Council for England 2003). Publishing, and involvement with the gatekeeping institutions in publishing, is one of the most important factors in shaping academic discourse (Morley and Walsh, 1995). Power and control within academic publishing is vested in the hands of 'gatekeepers' who determine what is deemed to be social knowledge (Smith 1978: 287).

Spender (1981: 187) identifies as gatekeepers editors of journals, referees, reviewers and advisors to publishers who, together, 'set the parameters in which individuals are encouraged to work if they wish to be at the centre of issues in their discipline' (Spender 1981: 186).

Engaging with the work of Morley and Walsh (1995), Smith (1978) and Spender (1981) previous research in leisure and tourism studies has sought to address these concerns by undertaking an analysis of the 'codification of knowledge' in a sample of international-refereed journals in leisure and tourism studies (Aitchison 2001e). Primary statistical analysis was developed from sex-segregation data in relation to six highly respected international refereed journals: *Leisure Studies, Journal of Leisure Research, Managing Leisure, Tourism Management, Annals of Tourism Research* and the *Journal of Sustainable Tourism*. The purpose of the research, however, was not to embrace or eschew Spender's radical feminist critique outlined at the end of the previous paragraph. Rather, the research investigated the complexity of the interrelationships between gender, power and knowledge and recognised the contribution of post-structural *and* structural feminist analyses to our understanding of the 'codification of knowledge' in leisure studies. This perspective acknowledged that, in universities and other 'modern professional organisations' (Weber 1922), power is used to maintain symbolic or cultural control as much, if not more than, material control (Etzioni 1964). The distributive research of the authorship of journal articles and the composition of journal editorial boards was undertaken to complement previous relational research and to accommodate Acker's (1994) call for a wide-ranging research programme related to gender, education and the production of knowledge. Although more usually associated with material analyses of gender relations, the quantitative data described in the study revealed that knowledge production is a product of both structural and cultural power and that both quantitative and qualitative data are required to theorise the social–cultural nexus of the gendered codification of knowledge.

The audit examining the authorship of all articles published by the six journals between 1982 and 1997 – a total of 1,784 articles – revealed that the ratio of male to female authors was four to one with men comprising 80.24 per cent of authors of refereed journal articles. Tourism journals demonstrated higher levels of sex-segregation than leisure journals and management journals displayed higher levels of sex-segregation than non-applied journals. The highest percentage of female authors (21.81) was found in the *Journal of Leisure Research* and the lowest percentage of female authors was found in *Tourism Management* (16.38). However, there was relatively little deviation from the averages outlined above and only a 3 per cent difference was recorded between the journal with the highest percentage of male authors (*Tourism Management*) and the journal with the lowest percentage of male authors (*Journal of Leisure*

Research). Men were also far more likely to be co-authors of refereed articles than women, raising questions of women's apparent isolation within the research environment, the more onerous task of achieving publication on one's own, and the subsequent effect upon women's research curricula vitae and future career progression. The more informal process of book reviewing displayed even greater levels of male dominance than the formal process of article refereeing, and men were authors of almost 90 per cent of all book reviews (Aitchison 2001).

The composition of editorial boards of the six leisure and tourism journals in 1997 showed that, in most cases, there was a close correlation between the percentage of men on the editorial board and the percentage of articles authored by men. For example, in the *Journal of Sustainable Tourism* both the percentage of men on the Editorial Board and the percentage of articles authored by men were identical at 81.8 per cent. In *Annals of Tourism Research*, 89.5 per cent of the editorial board was made up of men in 1997 while 87.8 per cent of published articles were authored by men in that year. In *Tourism Management*, however, 22.3 per cent of articles published in 1997 were authored by women whilst only 2.7 per cent of the editorial board were women. In the *Journal of Leisure Research*, which had the highest representation of women on an editorial board at 40.7 per cent, less than 30 per cent of articles were authored by women. Although these figures show varying patterns there is a clearly discernable trend of journal authorship reflecting the gender composition of the editorial board. Further research would be required to discern whether this is a straightforward correlation or whether other factors, such as percentage of articles submitted by women, are just as significant.

To contextualise further the sex-segregation data from leisure and tourism journals, comparative data were gathered from gender audits of publishing in cognate subject fields. On examining refereed journals from these subject areas it is apparent that leisure studies is less alert to gender issues, and the need for a reflexive approach towards gender and power in relation to the construction of knowledge, than many other subject fields. Looking at disciplines and subject fields that border leisure studies, it is possible to identify many examples of good practice in relation to gender scholarship. Two journals are highlighted here as providing data and analyses which offer useful frameworks for performance measurement, review, evaluation and monitoring of sex-segregation and gender relations in academic research and publishing. The contribution of social and cultural geography to leisure studies (outlined Chapter 4), is well established and the journal *Area* provides an illustration of a reflexive approach to gender scholarship in the social sciences. At the other end of the social–natural science continuum in leisure studies, the *Journal of Sport and Exercise Psychology* provides a similarly gender-aware approach.

In relation to geography, Rose (1993: 2) has previously stated 'Clearly, women have been and continue to be marginalised as producers of geographical knowledge. Nor are they prominent as the subjects of that knowledge'. Rose revealed that only 5 per cent of the papers in *Transactions of the Institute of British Geographers* were authored by women between 1974 and 1978, only 9 per cent of the papers in the *Australian Geographer* were authored by women between 1973 and 1978, and by 1989–90 only 13 per cent of papers in *Area* were authored by women. However, in spite of this picture of inequality and exclusion, it is possible to identify improvements in gender scholarship within geography over the last decade. Taking *Area* as an example of a journal that has introduced measures of good practice in relation to gender auditing, it is notable that the honorary editor of the journal is required to produce an annual report outlining the content and flow of the journal with particular reference to submission, acceptance and rejection rates together with cross-tabulations for gender and single and jointly authored articles. This report is published in the journal and demonstrates that the percentage of articles received from women rose from 10 per cent in 1990–91 to 33 per cent in 1996–97. In comparison, the percentage of articles authored by women and published in the selection of leisure and tourism journals outlined above only increased to 19.7 per cent in 1996 in spite of a higher starting point of 13.3 per cent in 1990. Painter (1998: 1) comments in his Editor's Report for *Area*'s 1996–97 publications that:

> Where the gender of authors is concerned, the largest single category of submissions continues to be sole male authors, although the proportion (38%) in this group marks a reduction from 53% in 1994–95 and 57% in 1995–96. Single male authors also topped the poll for the highest rejection rate, suggesting that, over time, *Area* may be moving slowly in the direction of greater equality in the gender distribution of published authors. There was also a marked increase in the proportion of papers submitted by joint female authors, from zero in 1994–95 and 2% in 1995–96 to 14% in 1996–97. The proportion of papers submitted by sole female authors has been more stable (21%, 16% and 19% in the same three years).

Within the *Journal of Sport and Exercise Psychology* each editor provides an extensive article at the end of their term of office. In 1992, Gill's thorough review presented comprehensive data on the gender of authors and illustrated that between 1985 and 1990 an average of 37.5% of articles had female authors.

> At the previous editorial change in 1985, Dan (Landers, Boutcher, & Wang, 1986) wrote an article presenting information on the editorial process and the journal submissions and status over the first 7 years.

At the same time, I (Gill, 1986) presented my views and plans as I began my editorial term. Now, as Dan did 5 years ago, I present information that may provide readers with further insight into journal editorial policies and practices and also provide an indication of the state of sport and exercise psychology as reflected by submissions to the journal over the past 5 years.

(Gill 1992: 1)

From both the journals outlined above, and from a number of other social science journals, the following examples of good practice in relation to promoting a more inclusive approach towards gender representation in academic publishing can be noted: the inclusion of an annual report; the provision of an editorial report at the end of each editor's period of office; the publication of submission figures by gender; the provision of publication figures by gender; the publication of figures relating to the number of single, joint and mixed authored papers; the publication of rejection rates by gender, single, joint and mixed authored submissions; the publication of timescales for the review of submitted papers; the publication of names of referees drawn from outside the journal's editorial board; the publication of gender statistics of referees; the publication of names of book reviewers drawn from outside the journal's editorial board; the publication of gender statistics of book reviewers; the publication of a statement on equal opportunities policy. However, the journal audit of gender representation and sex-segregation in leisure and tourism journals revealed that *none* of the practices outlined above had been adopted by *any* of the journals during the fifteen-year period covered by the audit.

Building a model of gender scholarship in leisure, tourism and sport education

Schuster and Van Dyne's (1984) and Packer's (1995) stages of gender scholarship, illustrated in Figure 1 (see p. 125), are echoed within leisure, tourism and sport where Henderson (1994), Swain (1995) and Talbot (1996) have identified five-phase typologies charting the development of unilinear chronologies of gender scholarship in leisure, tourism and sport research respectively. Each of these authors developed their chronology independently of the others, yet the similarities between the models and the stages of chronological development are clearly evident (Aitchison 2003e). Although poststructuralist interpretations might guard against the wholesale adoption of unilinear chronologies as a means of encapsulating the complexities of historical change, such a 'chronological classificatory framework' does serve a purpose in contributing to an understanding of the changing nature of gender scholarship (McDowell 1993a: 162).

Henderson's (1994: 122) typology was first presented in an article entitled 'Perspectives on analysing gender, women and leisure' published in the *Journal of Leisure Research*. Her typology progresses from an initial phase of *Invisible (womanless) scholarship* where 'little was written about women, let alone gender, in the leisure literature in the United States from 1940 until the early 1980s'. The typology concludes with a final phase of *Gender scholarship* denoting the shift from feminist scholarship and distributive research to gender scholarship informed by a relational approach. Resonating critiques by Stanley and Wise (1993), Henderson's second phase identifies *Compensatory (add women and stir) scholarship*. Phase three is identified by Henderson (1994: 125) as *Dichotomous (sex) differences scholarship* with an emphasis on biological determinism and essentialism and a neglect of culturally constructed difference. *Feminist (woman-centred) scholarship* forms phase four of Henderson's chronology and she attributes much of the 1980s socialist feminist leisure research discussed in Chapter 3 to this phase (Deem 1986; Green *et al.* 1987; Henderson and Bialeschki 1991).

Swain's (1995: 254) typology also identifies five distinct phases of scholarship related to the increasing visibility of gender issues within *Annals of Tourism Research*. Swain's typology mirrors Henderson's, demonstrating that gender scholarship in tourism studies appears to reflect the changes being experienced simultaneously in leisure studies. Phase one, identified as being an era of *No women*, ran from the first issue of the journal in 1973 to 1977 when 'the first articles on women in tourism appeared in volumes 4–8 (1977–1981)'. Phase two is then identified as *Add women* and phase three as *Descriptive differences*. Phase four is seen as being *Women centred* with phase five again reflecting *Gender scholarship*.

Talbot (1996) provides a further five-phase typology that follows a similar chronology to those presented by Henderson and Swain. Talbot's sport education typology, however, reflects a more pragmatic outcome to a transformed curriculum and research agenda in that she sees gender scholarship in sport education influencing gender equity in sport policy and practice. This interesting progression from theoretical research to policy development through to practical change is clearly one that affords scope for the development of integrated leisure theory, policy and practice. Talbot's model illustrates progression from an initial *Catching up* phase; a phrase used frequently in sport to reflect women's increasing times and distances in relation to men's. Here, the male benchmark is seen as the standard or the goal to be attained by women, something that would be questioned in feminist poststructural approaches. The second phase identified, like Henderson's and Swain's, is that of *Add women and stir* and again, like the previous two models, this is then followed by a third phase that increases women's *Visibility* in their own right. The fourth phase of Talbot's model is concerned with *Critique* of male norms and female compliance and this is then followed by a final phase of *Reconstruction* of sport research and sport itself.

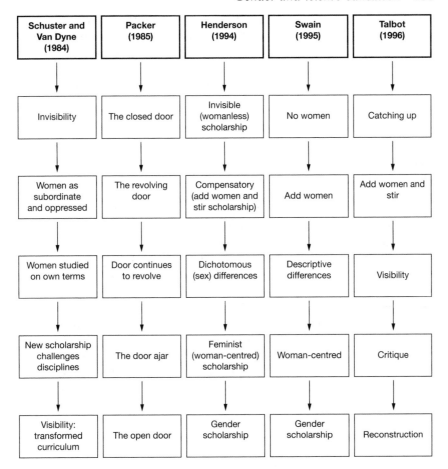

Figure 2 Models of gender scholarship in leisure, sport and tourism education
[Source: Devised from Schuster and Van Dyne (1984); Packer (1995); Henderson (1994); Swain (1995) and Talbot (1996).]

To assess the extent to which leisure and tourism journals have moved towards 'gender scholarship' and a more equitable research environment, as suggested by Henderson (1994), Swain (1995) and Talbot (1996), it is necessary to examine longitudinal change. The research of the leisure and tourism journals outlined above demonstrated that the percentage of female-authored papers published at five-year intervals in four journals that spanned the period 1982–97 did not follow a strictly linear progression. Whereas both *Tourism Management* and the *Journal of Leisure Research* demonstrated in excess of a 20 per cent increase in the number of published papers authored by women between 1982 and 1997, *Annals of Tourism Research* had only a 4 per cent rise and *Leisure Studies* actually recorded a 6 per cent fall. This indicates that the interrelationships between gender, power and knowledge in the construction of leisure, sport and tourism education and research are therefore more complex and more contested than previous unilinear models and typologies of research and curriculum change derived solely from structuralist perspectives might have suggested.

Overview

Whereas much of the research referred to in the feminist sociology of education literature is based on schools, and has been undertaken by researchers employed by universities, research into higher education is usually undertaken by those already employed within higher education. As feminists engaging in the sociology of higher education, we are locked within our own 'insider outsider' identity as we seek to critique the very world of which we are a part (Raymond 1986: 233).

The feminist sociology of higher education literature reveals that much of the research has been distributive rather than relational in nature and has focused on the employment and career progression patterns of women academics rather than the micro-structures or cultures that inform such patterns. Many of these research projects have resulted in recommendations for implementing equal opportunities policies, practices and procedures to encourage gender equity in staff recruitment, retention and career progression (Acker 1994). Although such distributive research is invaluable in demonstrating current inequality, and in focusing attention on strategies and targets for alleviating inequality, research addressing relational issues is also of importance in informing progress towards gender scholarship (Adler *et al.* 1993).

This book has been concerned with the construction of knowledge and theory within leisure studies and the ways in which such knowledge is translated into policy and practice. Within higher education, the subject field of leisure studies represents a key site and process of knowledge construction and the development of theory related to gender and leisure. This chapter has sought to review two models of gender scholarship in generic higher education and to contextualise three further models of gender scholarship within leisure, tourism and sport studies in relation to these broader feminist sociologies of education. The models were tested in relation to one site of engendered education: that of academic journals. The findings of the empirical research phase revealed that, while the models do provide a generalised trend towards gender scholarship, their rather structuralist approach masks the nuances of gender–power relations in higher education. Poststructuralist analysis, or a combination of structuralist and poststructuralist analysis, might therefore be advocated as a more sophisticated approach towards developing a critique of engendered education in leisure, tourism and sport studies.

7 Gender and leisure management

Introduction

The previous chapters have demonstrated how the cultural turn has recently transformed gender theory and methodology within social science. Gender studies, sociology, geography, social policy, education studies and, more recently, leisure studies have engaged with increasingly post-structural analyses of gender–power relations, albeit with varying degrees of acceptance. Within business and management studies too there has been growing recognition of the need to examine organisational cultures to supplement and complement previous analyses of organisational cultures.

Notwithstanding these developments, the research of gender–power relations in leisure management remains limited in volume and predominantly structuralist in approach. Consequently, cultural representations of gender–power relations in leisure management have remained largely untheorised (Aitchison 2000d). Structural, material or procedural 'improvements' in gender equity can be seen in the form of equal opportunities policies that are now enshrined in the legislation of many countries and implemented within many organisational structures. However, legacies of previous inequity often remain ingrained within the cultures of organisations. For example, compared to male colleagues on the same grade, and in spite of the presence of equal opportunities policies, women are still less likely to be seen as ready for promotion to a management role, less likely to be seen as suitable candidates to 'act up' into management roles, and less likely to be paid the same as male managers if they do achieve promotion to a management position.

Poststructural theory moves the critical eye from structures to cultures revealing the underpinning discourses and networks of power responsible for maintaining inequity or, indeed, for transforming equity policy into practice in everyday life. A focus on the social–cultural nexus recognises the mutually informing nature of structural and cultural power within organisations. It is argued here that further advances in gender equity require recognition of the interplay between structures and cultures within management. This approach seeks to build on the work of Adkins (1998:

47) who has also advocated research that combines cultural and structural analyses of gender–power relations in organisations. Such an approach, she states, is required at a time when our 'critical attention should be directed at the emerging gendered social/non-social nexus'.

This chapter attempts to combine cultural and structural analyses of gender–power relations in leisure management in an attempt to offer a more complete picture of the *sexuality of organisation* within leisure services (Hearn *et al.* 1989). By drawing on empirical research of *Gender Equity in Leisure Management*, undertaken in 1998/99, the chapter renders visible the social–cultural nexus of gender–power relations in leisure management (Aitchison, Brackenridge and Jordan 1999; Aitchison, Jordan and Brackenridge 1999; Aitchison 2000). Such a critique is constructed in relation to leisure management in general and the experiences of women members of the UK's Institute of Leisure and Amenity Management in particular.

The experiences narrated by women interviewees and respondents confirmed the presence of both structural and cultural constraints to achieving gender equity within leisure management. Previously, a clearly defined range of structural barriers such as lack of childcare provision have been documented in relation to women's inclusion in the workplace and their career progression within the workforce. Cultural resistance by both organisations and individuals to such inclusion and progression has been less visible within the discourses of management and leisure. This chapter documents the structural barriers recounted by women in leisure services within the wider context of cultural constraints experienced by women seeking career progression within leisure management. The aim of the chapter is neither to reiterate nor expand on the mass of empirical evidence that now exists in relation to sex discrimination in employment and vertical and horizontal sex-segregation in the workplace (Ledwith and Colgan 1996). Instead, an attempt is made to go beyond the statistical evidence on inequality within organisations and to examine the production and reproduction of gender–power relations within the workplace.

The chapter starts by defining the terms for the ensuing discussion on gender and management. It then outlines the origins and development of feminist theories related to gender and management including contemporary poststructural perspectives on the sexuality of organisation. Prior to discussing gender and leisure management, however, the chapter seeks to provide a contextual overview of gender equity research in relation to a series of other service sectors. The discussion then focuses on gender equity in leisure management by providing data and analysis from a series of research projects examining gender equity in leisure and sport management. The chapter then seeks to evaluate two specific aspects of gender–power relations in leisure management. First, structures and cultures of (un)equal opportunities in leisure management are explored and, second, gender equity and career progression in leisure management is evaluated. The discussion within the chapter therefore progresses from a focus on the workplace to a focus on the workforce and the interrelationships between the two.

Defining the terms in studies of gender and management

In their book entitled *The Sexuality of Organisation*, Hearn *et al.* (1989: 1) stated that 'Sexuality, gender, organisations, organisation: these concepts and their interrelationships are the central focus of this book'. An analysis of gender–power relations in organisations therefore necessitates acquaintance with the lexicon of the body of knowledge now referred to as the sexuality of organisation, a term coined by Hearn *et al.* (1989) following earlier work by Hearn and Parkin (1987) who developed the term 'organisation sexuality':

> Analysis of the ways in which organisations construct sexuality, and sexuality constructs organisations, are necessary conceptually and politically. In addition, the concept of 'organisation sexuality' has been developed to convey the paradoxical and powerful form of that interrelation.
>
> (Hearn et al. 1989: 25)

Sexuality, like gender and feminism, has a multiplicity of both positive and negative definitions. Most definitions make reference to the role of desire and the interconnections between power, knowledge and pleasure in constructing desire. The links between sexuality and power are perhaps most visible in the work of Foucault, who viewed sexuality as a fundamental communicative practice in the discourse of power. However, Foucault's 'concern with how sexuality is constituted in its construction generally ignored women and scholarship on women' (Hearn *et al.* 1989: 8). The complexity of sexuality as a conduit through which power is exercised and negotiated has been commented upon at length and from different feminist perspectives and these commentaries have recently been extended to embrace poststructural analyses. For example, Hearn *et al.* (1989: 13), from their self-identified pro-feminist perspective, call for a definition which views sexuality as 'an ordinary and frequent public process rather than an extraordinary feature of private life' or as 'one aspect of an all-pervasive "politics of the body" rather than a separable, discrete set of practices'.

It would be almost impossible to define sexuality without defining gender and many writers have merged the two categories by subsuming sexuality within gender. MacKinnon (1995), on the other hand, is one of few writers who have suggested that sexuality is the overarching framework within which gender is subsumed. Hearn *et al.* (1989: 2) state that:

The first and most important point to be made is that although gender and sexuality are conceptually distinct, they are also clearly closely related ... sexuality and gender are intimately interrelated with production and reproduction in and of society, and with the production and reproduction of organisations and organisation: hence a central element in that process is what we have called the sexuality of organisation.

Feminist writers have identified a number of different relationships between sexuality and power with many of these theories devised in relation to broad gender relationships rather than in reference to specific organisational cultures. As Chapter 4 revealed, French feminist philosophers and contemporary feminist social and cultural geographers have emphasised sexuality as the desire for the Other. Feminist writers from cultural and literary studies such as Kappeler (1986) have also provided critiques of sexuality as representation, and, as outlined in the previous chapter, writers such as Spender (1980) have emphasised the role of language as a mediator of sexuality and power in the construction of knowledge within and between organisations. What each of these writers has proposed is that sexuality is not confined to sexual practice but permeates culture at a much deeper level. For example, MacKinnon's (1995) more radical critiques have drawn attention to the ways in which the state condones the sexualisation of the non-sexual to maintain existing power structures within and between organisations.

Writings theorising power relationships within organisations can be traced back to Weber's *The Theory of Economic and Social Organisations* (1949). Weber examined the legitimacy of authority within different types of organisations which he classified into four categories: first, the *charismatic retinue* of followers or disciples of a leader; secondly, *feudal administration* by fief-holders; thirdly, *modern bureaucracies*, such as industrial manufacturing plants or government departments; and finally, *modern professional organisations* such as universities or hospitals (Stinchcombe 1967: 169). Stinchcombe goes on to comment that:

> The key difference that Weber noted among these organisations is the basis on which the organisation decides the truth of the theory on which planning is based. Since this theory is what justifies the exercise of authority and is what makes authority legitimate, Weber called these criteria of truth 'principles of legitimacy'.
>
> (Stinchcombe 1967: 169)

Etzioni (1964) presented a three-fold classification of means of control within organisations when he identified *physical* control as being reliant on *coercive power*, *material* control as being reliant on *utilitarian power*, and *symbolic* control as being reliant on *normative*, *normative–social* or *social power.* Drawing on both Weber's theory of economic and social organisation and Etzioni's theory of organisational control, it can be argued that leisure management organisations and the universities that educate leisure managers are modern professional organisations that utilise normative, normative–social or social power to exercise symbolic control. Analysis of the environment of symbolic control then requires analysis of the symbolic means of control in operation at both an organisational and individual level. At an individual level, the work of Mead (1934), as one of the 'founding fathers' of symbolic interactionism, is a significant starting point, while at the organisational or societal level Berger and Luckmann (1966) provide ideas and concepts that underpin many of today's theories relating to the sociology of knowledge. In an interesting passage from *The Social Construction of Reality*, Berger and Luckman (1966) point to the intersubjectivity of knowledge; a thread which is woven throughout this book. However, in common with much of the work of sociologists in the 1960s, they demonstrate an unconscious emphasis on *men's* sociology of knowledge rather than *our* sociology of knowledge:

> The reality of everyday life further presents itself to me as an intersubjective world, a world that I share with others. This intersubjectivity sharply differentiates everyday life from other realities of which I am conscious. I am alone in the world of my dreams, but I know that the world of everyday life is as real to others as it is to myself. Indeed, I cannot exist in everyday life without continually interacting and communicating with others. I know that my natural attitude to this world corresponds to the natural attitude to others, that they also comprehend the objectifications by which this world is ordered, that they also organise this world around the 'here and now' of *their* being in it and have projects for working in it. I also know, of course, that the others have a perspective on this common world that is not identical with mine. My 'here' is their 'there'. My 'now' does not fully overlap with theirs. All the same, I know that I live with them in a common world. Most importantly, I know that there is an ongoing correspondence between *my* meanings and *their* meanings in this world, that we share a common sense about this reality. The natural attitude is the attitude of commonsense consciousness precisely because it refers to a world that is common to many men. Common-sense knowledge is the knowledge I share with others in the normal, self-evident routines of everyday life.
>
> (Berger and Luckman 1966: 35)

Hearn *et al.* (1989: 10) point out that within organisational theory 'gender has either been ignored, treated implicitly as male, considered an organisational "variable", reduced to relative stereotypes, or been analysed in a blatantly sexist way'. While early studies of organisational culture pointed to 'organisation man' (Whyte 1956), 'corporate man' (Jay 1972) and 'bureaucratic man' (Kohn 1971), there are no equivalent studies that depict organisation, corporate or bureaucratic woman. Following a critique of the male domination of organisational studies, Hearn *et al.* (1989) attempted to shift the focus of organisational debate from organisations to organisation, in other words from the macro-level of the bureaucracy or professional institution to the micro-level of relationships and processes within the organisation and the ways in which sexuality and its associated power constructs such relationships and processes: 'The sexuality of organisation is a prime aspect of seen, yet often unnoticed, social processes within the organising of human interaction' (Hearn *et al.* 1989: 15).

Hearn *et al.* (1989: 26) go on to emphasise that gender and sexuality interlink to both produce and reproduce organisations. While what they term 'malestream' writing has focused on the production of organisations, and feminist writing has focused on reproduction, a new account of gender and sexuality in relation to organisation could be embraced within the term *(re)production of organisation*. Hearn *et al.* (1989: 14) outline five important principles within this conceptual framework: first, organisations are seen as problematic concepts; second, it is the concept and form of organisation rather than organisations which are of importance; third, there should be a questioning of the empiricist and pragmatic underpinning to the social science of organisations; fourth, the framework emphasises the non-linearity of history; and, fifth, research into the (re)-production of organisation should emphasise communal research networks rather than 'big science'.

Theorising gender (in)equity in management

Harding (1986) identified three broad perspectives from which research on gender had been undertaken: feminist empiricism, standpoint feminism and postmodern feminism. Many subsequent writers on gender, sexuality, organisations and organisation have drawn upon Harding's classification to situate their own research and to explain the perspective of other writers' research. For example, Harding's classification has also been labelled as gender as variable, feminist standpoint, and poststructuralist feminism (Alvesson and Billing 1997: 23). An alternative, but overlapping, classification is that offered by di Stefano (1990) who distinguished between feminist rationalism, feminist anti-rationalism and feminist post-rationalism.

Hearn *et al.* (1989) identified a four-fold classification for the conceptualisation of gender and sexuality and, again, these ideal types can be mapped onto the previous classificatory systems identified by Harding and others. While such a mapping exercise can be seen as a rather crude form of essentialism, it serves a purpose in clarifying and contextualising the different philosophical and methodological approaches to researching gender and management. Only three of Hearn *et al.*'s classifications are employed in other feminist typologies and discussed here as the first of Hearn *et al.*'s four classifications is that of biological explanations, which they view as essentialist and deterministic in seeing sexuality as biological, naturalised and normalised. This position conflates women's sexuality with the gender of women and with the female sex and, as a result of this essentialism, biological typologies do not feature in the feminist typologies produced by Harding or di Stefano.

The second category identified by Hearn *et al.* (1989) is that of gender and sexuality as the outcome of social roles and this can be equated with the 'gender as variable' perspective or with 'feminist rationalism'. The approaches outlined here have features in common with liberal feminism where equality is determined in numbers and measured quantitatively rather than qualitatively. This approach has been criticised for its reliance on distributive research, its inadequate analysis of social power, its exaggeration of individual power and its relatively ahistorical approach.

Analysing gender and sexuality as fundamental political categories forms the basis of Hearn *et al.*'s third category where 'sexuality and gender are seen as historically constructed, collectivities of interest and community, set within definite relations of power and dominance' (Hearn *et al.* 1989: 6). This approach focuses upon those factors that unite women as a category rather than anything that might emphasise difference and diversity among women. There are clear parallels here with the 'feminist standpoint' perspective and with 'feminist anti-rationalism', both of which can be seen as influenced by socialist and materialist feminism. Similarly, the view of men from feminist standpoint theory is of a category with more to unite than differentiate them as they have a set of common privileges and interests that rely on the collective subordination by men of the category 'women'. Connell (1987) cites this gendered material base of the dominant political, social and economic order as the major explanation for gendered relations in the workplace:

> It must now be accepted that gender divisions are not an ideological addition to the class–structural mode of production. They are a deep seated feature of production itself – not left over from feudalism or confined to domestic work or even to the division between unpaid domestic work and paid work in industry ... Gender divisions are a fundamental and essential feature of the capitalist system as fundamental as class divisions. Socialist theory can no longer evade the fact that capitalism is run by and mainly to the advantage of men.
>
> (Connell 1987: 103)

Such dual theories, combining capitalism and patriarchy, have underpinned the organisational analyses of Cockburn (1983, 1985, 1991), Hartman (1981) and Walby (1986, 1989, 1997). In addition to a socialist feminist approach, Cockburn also examines patriarchy as a useful over-arching theme thereby drawing on the radical feminist tradition. Indeed, she states: 'I believe that a study of equality strategies in organisations calls for a feminist approach that does not reject out of hand as heretical any of the three significant tendencies in feminism' (Cockburn 1991: 10). However, a historical materialist approach presents difficulties in analysing relationships at a micro-level within social institutions. This is particularly the case when that social institution can be identified as an example of one of Weber's (1949) modern professional organisations where, as Etzioni (1964) stressed, normative power is used to maintain *symbolic* rather than *material* control. The recognition of symbolic control then requires acknowledgement of both organisational and feminist theories that address symbolic power in addition to, material power.

This leads us to Hearn *et al.*'s (1989) fourth category of analysis where gender and sexuality are viewed as communicative practices and discourses of power. This perspective can be mapped onto 'poststructuralist feminism' and 'feminist post-rationalism', with their postmodernist emphasis on contextual specificity. The importance here is not to create unifying and generalising classifications and grand narratives, formed by either empirical data or socio-political categories, but to contextualise difference and diversity. Foucault (1980) can be criticised for generally ignoring women and research on women within his poststructural analysis of sexuality. However, his theories on discourse as the process through which sexuality and power are communicated have been usefully adopted and adapted by a number of feminist writers addressing issues of organisation and organisations (Oerton 1996). Alvesson and Billing (1997: 41) have argued that, 'to the extent that men and women are of interest to study, it is the discourses in which they are constituted that are relevant to explore'. They define a discourse as: 'a set of statements, beliefs and vocabularies that is historically and socially specific and that tends to produce truth effects – certain beliefs are acted upon as true and therefore become partially true in terms of consequences' (Alvesson and Billing 1997: 40).

Oerton (1996), who utilised discourse analysis in her research of the sexuality of organisation in non-hierarchical settings, has called for both structural and cultural analyses of gender–power relations. Similarly, Acker (1990, 1992) has called for an analysis of gender and organisations that addresses both the structural and the symbolic representations of gendered power across four intersecting processes. These she defines as: the construction of gender divisions and hierarchies within organisations represented by horizontal and vertical sex-segregation identified through distributive research; the symbolism related to such divisions and distinctions; the inter and intra-actions between men and women; and the nature of gender and sexuality in the construction of the self and individual identity in relation to, and in response to, such an organisational culture. In other words,

Acker emphasises the need to draw on both distributive (quantitative) and relational (qualitative) research (Dewar 1991). This approach stresses the need to examine symbolic interactions and the role of discourse in constructing what Hearn *et al.* (1989) identified as gender, sexuality, organisations, organisation and (re)production of organisation.

Gender–power relations, evident at both a structural and cultural level, have recently begun to be investigated in relation to sociological and gender critiques of *professions*. Witz (1992: 39) contends that 'the relationship between gender and professionalisation is a neglected one'. Part of the explanation for this neglect, she suggests, rests in the lack of recognition of the gendered nature of the professions themselves. Witz argues that 'it is necessary to speak of "professional projects", to gender the agents of these projects, and to locate these within the structural and historical parameters of patriarchal capitalism' (Witz 1992: 39).

Earlier research within the sociology of professions was undertaken from a largely functionalist perspective (Parsons 1949), or was concerned with demarcating those traits (Greenwood 1957) or processes which distinguished particular institutionalised occupations and areas of work. Later research, however, has reconceptualised professions as 'a mode of controlling an occupation' (Witz 1992: 40). For Witz, the 'central axis of the new critical sociology of the professions' was 'the conceptual indissolubility of the concepts of 'power' and 'profession''. Witz identifies Johnson (1972) as one of the first to reconceptualise professions as mechanisms of power rather than particular types of occupations. Following the work of Johnson, Parkin (1979) referred to both the strategic and exclusionary nature of professions. According to Parkin, the main purpose of a profession was to maintain/enhance the power of senior members of the occupation by limiting entry to the profession, thereby reducing labour supply and increasing market value, and, therefore, power. If Parkin's assertion is true, then the gender imbalance within the senior levels of professions is such that efforts to limit access will inevitably be made by men at the expense of women.

Gender (in)equity in service sector industries

Before examining gender equity within leisure management it is useful to contextualise the service sector of leisure within the wider service sector industries. This section therefore examines gender equity in a range of service sector industries in an attempt to give a wider comparative context for the leisure management data. An evaluation of published research is undertaken in relation to health services, education, retail services, financial services, and tourism and hospitality services.

Previously, *distributive research* has emphasised the numbers and positions occupied by men and women within particular industries and organisations. This approach has been associated with a liberal feminist analysis of equality of opportunity, one which relates equality to equal numerical representation. Distributive research maps patterns of sex-segregation to show men and women's vertical and horizontal positions in an organisation's structure. More recently, relational research has added to the distributive approach by exploring the construction and negotiation of gender relations within the workplace. This second approach recognises that gender and sexuality are not fixed categories but are culturally produced within industries and organisations. The discussion that follows therefore draws upon secondary sources that outline both distributive *and* relational research addressing issues of gender equity within the service sector.

So although it is not the purpose of this chapter to provide detailed empirical evidence relating to either sex discrimination or vertical and horizontal sex-segregation throughout the service sector, a brief summary is useful to contextualise leisure management in relation to other service sector industries. This summary draws on Stockdale's (1991: 57) definition of occupational sex-segregation which recognises that 'the jobs that women do are different from those done by men (horizontal segregation) and women work at lower levels than men in the occupational hierarchy (vertical segregation)'.

Further explanations for the differential pay and conditions experienced by women are provided by concepts of *sex-role spill-over* and *sex-role stereotyping*. Stockdale (1991: 57) defines *sex-role spill-over* as, 'the assumption that people in particular jobs and the jobs themselves have the characteristics of only one gender'. Both sex-role spill-over and sex-role stereotyping of women can have detrimental impacts on their working conditions and career prospects. Women may be viewed as committed primarily to the private/domestic sphere and thus less interested in pursuing a career (Kanter 1989; Cockburn 1985; Hicks 1990). Identifying women in biological terms as childbearers requiring career breaks may also adversely prejudice their chances of promotion (Skinner 1988). As Frean (1998: 5) comments, employers 'often write off pregnant women as too emotional and too woolly-headed to do their jobs properly'. These findings are supported by Buxton (1998) who points out that women with children also encounter prejudice, fuelled by media stereotypes, when they endeavour to return to the workforce. Some male (and female) employers still seem to disapprove of working mothers, believing that they are less effective employees, that they are putting children at risk or are simply bad mothers (Frean 1998; Buxton 1998). Brownell (1994) considers that this type of attitude can be prevalent in industries such as leisure, tourism and hospitality which are associated with having to work anti-social hours. *Sex-role stereotyping*, whereby decisions are made based on preconceptions of character traits or physical differences, may also have a negative impact on women's career progression. The appropriate characteristics of a manager are often deemed to be those associated with men such as leadership, objectivity and aggressiveness. Traits traditionally ascribed to women, such as caring and emotion, are not only considered to be irrelevant to leadership positions but actually detrimental to effective management.

Comparative information of both a distributive and relational nature, drawn from other service sector industries and organisations including education, health, retail services, and financial services serves to provide an overview of the gendered structure of work, sex-role spill-over, sex-role stereotyping, and related gender differences in power and pay (Acker 1994; Alvesson and Billing 1997; Broadbridge 1995; Cockburn 1983, 1985, 1991; Hearn *et al.* 1989; Ledwith and Colgan 1996; Morley and Walsh 1995; Savage and Witz 1992; Spencer and Podmore 1987; Walby 1986, 1997; Wearing 1996; Witz 1992). There is also a growing body of literature examining the gendered construction of employment and management within tourism and hospitality which has not been mirrored by similar literature reflecting the gendered nature of the leisure industry and leisure management (Adkins 1994; Bagguley 1990; Enloe 1989; Hicks 1990; Jordan 1997; Kinnaird and Hall 1994; Richter 1994). Across the professions in the UK, Perrons and Shaw (1995) assert that:

> women are under-represented in all the top jobs; for example, in 1992 only 5 out of 1,370 managing directors or chief executives were women, and in 1994 only 5 per cent of judges were women. Some 9 per cent of MPs and less than 6 per cent of university professors were women and, despite some notable exceptions, women are under-represented in the upper echelons of the civil service.
>
> (Perrons and Shaw 1995: 19)

While we can identify examples of progress, such as an increasing percentage of women MPs in the UK, with 119 women returned to parliament after the 1997 general election, advances towards gender equity in other spheres of management have been less obvious. Perrons and Shaw (1995: 28) point to an Institute of Management and Remuneration Economics survey which found that, 'the proportion of management jobs held by women fell from 10.2 per cent in 1993 to 9.5 per cent in 1994 and the proportion of directors has remained at 2.8 per cent'. Likewise, Holton (1995) revealed that only 4 per cent of directors of the UK's top 200 companies were women at the time of her research. These figures are illustrative of distributive data that demonstrate a lack of gender equity throughout management as a whole and the following section attempts to provide a more detailed analysis of gender equity in specific service sector industries in the UK.

In relation to Health Services, the Head of the UK's National Health Service's (NHS) Women's Unit, Caroline Langridge, commented that:

The 1991 Equal Opportunities Commission's highly critical report on Women's Employment in the NHS showed that, despite the widespread adoption by health authorities of equal opportunities policies, very little progress had occurred after a decade of such policies. Although women accounted for 79 per cent of NHS staff, they were heavily concentrated in the lowest managerial grades, with very few women in senior management. The position in medicine was even worse, with only 15 per cent of women achieving consultant status, although more and more women entered medical school following the outlawing by the Sex Discrimination Act of 1975 of restricting women to 30 per cent of medical school places.

(Wyatt and Langridge 1996: 213)

Following the publication of the 1991 report, the NHS became a founder member of Opportunity 2000, an initiative set up by Business in the Community in 1991 in an attempt to improve both the quality and quantity of women's employment conditions and prospects throughout British industry and to meet European Community targets for women's economic development. The Department of Health became the first government department to sign up to Opportunity 2000 and in 1991 the NHS Management Executive for England established the NHS Women's Unit together with a series of eight goals designed to improve women's careers within the NHS. Wyatt and Langridge (1996) stated that:

The result has been a shift from a traditional equal opportunities policy framework with its concepts of social justice embedded in the language of rights, to a new business-focused approach based on competitive advantage, seeing women as a resource and not a problem. An early priority was to identify and publicise the existence of credible role models, especially increasing the percentage of top women managers and of women medical consultants. To enhance visibility a profile of 27 top women managers was published, together with guidelines for aspiring women managers.

(Wyatt and Langridge 1996: 213–214)

Although retail services employ more women than men, the culture of retailing has been variously described as masculine and paternalistic or dominated by women and managed by men (Brockbank and Traves 1996; Howe *et al.* 1992). There is significant vertical and horizontal sex-segregation within the retail sector with women concentrated in low-paid, part-time positions and in particular sectors such as food and clothing where sex role spill-over from domestic roles is evident. Collins (1990) emphasised that in Sainsbury's 291 stores there were only 5 women store managers and in 461 stores operated by WH Smith there were only 26 women store managers. A high street retail operation was one of four organisational case studies in which Cockburn investigated 'men's resistance to sex equality in organisations'. Here, Cockburn was more concerned with relational data than distributive data. Cockburn (1991: 69) pointed out that where women had made it into management positions their 'relation to power was problematised'. This situation came about, she states, because women were positioned in a type of Catch-22 situation where men either perceived them as being too authoritative or not being sufficiently authoritative. There are, however, some examples of good practice, with 50 per cent of management positions in Littlewoods held by women following the introduction of job sharing, flexible working, career breaks and a nursery at its head office, while Boots introduced job sharing at supervisory and management levels in 1989 (Brockbank and Traves 1996; MccGwire 1992). In addition, many retail employers have signed up to Opportunity 2000.

While the financial services sector continues to be a major employer of women, the proportion of full-time posts occupied by women decreased from 53 per cent in 1980 to 42 per cent in 1994 (Equal Opportunities Commission 1995). This change is reflective of a casualisation of the female labour force across the service sector where part-time workers often do not enjoy the same rates of pay or employment benefits as full-time workers. While retail services have also been subject to casualisation, it is the financial service sector that has witnessed the highest levels of restructuring in recent years. Several research studies have demonstrated that restructuring within the financial services sector has had a negative impact on women with men's careers promoted and prioritised over women's (Crompton and Sanderson 1990, 1994; Halford *et al.* 1997). McInnes (1988), for example, has argued that in banking it has now become more important to be employed at head office than as a branch manager in order to ensure career progression. As the status of branch manager has become reduced, so more women have begun to occupy this role thereby creating a *feminisation* of the role of branch manager. It can be argued that while women have entered management positions in increasing numbers, many of these management positions have been restructured in such a way as to reduce their status.

Like retail services, tourism and hospitality are sectors which are dominated by women and managed by men (Bagguley 1990; Hicks 1990; Jordan 1997; Wood 1992). Diaz and Umbreit (1995: 48) point out that, although the American hospitality industry 'has virtually achieved gender neutrality' in lower and middle management, less than 0.5 of 1 per cent of senior managers are women. Similarly, research undertaken in the UK revealed that only 4 per cent of middle/senior management and only 1 per cent of top management are women (Jones 1992: 12). However, research by Burnell *et al.* (1997), comparing equality of opportunity in hospitality employment for women in four European countries, found that the situation in the UK was relatively favourable, with a small majority of women in supervisory and lower level management positions. They point out that this reflects the findings of the Labour Force Survey which showed that, in 1992, 54 per cent of hotel managers and 49 per cent of restaurant managers were women (Burrell *et al.* 1997: 174). However, Brownell (1994) argues that while the number of women managers is increasing, women are concentrated in the management of smaller properties in comparison with their male counterparts. The area of tourism employment has 'not been subjected to widespread academic analysis' (Baum 1994: 259). Thus, there is limited empirical evidence concerning the position of women. However, studies that have been carried out reveal employment patterns which mirror those in hospitality (Adkins 1994; Ireland 1993; Richter 1994). Kinnaird and Hall (1994) comment that women fulfil the majority of jobs in tourism, especially those which are poorly paid, low skilled and part-time. They point out that this situation has been created and supported by gender stereotyping and traditional notions of what constitutes appropriate work for women. Jordan (1997) has presented both distributive and relational findings which illustrate the sex-segregated nature of the tourism industry and the impact of the *sexuality of organisation* upon women's careers (Hearn *et al.* 1989). Summarising the status of women across tourism and hospitality Jordan (1997: 532) put forward conclusions from her research that 'suggest that the majority of the tourism organisations studied do reproduce and rationalise sex segregation'.

This section has outlined the status of gender equity in five sectors of the service industry: health services, education, retail services, financial services, and tourism and hospitality services. Distributive research has identified similar patterns of *vertical* and *horizontal sex-segregation* within each industry while relational research has highlighted the presence and influence of *sex-role stereotyping* and *sex-role spill-over* in determining women's employment patterns and career paths. The remainder of this chapter examines issues of gender equity and employment in relation to leisure services and leisure management.

Professionalism and leisure management

In 1998, the UK's Institute of Leisure and Amenity Management (ILAM) commissioned a research project entitled *Gender Equity in Leisure Management*. The research formed part of the work programme of ILAM's Equal Opportunities Working Party, formed in 1995 with a broad remit of recommending further research and initiatives designed to enhance gender equity within ILAM and the wider leisure industry. The Equal Opportunities Working Party was established four years after ILAM's first piece of commissioned research into gender equity in leisure management (Bacon 1991). The 1998 research had four main aims: first, to contextualise gender equity in leisure management in relation to other service sector industries; second, to compile occupational data relating to the female ILAM membership; third, to determine and review constraints to women's career progression within leisure management; and finally, to analyse the effectiveness of ILAM in assisting the career development of women within leisure management. This chapter has already contextualised gender equity in relation to other service sector industries and the remaining focus of the chapter seeks to outline and evaluate findings related to the remaining aims of the research by focusing on the structural and cultural constraints to women's inclusion in the workplace and their career progression within the workforce.

ILAM defines itself as 'the professional Institute for the leisure industry'. Together with the Institute of Sport and Recreation Management (ISRM), ILAM aims to represent the broad spectrum of management services and managers across the leisure industry. ILAM was formed in 1983 following the amalgamation of four leisure and recreation associations/institutes: the Association of Recreation Managers, the Institute of Municipal Entertainment, the Institute of Park and Recreation Administration, and the Institute of Recreation Management. Alongside ILAM and ISRM, there are numerous professional associations that aim to represent specific segments of the leisure industry. These include, for example, the Museums Association, the Tourism Society, and the British Association of Sport and Exercise Sciences. In addition, there are other organisations, such as the Chief Leisure Officers Association (CLOA) that represent employees at specific levels within the leisure industry. These professional divisions are therefore constructed along lines of both horizontal and vertical segregation. The results of the 1998 research, together with previous research findings, confirm that these horizontal and vertical divisions also reflect *sex-segregation*.

A combination of quantitative and qualitative data capture methods was employed in the research. These included a self-administered postal questionnaire of all women members of ILAM, collation and analysis of data from returned questionnaires, secondary research relating to leisure management, secondary research relating to gender equity in other service sector industries and qualitative research in the form of individual interviews with middle and senior women leisure managers not in membership of ILAM or whose membership had lapsed.

Although there was an increase from 568 women members in 1991 to 1,151 in 1998, the respondents to the ILAM survey still testified to isolation, discrimination and harassment within the organisational culture of leisure management. Moreover, in spite of the increasing number of women entering junior management, there remained evidence of a 'glass ceiling' within the industry. While many of the structural inequalities, identified in the 1991 research, had been addressed, the glass ceiling appeared to have been maintained by cultural constraints or the interplay between the remaining structural constraints and cultural constraints which had yet to be recognised and/or addressed.

Prior to the 1991 research, ILAM did, however, recognise the presence of gender inequity within the leisure profession, acknowledging the role that ILAM itself played in shaping gender–power relations within leisure management. In spite of this recognition, however, the 1991 research stated that: 'We are witnessing the onset of a slow but inexorable revolution in that women are beginning to colonise managerial work in ever increasing numbers. By the end of the century, given present trends, it is probable that half of all leisure managers will be women' (Bacon 1991: 7). Such a vision, now demonstrated to be overoptimistic and inaccurate, was influenced by statistical trends indicating that 'very large numbers of younger women have either moved into junior management training roles, or certainly aspire to make a career within the leisure industry once they complete their college training' (Bacon 1991: 2).

At the time of the 1991 research, women in leisure management reported discrimination and harassment in relation to four aspects of their work. These were identified as: inequality in the working conditions experienced by women and men; unfavourable treatment for women attempting to balance paid work and domestic responsibilities; negative perceptions about women as managers; and the use of sexist language and behaviour by male colleagues. By 1998 female membership of ILAM had, indeed, increased to over 20 per cent of total membership from less than 10 per cent in 1991. One of the tasks of the 1998 research was, therefore, to gauge the extent to which these structural and cultural constraints, identified at the beginning of the decade, had been addressed by the end of the decade.

Structures and cultures of (un)equal opportunities in leisure management

Previous research has demonstrated that many service sector industries, including tourism and hospitality, are 'dominated by women but managed by men' (Brockbank and Traves 1996). Within the leisure industry, however, the legacy of male-dominated sports provision and public sector leisure provision's historical incorporation within male-dominated technical services departments has ensured the maintenance of male domination within the leisure services.

There are, however, indications of structural changes in the sex-segregation of the leisure industry's labour force. Within the leisure industry it is estimated that the UK sector, encompassing recreational, cultural and sporting services, now provides 305,300 full-time jobs (increased from 289,600 in 1995) and a further 222,000 part-time jobs (increased from 209,600 in 1995) (Office for National Statistics 1998). Although leisure services now employ approximately equal numbers of men and women, the industry continues to be sex-segregated in type and level of employment. Examination of labour market data over the last four years does, however, demonstrate that the gender gap is beginning to lessen. Across all recreational, cultural and sporting services men occupy 47 per cent of all jobs (down from 48.3 per cent in 1995) but 59 per cent of all full-time jobs (down from 62.2 per cent in 1995) while women occupy 53 per cent of all jobs (up from 51.6 per cent in 1995) but only 41 per cent of all full-time jobs (up from 37.7 per cent) (Office for National Statistics 1998). There appears to be widespread variation in the degree of sex-segregation, with sporting and recreational services providing a lower proportion of full-time posts occupied by women than entertainments and cultural services. Only 22 per cent of the sport and recreation labour force is made up of full-time female employees (although this figure has increased from just 16.7 per cent in 1995) whereas 31 per cent of full-time posts are occupied by men (Office for National Statistics 1998). Even in the area of cultural services, libraries and museums – areas traditionally seen as favouring female employees – women and men occupy roughly equal numbers of full-time posts but women are four times more likely to be employed in part-time posts than their male colleagues (CSO 1995).

In addition to horizontal sex-segregation, leisure services are also sex-segregated by vertical level of employment. Within the public sector as a whole women occupy only 4.9 per cent of chief executive posts – the most senior positions in local government – and only 6.9 per cent of chief officer posts (Local Government Management Board 1995). In UK leisure services only seven out of 146, or less than five per cent, of local authority Leisure Services Departments are headed by women (Local Government Management Board 1995). At the level of facility management men still dominate and there is evidence to suggest that up to 80 per cent of posts such as client manager which are related specifically to management changes introduced as a result of compulsory competitive tendering a decade ago, were awarded to men (Aitchison 1997).

By 2003, female membership of ILAM had increased from just over 20 per cent in 1998 to just over 27 per cent. However, more detailed scrutiny of these total membership figures reveals distinct levels of gender inequity at different levels within the organisation. At each increasing level of membership status the representation of women decreases significantly such that 45 per cent of student members were women, 37 per cent of associate members were women but only 18 per cent of those with full-member status were women, thus indicating that men continue to dominate the senior ranks within ILAM where only 4 out of 93 members holding the prestigious fellow category were women (Institute of Leisure and Amenity Management 2003).

In 1991, Bacon commented that the dominant culture of the leisure industry served to exaggerate gender inequity identified in other sectors of the service industry. The characteristics of sport and leisure services include their association with informality, sociability, alcohol, and different states of dress and undress. Sport was singled out as the area where women experienced most discrimination and harassment as a result of what McKay (1996) defines as 'corporate masculinity' or what we might define here as the 'locker room culture' of masculinity prevalent in sport (Messner 1998).

To address these inequalities, many local authorities have been eager to implement equal opportunities policies. The research conducted for ILAM found that 86.6 per cent of respondents stated that their employing organisation had an equal opportunities policy. However, only 55.7 per cent of these respondents felt that their policy was effective. Reasons for thinking the policy was effective centred around material or quantitative evidence of change: workforce statistics showing equal numbers of male and female employees, evidence that management took the policy seriously, and evidence that awareness of equal opportunities had been raised. Reasons given for thinking that their organisation's policy was ineffective were more likely to be related to organisational culture: lack of value and respect for the policy within the organisation, lack of visibility of the policy, and minimal implementation of the policy.

While structural change in the form of policy formulation and implementation may have taken place, the perception of many women was that such policies had not effected change in relation to the cultural practices of their organisations. One-third of respondents agreed that their organisation had a 'glass ceiling' and 15 per cent claimed to have had personal experience of sex discrimination within their current organisation. Rather than identifying discriminatory structures within their organisation, however, many respondents referred to organisational cultures as colluding with discriminatory practices:

> Discrimination is difficult to identify in a 'recruitment, selection and promotion' situation as there are many reasons which could be 'smoke screens'. I feel that discrimination takes place in a more informal day-to-day manner, such as in attitudes of (usually elderly) males to women in more senior positions. Respect is often slow in coming – you are likely to be treated as 'fluff'. There is often an underlying attitude of 'don't worry your pretty little head about it'.
>
> (Survey respondent)

In spite of the identification of working cultures that contravened equal opportunities structures, the most common response to personal experience of sex discrimination was for the complainant to make an informal verbal complaint to her manager(s). The least common response was to make a formal written complaint to a manager. These actions (or in-actions) could be seen as indicating a lack of confidence in the structural

procedures designed to enforce equal opportunities legislation and organisational policy.

McKay (1996) has demonstrated that women have substantially reduced
confidence in the ability of organisations to demonstrate gender equity.
In his research of gender equity in sports organisations in Australia, New
Zealand and Canada, he found that 90 per cent of men believed their
organisations promoted the 'best person for the job' and that 'sex was
irrelevant to gatekeepers'. In contrast:

> only about 10 per cent of women identified their organisation as
> looking like this, and most reported intense feelings of exclusion and
> isolation. They used a variety of metaphors to describe their situation:
> 'glass ceilings', 'brick walls', 'hoops', 'blockages', 'hurdles', 'ghettos',
> 'on the outside looking in', 'passing the ball but never having it passed
> back', 'frozen out', 'kept in the dark'.
>
> (McKay 1996: 64)

In the United States, Henderson (1992), Bialeschki and Henderson
(1984) and Henderson and Bialeschki (1993, 1995) examined the status
of women and their career development in leisure management. In their
earlier research, they found that women reported a number of structural
factors related to gender that made competition for senior management
posts problematic. These factors included low pay, inadequate childcare
and family conflicts. Frisby and Brown (1991) then indicated the presence of organisational cultures as well as structures in their research which
found that women had lower aspirations of their career progress than
their male colleagues. Later research by Henderson and Bialeschki (1993)
concurred with this finding with over half of women respondents stating
that they perceived that they had fewer opportunities for career advancement than their male colleagues. Many of these findings were again
reiterated in the research of *Gender Equity in the Leisure Services Field*
conducted by Shinew and Arnold (1998) and Bialeschki and Henderson
(2000).

The findings from Australia, New Zealand, Canada and the United
States, together with the Aitchison *et al.* research, demonstrate that the
discursive practices of organisations may serve to enforce gender–power
relations as much, if not more than, the structural barriers identified by
previous feminist research.

Gender equity and career progression in leisure management

Somewhat surprisingly, and in spite of acknowledging discrimination
within their organisations, women remained optimistic about their career
progression. Overall, respondents endured deflated salaries and increased

responsibilities compared with other service sector industries. Whereas 13 per cent of respondents had responsibility for over fifty staff, only 3 per cent earned more than £40,000 per annum. Over one-third of respondents earning less than £20,000 had line management responsibility, and many women identifying themselves as middle and senior management had responsibility for between ten and fifty staff yet earned less than £30,000. There was clear evidence that many women were taking on middle management responsibilities for junior management salaries and senior management responsibilities for middle management salaries.

Previous research in both organisational behaviour and employee relations has demonstrated that 'the degree to which women accept, conform to or challenge gendered patterns of organisational segregation and gender politics within their organisation will depend on a balance between their consciousness of discrimination and career barriers; their reading of organisational politics and their willingness to adopt individualist, collectivist and/or separatist strategies, (Ledwith and Colgan 1996: 23). Within leisure management, Yule (1997a, 1997b, 1998), drawing on the work of Connel (1987) and Sheppard (1989), has pointed to a four-fold typology of subcultural strategies employed by women and ranging from 'compliance' to 'resistance'. The ILAM survey results demonstrated that the dominant strategy within leisure management was one of 'compliance' or 'blending in' (Sheppard 1989) but with some women adopting an 'individual strategy of resistance' (Yule 1998). These individualistic strategies accord with what Arroba and James (1987) termed 'clever' behaviour. Such strategies serve to enhance women's career aspirations and opportunities in the short-term through opportunistic behaviour of an individualist nature. In the case of the women respondents, this attempt at meshing with the dominant organisational culture was evident in their continual search for career-related information and training opportunities together with their high levels of participation in continuing professional development and part-time education.

Over 60 per cent of respondents stated that their career plan for the next three to five years was to secure promotion. One-third of respondents were looking externally for promotion and a quarter of respondents had their sights on internal promotion opportunities. When asked to identify multiple reasons for seeking a change in employment the responses indicated an overwhelming enthusiasm and optimism for the leisure industry. 'To gain more experience', 'to gain a higher salary', 'to have a more challenging job' and 'to have more responsibility' were all cited as explanations by more than half of the women seeking a change in their job. 'I don't like my job', 'I want to spend more time with my family', 'I don't get on with my superiors', 'my current job is too stressful', and 'to get away from sexual harassment and discrimination' were each cited by less than 10 per cent of respondents as reasons for seeking change.

Notably, sexual harassment and discrimination, although experienced by 15 per cent of respondents, was only cited by 2.8 per cent as a reason for seeking a change of job. In other words, the majority of women who experienced sexual harassment in their current jobs seemed resigned to tolerating this type of behaviour in the workplace.

Women placed a high emphasis on education and training to achieve promotion. Ninety per cent of respondents stated that one of the reasons they had joined ILAM was 'to receive information about job opportunities', 80 per cent 'to improve my career prospects' and 70 per cent 'to make use of training opportunities'. Similarly, the most important aspect of ILAM membership was seen as 'information on job opportunities/careers (contained within ILAM's weekly publication *Leisurenews*). Less than a third of respondents stated that 'information on leisure issues' was an important aspect of their membership. Women's desire to receive training did appear to be met by many employers. At least 70 per cent of employers provided funding for both external training opportunities and in-house training for professional development. In contrast, less than half of the respondents' employers provided job share opportunities, and less than 20 per cent provided career breaks, crèche facilities or childcare provision. Although the majority of respondents' employers provided education and training opportunities designed to enhance women's career prospects, only a minority of employers provided the support required to enable women, and particularly women with children, to progress in their careers once they had taken advantage of such education and training.

Over half of the respondents agreed with the statement that 'women work harder than men to achieve equal recognition in my organisation'. Moreover, there was clear evidence that many women were deferring starting a family in order to further their leisure management career. Although almost 80 per cent of respondents were aged between 21 and 40, only 21 per cent of all respondents had children under the age of 18 and only 13 per of all respondents cent had children under 5 years of age. The combination of career and family was seen by many women to be both incompatible and unsustainable. These generalisations, however, serve to give the impression that women in leisure management can be seen as a homogenous group. The diversity and difference in degree of disadvantage experienced by women was evident:

> Unfortunately, my own desire to spend more time with my children will probably ensure that I stay where I am for convenience. I guess many capable women will not make it into the positions of influence for these reasons. Unfortunately, the women making it are usually childless and are therefore less aware of the work conditions that need to change.
>
> (Survey respondent)

Cultural analyses of organisational power can be seen as accommodating these fractured and fragmented experiences and narratives. As
outlined in the Introduction and reiterated throughout many of the chapters of this book, Cooper (1994) has emphasised that power is 'productive,
relational and everywhere' and this emphasis on social construction, rather
than material determinacy, builds on Elshtain's (1981) critique of socio-
structural theories as 'narratives of closure'. In management, just as in
other social and cultural relations, the totalising explanations offered by
the meta-narratives of structural theories are seen as 'narratives of closure'
because of their emphasis on organisational power as repressive and
dominating, rather than productive and relational. By acknowledging the
interrelationships between social and cultural power, or between structural and symbolic power, a more complete interpretation of gender–power
relations in organisations may be possible. For example, Oerton (1996)
notes that socio-cultural critiques emphasise that:

> workers cannot be reduced to commodified objects of managerial
> control or their experiences simply 'read off' from their structural
> positions within a capitalist, patriarchal society. In other words,
> women and men's working lives cannot be fully theorised without
> taking into account the ways in which they negotiate and manoeuvre
> within dominant social structures and discourses. This involves analys-
> ing the complex interconnections between, for example, women's
> commitments and motives to work, the ways in which they construct
> and manage their work profiles and careers, and their opportunities
> for progression in a range of traditionally male-dominated occupa-
> tions and organisations.
>
> (Oerton 1996: 51)

When asked to suggest additional measures that their employers could
take to enhance women's prospects of career progression, responses were
made in relation to three broad categories. Two of the three categories
reflect the findings outlined above and can be loosely described as *working
conditions* and *training-related measures* to enhance career prospects.
The third category of additional measures can be classified as *cultural
change*. Here, women referred to the need for better consultation and
communication, more respect and recognition for women employees from
senior management and local authority councillors, more encouragement
to women returners to work, more encouragement for personal development and greater opportunities for informal networking. These measures
relate to changes in organisational culture and discursive practice and
were seen by many respondents to be an essential prerequisite to structural
change.

As organisational structures are more visible than cultures, it is possible
that organisations can give the impression of being more egalitarian in

their employment and promotion practices than scrutiny of their organisational cultures would suggest. The narratives of the women who participated in the ILAM *Gender Equity in Leisure Management* research suggest that a combination of measures, designed to address both structural and cultural inequities, is required to improve the experience of women within the leisure management workplace and to enhance the position of women within the leisure management workforce. The ILAM is currently implementing an action plan designed to address these recommendations.

Overview

This chapter has sought to identify and explain the origins and nature of terms, concepts and theories that address the interrelationships of gender, sexuality, organisations and organisation in relation to leisure management. The chapter introduced Hearn *et al*.'s (1989) concept of the sexuality of organisation to emphasise a shift in thinking from structural constraints to cultural relations. Similarly, theories of gender relations that distinguished between gender as a variable, standpoint feminism and poststructural feminism (Alvesson and Billing 1997) were outlined and evaluated to demonstrate the shift in feminist theory from liberal to socialist to poststructural. This shift in research philosophy or epistemology was mirrored by a shift in the focus of research methodology from distributive to relational research and a commensurate shift in research methods from quantitative to qualitative. Stockdale's conceptualisation of sexrole spill-over and sex-role stereotyping were introduced and explained together with illustrations of vertical and horizontal sex-segregation within organisations.

The chapter then explored research into gender equity in the service sectors of health, retail, finance, hospitality and tourism to contextualise research of gender and leisure management within the wider service sector. This section also served to complement and supplement the earlier accounts of gender equity in the educational sector that were provided in the previous chapter. The research findings from the ILAM project entitled *Gender Equity in Leisure Management* (Aitchison *et al.* 1999) were then discussed in detail and the chapter focused upon structures and cultures of (un)equal opportunities in leisure management and career progression in leisure management. Throughout the discussion of gender equity in UK leisure management comparative data from international studies of gender equity in sport and leisure management were used to evaluate the findings in a wider context. Of particular note here was the study of gender equity in sports organisations in Australia, New Zealand and Canada conducted by McKay (1996) and the work of Bialeschki and Henderson (1984) and Henderson and Bialeschki (1993, 1995) examined the status of women and their career development in leisure management in the US and Shinew and Arnold's (1998) study *Gender Equity in the Leisure Services Field*, again in the US.

Across all of the research studies cited there was strong evidence to demonstrate that women's experience of leisure management was shaped by both structural and cultural factors. Indeed, there was evidence to show that the interrelationship between structures and cultures was often what consolidated or maintained the social–cultural nexus of gender inequity within leisure management organisations.

8 Gender and leisure: the social–cultural nexus

This book has sought to offer a critical appraisal of a range of different perspectives on gender and leisure. The focus of the book has been on social and cultural perspectives drawn from: social, cultural and gender theory; sociology; social and cultural geography; social and public policy; the sociology of education and management studies. The text has encouraged the reader to think across disciplines and subject fields to form interdisciplinary analyses of gender and leisure relations at work in everyday life. In addition to stressing the importance of understanding both social and cultural relations, each chapter has emphasised the inter-relationships *between* the social and the cultural.

If there were to be a conclusion to this book it would be that it is at the site and process of the social–cultural nexus that gender and leisure relations are often formed and reformed within leisure theory, leisure studies, leisure spaces, leisure policy, leisure education and leisure management. However, poststructural theory warns against 'closure' in the form of a definitive conclusion. By revealing the webs, networks and circuits of culture that are continually at work and being reworked by our knowledge and actions it is evident that our social and cultural perspectives of gender and leisure are too fluid to be dammed by a conclusion. It is therefore perhaps more appropriate to end this book with a series of summaries and questions relating to each of the chapters.

The book started from the premise that particular leisure policies and practices are the outcome of equally particular leisure perspectives and philosophies and that our view of the world, and the place of gender and leisure within the world, shapes the way in which our gender and leisure relations are produced and understood. To understand relations of gender and leisure therefore requires an understanding of the perspectives, philosophies, values and beliefs upon which these relations are based. Chapter 2 'Gender and leisure theory', therefore sought to identify and explain a series of social science perspectives that has served to shape our understanding of social relations including leisure relations. The chapter then identified and explained a range of perspectives from feminist and gender theory that has shaped our understanding of the role of gender relations in forming wider social relations. The chapter therefore introduced the theoretical foundations upon which more detailed discussions of gender and leisure were developed throughout the book. But the chapter also raised a series of epistemological questions that were then to be revisited in later chapters: How have different kinds of knowledge been constructed within social science in general and gender studies in particular? How have these ways of knowing shaped our understandings of gender and leisure? What do we know of and what do we consider as leisure? How do we come to know about gender–power relations within leisure sites and processes? How do our beliefs and values shape what we know? What 'evidence' is there is to support or refute our claims to knowledge? How do we come to have this knowledge rather than or in addition to other kinds of knowledge?

Chapter 3 'Gender and leisure studies', attempted to illustrate how the subject field of leisure studies has evolved over the course of the last four decades and how some forms of knowledge have been developed rather than others or have been developed at different times from others. The chapter asked: how significant have sociological perspectives been to the study of leisure? In what ways have dominant definitions of leisure been informed by different sociological perspectives? How have the parameters of the subject field been defined by these sociologists and their sociological perspectives? How have both the feminist research of the 1980s and the poststructural research of the 1990s challenged the sociological orthodoxies of the 1970s? Will the development of cultural sociology as a subdiscipline of sociology serve to strengthen or weaken the subject field of leisure studies and its analysis of gender and leisure relations?

Chapter 4 'Gender and leisure places', asked similar questions to those posed in Chapter 3 but in relation to geographical rather than sociological perspectives. Here, the recent discourses of social and cultural geography have served to complement and supplement our knowledge of gender and leisure relations by seeking answers to such questions as: how can contemporary geographical theory inform our understanding of the interrelationships between the social, cultural and spatial relations of gender and leisure? In what ways do the concepts of 'the gaze', 'the dualism' and 'the Other' assist in theorising the spatial dynamics of gender and leisure? How do relations of productive consumption inform the ways in which we experience gender and leisure?

Chapter 5 'Gender and leisure policy', evaluated the ways in which leisure policy has acted as a vehicle for the implementation of different perspectives or value systems in practice. In providing a historical context to such a discussion the chapter revealed the changing nature of both leisure policy and the incorporation of feminist and gender perspectives to such policies. The chapter therefore asked: how has leisure policy been informed by socialist feminist critiques? In what ways has leisure policy reflected the views and needs of women? Is the inclusion of women as a homogenous group really an appropriate way in which to achieve social inclusion? What have been the roles and policies of national and local leisure and sport organisations in delivering social inclusion for women in and through leisure? How have strategic approaches been influenced by wider discourses of public policy and political economy?

Chapter 6 'Gender and leisure education', then sought to explore ways in which leisure studies knowledge is formed within higher education and research. The chapter evaluated leisure studies education as a series of sites and processes that are significant in the production, legitimation, reproduction and reworking of perspectives on gender and leisure that, in turn, inform leisure policy and practice. The chapter questioned: how is our knowledge of leisure constructed, legitimated, reproduced and reworked? Who influences what counts as knowledge? What are the mechanisms within higher education that contribute to the formation of leisure studies knowledge, gender scholarship and gender (in)equity? What contributions have feminist and gender critiques within leisure, sport and tourism studies made towards the development of gender scholarship and gender equity in education?

Chapter 7 'Gender and leisure management', then explored the translation of theory, policy and education into leisure management practice. It sought to identify and explain the origins and nature of terms, concepts and theories that address the interrelationships of gender, sexuality and organisation in leisure management. The chapter considered: What role do sex-role spill-over, sex-role stereotyping, vertical and horizontal sex-segregation play in constructing the leisure services sector and the leisure management profession? What has distributive and relational feminist and gender research revealed of the gender–power relations in leisure management? How have such relations been experienced by women leisure managers in the UK? How do these experiences of gender relations compare with those of women from other countries where there are also well-established leisure services sectors?

In all of the chapters the central concern has been to explore the ways in which gender and leisure relations are shaped by both social *and* cultural relations. Rather than coming down on the side of structural or post-structural analyses as providing the key to unlock the answers to questions of gender and leisure, all of the chapters have stressed the importance of structural and poststructural critiques. Moreover, many of the chapters have demonstrated that it is the interrelationship between structures and cultures that frequently serves to consolidate or maintain gender inequity within and through leisure relations. Thus, the site and process of the social–cultural nexus is revealed as pivotal in the formation of gender and leisure relations. This site and process requires further and closer scrutiny to explore gender and leisure relations in greater depth and across a wider breadth of arenas than those considered within this book. How everyday cultures of gender and leisure interact with the macro-structures of patriarchy and capitalism that have previously been rendered visible by structuralist analyses is an ongoing research project for feminist and gender leisure studies.

References

Acker, S. (ed.) (1989) *Teachers, Gender and Education*, London: Falmer.

Acker, S. (1990) 'Hierarchies, jobs, bodies: a theory of gendered organisations', *Gender and Society* 4, 2: 139–158.

Acker, S. (1992) 'New perspectives on an old problem: the position of women academics in British higher education', *Higher Education* 24, 1: 57–75.

Acker, S. (1994) *Gendered Education*, Buckingham: Open University Press.

Acker, S. and Warren Piper, D. (1984) *'Is Higher Education Fair to Women?'*, Guildford: Society for Research into Higher Education.

Adkins, L. (1994) *Gendered Work: Sexuality, Family and the Labour Market*, Open University Press: Milton Keynes.

Adkins, L. (1998) 'Feminist theory and economic change', in S. Jackson and J. Jones (eds) *Contemporary Feminist Theories*, Edinburgh University Press: Edinburgh.

Adler, S. Laney, J. and Packer, M. (1993) *Managing Women: Feminism and Power in Educational Management*, Buckingham: Open University Press.

Adorno, T. and Horheimer, M. (1944) *Dialectic of Enlightenment*, London: Verso.

Aitchison, C.C. (1995) 'Women's access to leisure provision: the impact of Compulsory Competitive Tendering (CCT) in London', in D. Leslie (ed.) *Tourism and Leisure: Perspectives on Provision*, Eastbourne: Leisure Studies Association.

Aitchison, C.C. (1997a) 'A decade of Compulsory Competitive Tendering (CCT) in UK sport and leisure services: some feminist reflections', *Leisure Studies* 16, 2: 85–105.

Aitchison, C.C. (1997b) 'Patriarchal paradigms and the politics of pedagogy: a framework for a feminist analysis of leisure and tourism studies', *World Leisure and Recreation* 38, 2: 38–41.

Aitchison, C.C. (1998a) 'Gendered space: the contribution of feminist geography to discourses of gender and leisure', paper presented at Leisure in a Globalised Society: Inclusion or Exclusion, World Leisure and Recreation Association 5th World Congress, Sao Paulo, Brazil: October.

Aitchison, C.C. (1998b) 'Gender and power: (re)constructing knowledge in leisure and tourism studies', paper presented at The Big Ghetto: Gender, Sexuality and Leisure, Leisure Studies Association 4th International Conference, Leeds Metropolitan University, Leeds: July.

Aitchison, C.C. (1999a) 'New cultural geographies: the spatiality of leisure, gender and sexuality', *Leisure Studies* 18, 1: 19–39.

Aitchison, C.C. (1999b) 'Heritage and nationalism: gender and the performance of power', in D. Crouch (ed.) *Leisure/Tourism Geographies: Leisure Practices and Geographical Knowledge*, London: Routledge.

Aitchison, C.C. (2000a) 'Poststructural feminist theories of representing Others: a response to the "crisis" in leisure studies' discourse', *Leisure Studies* 19, 3: 127–144.

Aitchison, C.C. (2000b) 'Young disabled people, leisure and everyday life: reviewing conventional definitions for leisure studies', *Annals of Leisure Research* 3, 1: 1–20.

Aitchison, C.C. (2000c) 'Leisure and urban exclusion: developing leisure geographies and geographies of leisure', *North West Geographer* 3, 2: 13–20.

Aitchison, C.C. (2000d) 'Women in leisure services: managing the social–cultural nexus of gender equity', *Managing Leisure* 5, 4: 81–91.

Aitchison, C.C. (2000e) 'Locating gender: space, place and heritage tourism', in K. Atkinson, S. Oerton and G. Plain (eds) *Feminisms on Edge: Politics, Discourses and National Identities*, Cardiff: Cardiff Academic Press.

Aitchison, C.C. (2000f) 'Gender equity in leisure management: a comparative international study', paper presented at Leisure and Human Development, World Leisure 6th World Congress, University of Duesto, Bilbao, Spain: July

Aitchison, C.C. (2001a) 'Theorising Other discourses of tourism, gender and culture: can the subaltern speak (in tourism)?', *Tourist Studies* 1, 2: 133–147.

Aitchison, C.C. (2001b) 'A disabled leisure studies: theorising dominant discourses of the employed body, the able body and the active body?' in G. McPherson (ed.) *Leisure and Social Inclusion: New Challenges for Policy and Provision*, Eastbourne: Leisure Studies Association.

Aitchison, C.C. (2001c) 'Deconstructing the tourist gaze: theorising disability's lack of embodiment in tourism studies', paper presented at Leisure: Global Perspectives, Australia and New Zealand Leisure Studies Association Conference, Edith Cowan University, Australia: July

Aitchison, C.C. (2001d) *Women and Sport*, London: Women's Sports Foundation

Aitchison, C.C. (2001e) 'Gender and leisure research: the "codification of knowledge"', *Leisure Sciences* 23, 1: 1–19.

Aitchison, C.C. (2002a) 'Leisure studies: discourses of knowledge, power and theoretical "crisis"', keynote paper presented at Journeys in Leisure: New Theoretical Directions, Leisure Studies Association Annual Conference 2001, University of Luton, UK, July and published in L. Lawrence and S. Parker (eds) *Leisure Studies; Trends in Theory and Research*, Eastbourne: Leisure Studies Association.

Aitchison, C.C. (2002b) 'Cultural identity and community development: UK local cultural strategies as responses to national policies and discourses', paper presented at Global Forces and Local Responses: Leisure, Sport, Tourism, Kuala Lumpur, Malaysia: October.

Aitchison, C.C. (2003a) 'When East meets West: cultural difference, gender and global sports movements', keynote paper presented at The National Olympic Committee and Physical Education and Sport Scientific Association 5th National Congress on Physical Education and Sport Sciences, Ahvaz, Iran, February published in *Research in Sport Science* (in press).

Aitchison, C.C. (2003b) 'From leisure and disability to disability leisure: developing data, definitions and discourses', *Disability and Society* (in press).

Aitchison, C.C. (2003c) 'Local Cultural Strategies: critiques and challenges', in B. Snape, R. Thwaites and C. Williams (eds) *Access and Inclusion in Leisure and Tourism*, Eastbourne: Leisure Studies Association.

Aitchison, C.C. (2003d) 'Venturing into Other territories: theoretical journeys of social and cultural inclusion in outdoor environments', keynote paper presented at Whose Journeys? Where and Why? The 'Outdoors' and 'Adventure' as Social and Cultural Phenomena, Buckinghamshire Chilterns University College, UK, April 2002 and published in B. Humberstone (ed.) *Whose Journeys? The 'Outdoors' and 'Adventure' as Social and Cultural Phenomena*, Penrith: Institute for Outdoor Learning.

Aitchison, C.C. (2003e) 'Engendered education: adapting models from the sociology of education for leisure, sport and tourism in higher education', *Journal of Hospitality, Leisure, Sport and Tourism Education* 2, 1: 93–106.

Aitchison, C.C. (2004) 'From policy to place: theoretical explorations of gender–leisure relations in everyday life', in R. Bunton, E. Green and W. Mitchell (eds) *Youth, Risk and Leisure: Constructing Identities in Everyday Life*, London: Palgrave.

Aitchison, C.C., Brackenridge, C. and Jordan, F. (1999) *Gender Equity in Leisure Management*, Reading: Institute of Leisure and Amenity Management.

Aitchison, C.C. and Evans, T. (2003) 'The cultural industries and a model of sustainable regeneration: manufacturing "pop" in the Rhondda Valleys of South Wales', *Managing Leisure* 8, 3: 133–144.

Aitchison, C.C. and Jordan, F. (eds) (1998) *Gender, Space and Identity: Leisure, Culture and Commerce*, Eastbourne: Leisure Studies Association.

Aitchison, C.C., Jordan, F. and Brackenridge, C. (1999) 'Women in leisure management: a survey of gender equity', *Women in Management Review*, 14, 4: 121–127.

Aitchison, C.C., MacLeod, N. and Shaw, S. (2000) *Leisure and Tourism Landscapes: Social and Cultural Geographies*, Routledge, London.

Aitchison, C.C. and Reeves, C. (1998) 'Gendered (bed)spaces: the culture and commerce of women only tourism', in C. Aitchison and F. Jordan (eds) *Gender, Space and Identity: Leisure, Culture and Commerce*, Eastbourne: Leisure Studies Association.

Alonso, W. (1960) 'A theory of the urban land market', *Papers and Proceedings of the Regional Science Association* 6, 149–158.

Althusser, L. (1971) *Lenin and Philosophy and Other Essays*, London: New Left Books.

Alvesson, M. and Billing, Y.D. (1997) *Understanding Gender and Organizations*, London: Sage.

Appiah, K.A. (1996) 'Is the post in postmodernism the post in postcolonialism?', in P. Mongia (ed.) *Contemporary Postcolonial Theory: A Reader*, London: Arnold.

Appleton, D. (2002) *A Place at the Table: Culture and Leisure in Modern Local Government*, London: Local Government Association.

Arnold, M.L. and Shinew, K.J. (1998) 'The role of gender, race and income on park use constraints', *Journal of Park and Recreation Administration* 16, 4: 39–56.

Arnot, M. and Weiner, G. (eds) (1987) *Gender and the Politics of Schooling*, London: Hutchinson.

Arroba, T. and James, K. (1987) 'Are politics palatable to women managers: how women can make wise moves at work?', *Women in Management Review* 3, 3: 123–130.

Audit Commission (1989) *Sport for Whom*, London: HMSO.

Bacon, W. (1991) *Women's Experiences in Leisure Management*, Reading: Institute of Leisure and Amenity Management.

Bagguley, P., (1990) 'Gender and labour flexibility in hotel and catering', *Service Industries Journal*, 10, 4: 737–747.

Bagilhole, B. (1993) 'How to keep a good woman down: an investigation of the institutional factors in the process of discrimination against women academics', *British Journal of Sociology of Education* 14, 3: 262–274.

Bailey, P. (1978) *Leisure and Class in Victorian England: Rational Recreation and the Contest for Control, 1830–1885*, London: Routledge.

Bailey, P. (1989) 'Leisure, culture and the historian: reviewing the first generation of leisure historiography in Britain', *Leisure Studies* 8, 2: 102–127.

Ball, S. J. (1987) *The Micro-Politics of the School*, London: Methuen.

Barbier, B. (1984) 'Geography of tourism and leisure', *Geojournal* 9, 1: 5–10.

Barnes, T. and Gregory, D. (1997) *Reading Human Geography: The Poetics and Politics of Inquiry*, Arnold: London.

Baron, S., Field, J. and Schiller, T. (eds) (2000) *Social Capital: Critical Perspectives*, Oxford: Oxford University Press.

Barrett, M. (1988) *Women's Oppression Today: The Marxist Feminist Encounter*, London: Verso.

Barton, L. and Walker, S. (eds.) (1983) Gender, Class and Education, Lewes: Falmer Press.

Baum, T. (ed.) (1994) *Human Resource Issues in International Tourism*, Oxford, Butterworth-Heinemann.

Bauman, Z. (1998) *Work, Consumerism and the New Poor*, Buckingham: Open University Press.

de Beauvoir, Simone (1949) *The Second Sex*, Harmondsworth: Penguin.

Bell, Daniel (1973) *The Coming of Post-Industrial Society*, Harmondsworth: Penguin.

Bell, David (1991) 'Insignificant others: lesbian and gay geographies', *Area* 23, 4: 323–329.

Bell, David and Binnie, J. (1998) 'Theatres of cruelty, rivers of desire: the erotics of the street', in N. R. Fyfe (ed.) *Images of the Street: Planning, Identity and Control in Public Space*, London: Routledge.

Bell, David, Binnie, J., Cream, J. and Valentine, G. (1994) 'All hyped up and no place to go', *Gender, Place and Culture* 1, 1: 31–47.

Bell, David and Valentine, G. (eds) (1995) *Mapping Desire: Geographies of sexualities*, London: Routledge.

Bender, B. (1993) *Landscape: Politics and Perspectives*, Oxford: Berg.

Bennett, T. and Watson, D. (eds) (2002) *Understanding Everyday Life*, Oxford: Blackwell.

Berger, P. (1963) *Invitation to Sociology: A Humanistic Perspective*, Harmondsworth: Penguin.

Berger, P. and Luckman, T. (1966) *The Social Construction of Reality*, London: Penguin.

Bhabha, H. (1983) 'The other question: the stereotype and colonial discourse', *Screen* 24, November/December: 18–36.

Bialeschki, D. and Henderson, K. (1984) 'The personal and professional spheres: complement or conflict for women leisure service professionals', *Journal of Park and Recreation Administration* 2, 1: 45–54.

Bialeschki, D. and Henderson, K. (1986) 'Leisure in the common world of women', *Leisure Studies* 5, 4: 299–308.

Bialeschki, D. and Henderson, K. (2000) 'Gender issues in recreation management', in M.T. Allison and E. Schneider (eds) *Diversity and the Recreation Profession*, State College, Pennsylvania: Venture Press.

Bianchini, F. and Parkinson, M. (eds) (1993) *Cultural Policy and Urban Regeneration: The West European Experience*, Manchester: Manchester University Press.

Blair, S.L. and Lichter, D.T. (1991) 'Measuring the division of household labour: gender segregation of housework among American couples', *Journal of Family Issues* 12, 1: 91–113.

Bland, L. (1995) *Banishing the Beast: Sexuality and Early Feminists*, London: Penguin.

Bondi, L. (1992a) 'Gender and dichotomy', *Progress in Human Geography* 16, 1: 98–104.

Bone, V. and Mitchell, B. (2000) *101 Ways to Develop a Local Cultural Strategy*, Reading: Institute of Leisure and Amenity Management.

Boorstin, D.J. (1964) *The Image: A Guide to Pseudo-events in America*, New York: Harper & Row.

Bourdieu, P. (1973) 'Cultural reproduction and social reproduction', in R. Brown (ed.) *Knowledge, Education and Cultural Change*, London: Tavistock.

Bourdieu, P. (1984) *Distinction: A Social Critique of the Judgement of Taste*, London: Routledge.

Bowles, S. and Gintis, H. (1976) *Schooling in Capitalist America*, London: Routledge & Kegan Paul.

Brackenridge, C. (2001) *Spoilsports: Understanding and Preventing Sexual Exploitation in Sport*, London: Routledge.

Brah, A. (1991) 'Questions of difference and international feminism', in J. Aaron and S. Walby (eds) *Out of the Margins*, London: Sage.

Bramham, P. (1989) *Leisure and Urban Processes*, London: Routledge.

Broadbridge, A. (1995) 'Female and male earnings differentials in retailing', *Service Industries Journal* 15, 1: 14–34.

Brockbank, A. and Traves, J. (1996) 'Career aspirations – women managers and retailing', in Ledwith and F. Colgan (eds) *Women in Organisations: Challenging Gender Politics*, Basingstoke: Macmillan.

Brooks, A. (1997) *Postfeminism, Feminism: Cultural Theory and Cultural Forms*, London: Routledge.

Brown, R.M. (1935) 'The business of recreation' *Geographical Review* 25: 467–475.

Brownell, J. (1994) 'Women in hospitality management: general managers' perceptions of factors related to career development', *International Journal of Hospitality Management*, 13: 2: 101–117.

Bryson, V. (1992) *Feminist Political Theory*, Basingstoke: Macmillan.

Bryson, V. (1999) *Feminist Debates: Issues of Theory and Political Practice*, Basingstoke: Macmillan.

Burnell, J., Manfredi, S. and Rollin, H. (1997) 'Equal opportunities for women employees in the hospitality industry: a comparison between France, Italy, Spain and the UK' *International Journal of Hospitality Management*, 16, 2: 161–179.

Burnett, P. (1973) 'Social change, the status of women and models of city form and development', *Antipode 5*, 1: 57–61.

Burton, T.L. (1996) 'Safety nets and security blankets: false dichotomies', *Leisure Studies 15*, 1: 17–19.

Butler, J. (1990) *Gender Trouble: Feminism and the Subversion of Identity*, London: Routledge.

Butler, J. (1993) *Bodies that Matter*, London: Routledge.

Butler, R.W. (1980) 'The concept of a tourism area cycle of evolution: implications for management of resources', *Canadian Geographer 24*, 1: 5–12.

Byrne, D. (1999) *Social Exclusion*, Buckingham: Open University Press.

Byrne, E. (1978) *Women and Education*, London: Tavistock.

Cabinet Office (1998) *Bringing Britain Together: A National Strategy for Neighbourhood Renewal*, London: HMSO.

Carlson, A.W. (1980) 'Geographical research on international and domestic tourism', *Journal of Cultural Geography 1*, 1: 149–160.

de Certeau, M. (1984) *The Practice of Everyday Life*, Berkeley. CA: University of California Press.

Chambers, D. (1986) 'The constraints of work and domestic schedules on women's leisure', *Leisure Studies 5*, 4: 309–325.

Choi, P.Y.L. (2000) *Femininity and the Physically Active Woman*, London: Routledge.

Chomsky, N. (2003) *On Nature and Language*, A. Belletti and Luigi Rizzi (eds) Cambridge: Cambridge University Press.

Cixous, Hélène (1983/92) 'The Laugh of the Medusa', in E. Abel and E.K. Abel (eds) *The Signs Reader: Women, Gender and Scholarship*, Chicago: University of Chicago Press.

Clarke, J. and Critcher, C. (1985) *The Devil Makes Work: Leisure in Capitalist Britain*, London: Macmillan.

Clifford, J. and Marcus, G.E. (1986) *Writing Culture*, University of California Press, Berkeley, CA: California.

Coalter, F. (ed.) (1989) *Freedom and Constraint: The Paradoxes of Leisure*, London: Routledge.

Coalter, F. (1997) 'Leisure sciences and leisure studies: different concept, same crisis?', *Leisure Sciences 19*, 4: 255–268.

Coalter, F. (1998) 'Leisure studies, leisure policy and social citizenship: the failure of welfare or the limits of welfare', *Leisure Studies 17*, 1: 21–36.

Coalter, F. (2001) *Realising the Potential of Cultural Services: Making a Difference to the Quality of Life*, London: Local Government Association.

Coalter, F. (2002) 'Cultural services and social inclusion', paper presented at the 7th World Leisure Congress, Kuala Lumpur, Malaysia: October 2002.

Coalter, F., Long. J. and Duffield, B. (1988) *Recreational Welfare: The Rationale for Public Leisure Provision*, Avebury: Aldershot.

Coalter, F. and Parry, N. (1982) *Leisure Sociology or the Sociology of Leisure*, London: Polytechnic of North London.

Cochrane, A. (1993) *Whatever Happened to Local Government?*, Milton Keynes: Open University Press.

Cockburn, C. (1983) *Brothers: Male Dominance and Technological Change*, London: Pluto Press.

Cockburn, C. (1985) *Machinery of Dominance: Women, Men and Technical Knowhow*, London: Pluto Press.

Cockburn, C. (1991) *In The Way of Women: Men's Resistance to Sex Equality in Organisations*, Basingstoke: Macmillan.

Code, L. (1981) 'Experiences, knowledge and responsibility', in A. Garry and M. Pearsall (eds) *Women, Knowledge and Reality*, London: Allen & Unwin, 245–264.

Cole, J. (1979) *Fair Science: Women in the Scientific Community*, New York: The Free Press.

Collins, M. (1995) *Sports Development Locally and Regionally*, Reading: Institute of Leisure and Amenity Management.

Connell, R.W. (1987) *Gender and Power*, Oxford: Polity Press.

Cooper, D. (1994) 'Productive, relational and everywhere? Conceptualising power and resistance within Foucauldian feminism', in *Sociology* 28, 3: 435–454.

Cooper-Chen, A. (1994) 'Global games, entertainment and leisure: women as TV spectators', in C. Creedon (ed.) *Women, Media and Sport: Challenging Gender Values*, London: Sage.

Coppock, J.T. (1982) 'Geographical contributions to the study of leisure', *Leisure Studies* 1, 1: 1–27.

Coward, R. (1977) *Language and Materialism*, London: Routledge & Kegan Paul.

Crang, M., Crang, P. and May, J. (1999) *Virtual Geographies: Bodies, Spaces, Relations*, London: Routledge.

Crawford, D., Jackson, E. and Godbey, G. (1991) 'A Hierarchical model of leisure constraints', *Leisure Sciences* 9, 2: 119–127.

Critcher, C. (1988) 'A socialist leisure theory', in A. Clarke and B. Bacon (eds) *Leisure Theory: Four Perspectives*, Sheffield: Working Papers in Leisure and Tourism, University of Sheffield.

Crompton, R. and Sanderson, K. (1990) *Gendered Jobs and Social Change*, London: Unwin Hyman.

Crompton, R. and Sanderson, K., (1994) 'The Gendered Restructuring of Work in the Finance Sector', in Scott, A.M. (ed.), *Gender, Segregation and Social Change*, Oxford: Oxford Press.

Csikszentmihalyi, M. (1975) *Beyond Boredom and Anxiety*, San Francisco, CA: Jossey-Bass.

Csikszentmihalyi, M. (1990) *Flow: The Psychology of Optimal Experience*, New York: Harper & Row.

Cunningham, H. (1980) *Leisure in the Industrial Revolution, 1780–1880*, London: Croom Helm.

Currie, J., Harris, P. and Thiele, B. (2000) 'Sacrifices in "greedy universities": are they gendered?', *Gender and Education* 12, 3: 269–291.

Daly, M. (1973) *Beyond God The Father: Towards a Philosophy of Women's Liberation*, Boston: Beacon Press.

Daly, M. (1978) *Gyn/Ecology: The Metaethics of Radical Feminism*, Boston: Beacon Press.

Daniels, S. and Cosgrove, D. (eds) (1988) *The Iconography of Landscape: Essays on the Symbolic Representation, Design and Use of Past Environments*, Cambridge University Press: Cambridge.

Dann, G. (1981) 'Tourism motivation', *Annals of Tourism Research* 8, 2: 187–219.

Dann, G. (1993) 'Advertising in tourism and travel: travel brochures', in M. Khan, M. Olsen and T. Var (eds) *VNR's Encyclopedia of Hospitality and Tourism*, New York: Van Nostrand Reinhold.

David, M. (1989) 'Prima donna *inter pares?* Women in academic management', in S. Acker (ed.) *Teachers, Gender and Careers*, London: Falmer Press.

David, M (1994) 'Critical introduction: engendering education – feminism and the sociology of education', in S. Acker (ed.) *Gendered Education*, Buckingham: Open University Press.

Davies, A. (1992) *Leisure, Gender and Poverty: Working Class Culture in Salford and Manchester 1900–1939*, Buckingham: Open University Press.

Davies, C. and Holloway, P. (1995) 'Troubling transformations: gender regimes and organisational culture in the academy', in L. Morley and V. Walsh (eds) *Feminist Academics: Creative Agents for Change*, London: Taylor and Francis.

Davis, M. (1990) *City of Quartz: Excavating the Future in Los Angeles*, Verso: London.

Deem, R. (1978) *Women and Schooling*, London: Routledge & Kegan Paul.

Deem, R. (1986). *All Work and No Play: The Sociology of Women and Leisure*, Milton Keynes: Open University Press.

Deem, R. (1988) 'Feminism and leisure studies: opening up new directions', in E. Wimbush and M. Talbot (eds) *Relative Freedoms: Women and Leisure*, Milton Keynes: Open University Press.

Deem, R. (1999) 'How do we get out of the ghetto? Strategies for research on gender and leisure for the twenty-first century', *Leisure Studies* 18, 3: 161–177.

Department for Culture, Media and Sport (1999) *Arts and Sport: A Report to the Social Exclusion Unit*, London: HMSO.

Department for Culture, Media and Sport (2002) *The Role of the DCMS: Government Policy and Local Government*, London: DCMS. Online: (www.culture.gov.uk/role/local_govt.html) (10 October 2002).

Department of Health (1992) *The Health of the Nation*, London: Department of Health.

Department of Health (1999) *Saving Lives: Our Healthier Nation*, London: Department of Health.

Dewar, A.M. (1991) 'Incorporation of resistance?: towards an analysis of women's responses to sexual oppression in sport', *International Review for the Sociology of Sport* 26, 1: 15–22.

Diaz, P.E. and Umbreit, W.T. (1995) 'Women leaders – a new beginning', *Hospitality Research Journal*, 18, 3 and 19, 1 (double issue): 49–60.

Dirlik, A. (1994) 'The postcolonial aura: third world criticism in the age of global capitalism', *Critical Inquiry* 20, 328–356.

Dixey, R. and Talbot, M. (1982) *Women, Leisure and Bingo*, Leeds: Trinity and All Saints College.

Duffield, B.S. and Owen, M.L. (1970) *Leisure + Countryside = A Geographical Appraisal of Countryside Recreation in Lanarkshire*, Edinburgh: Tourism and Recreation Research Unit, University of Edinburgh.

Dumazadier, J. (1967) *Toward a Society of Leisure*, New York: Free Press.

Dumazadier, J. (1974) *Sociology of Leisure*, Amsterdam: Elsevier.

Duncan, N. (ed) (1996) *BodySpace: Destabilising Geographies of Gender and Sexuality*, London: Routledge.

Dunleavy, P. (1986) 'Explaining the privatisation boom: public choice versus radical explanations', *Public Administration* 64, 1: 13–34.

Durkheim, E. (1895) *The Rules of Sociological Method*, New York: Free Press.

Dworkin, A. (1981) *Pornography: Men Possessing Women*, New York: Perigree.

Dworkin, A. (1982) *Our Blood: Prophesies and Discourses on Sexual Politics*, London: Women's Press.

Dyck, I. (1993) 'Ethnography: a feminist method', *Canadian Geographer* 20, 4: 410–413.

Dyer, K. (1982) *Catching Up the Men: Women in Sport*, London: Junction Books.

Easterby Smith, M., Thorpe, R. and Lowe, A. (1991) *Management Research*, London: Sage.

Eco, U. (1994) *Apocalypse Postponed*, Bloomington, IN: Indiana University Press.

Edensor, T. (2000) 'Staging tourism: tourists as performers' *Annals of Tourism Research*, 27, 2: 322–344.

Edwards, E. (1996) 'Postcards: greetings from another world', in T. Selwyn (ed.) *The Tourist Image: Myths and Myth Making in Tourism*, Chichester: Wiley.

Eisenstein, Z. (1982) *The Radical Future of Liberal Feminism*, Boston: Northeastern University Press.

Elshtain, J.B. (1981) *Public Man, Private Woman*, Princeton, NJ: Princeton University Press.

Enloe, C. (1989) *Bananas, Beaches and Bases: Making Feminist Sense of International Politics*, London: Pandora.

Equal Opportunities Commission (1995) *The Impact of Compulsory Competitive Tendering*, Manchester: Equal Opportunities Commission.

Etzioni, A. (1964) *Modern Organisations*, London: Prentice-Hall.

Evans, J. (1995) *Feminist Theory Today: An Introduction to Second-wave Feminism*, London: Sage.

Farnham, D. and Horton, S. (eds) (1993) *Managing the New Public Services*, Basingstoke: Macmillan.

Farran, D. (1990) ' "Seeking Susan": producing statistical information on young people's leisure', in L. Stanley (ed.) *Feminist Praxis: Research, Theory and Epistemology in Feminist Sociology*, London: Routledge.

Firestone, S. (1979) *The Dialectic of Sex*, London: Women's Press.

Flax, J. (1990) 'Postmodernism and gender relations in feminist theory', in L. Nicholson (ed.) *Feminism/Postmodernism*, London: Routledge.

Foucault, M. (1976) *The Birth of the Clinic*, London: Tavistock.

Foucault, M. (1977) *Discipline and Punish: The Birth of the Prison*, Harmondsworth: Peregrine.

Foucault, M. (1979) *Power, Truth and Strategy*, (eds) M. Morris and P. Patton Sydney: Feral Publications.

Foucault, M. (1980) *Power/Knowledge: Selected Interviews and Other Essays 1972–1977*, Brighton: Harvester.

Fowler, D.D. and Hardesty, D.L. (1994) *Others Knowing Others: Perspectives on Ethnographic Careers*, Washington, DC: Smithsonian Institute Press.

Frisby, W. and Brown, B. (1991) 'The balancing act: women leisure service managers', *Journal of Applied Recreation Research* 16, 4: 297–321.

Fullagar, S. (2002) 'Narratives of travel: desire and the movement of subjectivity', *Leisure Studies* 21, 1: 57–74.

Fyfe, N.R. (1998) *Images Of The Street: Planning, Identity and Control in Public Space*, London: Routledge.

Fyfe, N.R. and Bannister, J. (1998) 'Eyes upon the street', in N.R. Fyfe (ed.) *Images of the Street: Planning, Identity and Control in Public Space*, London: Routledge.

Gamble, A. (1994) *The Free Economy and the Strong State: The Politics of Thatcherism* (second edition), Basingstoke: Macmillan.

Garcia-Ramon, M.D., Castener, M., and Centelles, N. (1988) 'Women and Geography in Spanish Universities', *Professional Geographer* 40, 307–315.

Garfinkel, H. (1967) *Studies in Ethnomethodology*, New Jersey: Prentice-Hall.

Gatens, M. (1992) 'Power, bodies and difference', in M. Barret and A. Phillips (eds) *Destabilising Theory: Contemporary Feminist Debates*, Cambridge: Polity.

Gatens, M. (1996) *Imaginary Bodies*, London: Routledge.

Giddens, A. (1984) *The Construction of Society: Outline of a Theory of Structuration*, Cambridge: Polity Press.

Gilbert, E.W. (1939) 'The growth of inland and seaside health resorts in England', *Scottish Geographical Magazine* 55, 1: 16–35.

Gill, D.L. (1992) 'Status of the journal of sport and exercise psychology', *Journal of Sport and Exercise Psychology* 14, 1, 1–14.

Gillborn, D. and Yondell, D. (2000) *Rationing Education*, Buckingham: Open University Press.

Gilligan, C. (1982) *In A Different Voice*, Cambridge, MA: Harvard University Press.

Glasser, R. (1970) *Leisure: Penalty or Prize*, New York: Macmillan.

Gleeson, B. (1999) *Geographies of Disability*, London: Routledge.

Gluckman, A. and Reed, B. (eds) (1997) *Homo Economics: Capitalism, Community and Lesbian and Gay Life*, New York: Routledge.

Glyptis, S. (1991) *Countryside Recreation*, Harlow: Longman/ILAM.

Goodale, T. and Godbey, G. (1988) *The Evolution of Leisure*, State College Pennsylvania: Venture.

Gramsci, A. (1978) *Selections From Political Writing: 1921–1926*, trans. Q. Hoare, New York: International Publishers.

Gramsci, A. (1985) *Prison Notebooks: Selections*, New York: International Publishers.

Gray, A. (1997) 'Learning from experience: cultural studies and feminism', in J. McGuigan (ed.) *Cultural Methodologies*, London: Sage.

de Grazia, S. (1962) *Of Time, Work and Leisure*, New York: The Twentieth Century Fund.

Green, E. (1998) 'Women doing friendship: an analysis of women's leisure as a site of identity construction, empowerment and resistance', *Leisure Studies* 17, 3: 171–186.

Green, E., Hebron, S. and Woodward, D. (1985) 'A woman's work', *Sport and Leisure*, July/August: 36–38.

Green, E., Hebron, S. and Woodward, D. (1987) *Leisure and Gender: A Study of Sheffield Women's Leisure Experiences*, Sheffield: The Sports Council/ Economic and Social Research Council.

Green, E., Hebron, S. and Woodward, D. (1990) *Women's Leisure, What Leisure?* Basingstoke: Macmillan.

Greenwood, E. (1957) 'The attributes of a profession', *Social Work* 2, 1: 44–55.

Gregory, D., Martin, R. and Smith, G. (1994) *Human Geography: Society, Space and Social Science*, Basingstoke: Macmillan.

Griffin, S. (1981) *Pornography and Silence: Culture's Revenge Against Nature*, London: Women's Press.

Grosz, E. (1994) *Volatile Bodies: Towards a Corporeal Feminism*, Sydney: Allen & Unwin.

Grosz, E. (1995a) *Space, Time and Perversion: The Politics of Bodies*, Sydney: Allen & Unwin.

Grosz, E. (1995b) 'Women, chora, dwelling', in S. Watson and K. Gibson (eds) *Postmodern Cities and Spaces*, Oxford: Blackwell.

Guttman, A. (1991) *Women's Sports: A History*, New York: Colombia University Press.

Habermas, J. (1962) *The Structural Transformation of the Public Sphere*, Cambridge: Polity Press.

Habermas, J. (1989) *The New Conservatism: Cultural Criticism and the Historians' Debate*, Cambridge: Polity Press.

Habermas, J. (1971) *Knowledge and Human Interests*, London: Hutchinson.

Halford, S., Savage, M. and Witz, A. (1996) 'Organised bodies: gender, sexuality and embodiment in contemporary organisations', in L. Adkins and V. Merchant (eds) *Sexualising the Social: Power and the Organisation of Sexuality*, Basingstoke: Macmillan.

Hall, V. (1996) *Dancing on the Ceiling: A Study of Women Managers in Education*, London: Paul Chapman Publishing.

Hantrais, L., Clark, P. and Samuel, N. (1984) 'Time–space dimensions of work, family and leisure in France and Great Britain', *Leisure Studies* 3, 4: 301–317.

Haraway, D. (1985) 'Class, race, sex, scientific objects of knowledge: a socialist feminist perspective on the construction of productive knowledge and some political consequences', in V. Haas and C. Perucci (eds) *Women in Scientific and Engineering Professions*, Michigan: University of Michigan Press.

Harding, S. (1986) *The Science Question in Feminism*, Milton Keynes: Open University Press.

Harding, S. (ed.) (1987) *Feminism and Methodology*, Milton Keynes: Open University Press.

Hardy, S., Maldon, B. and Taverner, C. (eds) (1996) *The Role of Art and Sport in Local and Regional Economic Development*, London: Regional Studies Association.

Hargreaves, J. (1994) *Sporting Females: Critical issues in the History and Sociology of Women's Sports*, London: Routledge.

Hartman, H. (1981) 'The unhappy marriage of Marxism and feminism: towards a more progressive union', in L. Sargent (ed.) *Women and Revolution: the Unhappy Marriage of Marxism and Feminism*, London: Pluto Press.

Hartsock, N. (1990) 'Foucault on Power', in L. Nicholson (ed.) *Feminism/ Postmodernism*, London: Routledge.

Harvey, D. (1969) *Explanation in Geography*, London: Edward Arnold.

Harvey, D. (1973) *Social Justice and the City*, London: Edward Arnold.

Haywood, L. (1994) *Community Leisure and Recreation*, Oxford: Butterworth-Heinneman.

Haywood, L., Kew, F. and Bramham, P. (1989) *Understanding Leisure*, London: Hutchinson.

Health Promotion Research Trust (1987) *Women's Leisure and Well-being: Interim Report*, Edinburgh: Centre for Leisure Research, Moray House College of Education.

Hearn, J. and Parkin, W. (1987) *'Sex' at 'Work': The Power and Paradox of Organisation Sexuality*, Brighton: Wheatsheaf.

Hearn, J., Sheppard, D.L., Tancred-Sherrif, P. and Burrell, G. (1989) *The Sexuality of Organisation*, London: Sage.

Heidi, J. and Pile, S. (1998) *Places Through the Body*, London: Routledge.

Hemingway, J. (1995) 'Leisure studies and interpretative social inquiry', *Leisure Studies* 14, 1: 32–47.

Henderson, K.A. (1992) 'Being female in the recreation and park profession in the 1990s: issues and challenges', *Journal of Park and Recreation Administration* 10, 2: 15–30.

Henderson, K.A. (1994) 'Perspectives on analysing gender, women and leisure', *Journal of Leisure Research* 26, 2: 119–37.

Henderson, K.A. and Ainsworth, B.E. (2001) 'Researching leisure and physical activity with women of colour: issues and emerging questions', *Leisure Sciences* 23, 1: 21–34.

Henderson, K.A. and Allen, K.R. (1991) 'The ethic of care: leisure possibilities and constraints for women', *Leisure and Society* 14, 1: 97–113.

Henderson, K.A. and Bialeschki, D. (1991) 'A sense of entitlement to leisure as constraint and empowerment for women', *Leisure Sciences* 13, 1: 51–65.

Henderson, K.A. and Bialeschki, D. (1993) 'Professional women and equity issues in the 1990s', *Parks and Recreation* 28, 3: 54–59.

Henderson, K.A. and Bialeschki, D. (1995) 'Career development and women in the leisure services profession', *Journal of Park and Recreation and Administration* 13, 1: 26–42.

Henderson, K.A., Bialeschki, D., Shaw, S.M. and Freysinger, V.J. (1989) *A Leisure of One's Own: A Feminist Perspective on Women's Leisure*, College Park, Pennsylvania: Venture Publishing.

Henderson, K.A., Bialeschki, D., Shaw, S.M. and Freysinger, V.J. (1996) *Both Gains and Gaps: Feminist Perspectives on Women's Leisure*, College Park, Pennsylvania: Venture Publishing.

Henry, I. (1993) *The Politics of Leisure Policy*, Basingstoke: Macmillan.

Henry, I. (1997) 'The politics of sport and symbolism in the city: a case study of the Lyon conurbation', *Managing Leisure*, 2, 1: 65–81.

Hicks, L. (1990) 'Excluded Women: how can this happen in the hotel world?', *Service Industries Journal*, 10, 2: 348–363.

Higher Education Funding Council for England (2003) *Higher Education Funding Council for England Draft Strategy 2003–2008*, Bristol: HEFCE.

Higher Education Statistics Agency Limited (2002) *Resources of Higher Education Institutions 1999/2000*, Cheltenham: HESA. Online (www.hesa.ac.uk/holisdoc/pubinfo/staff/st90.htm) (18 October 2002).

Hochschild, A. and Machung, A. (1989) *The Second Shift*, New York: Viking.

Holt, R. (1989) *Sport and the British: A Modern History*, Oxford: Clarendon Press.

Holton, V. (1995) 'Women on the boards of Britain's top 200 companies', *Women in Management Review* 10, 3: 16–21.

hooks, b. (1990) *Yearning: Race, Gender and Cultural Politics*, Boston: South End Press.

Horna, J. (1989) 'The dual asymmetry in the married couple's life: the gender differentiated work, family and leisure domains', *International Journal of Sociology of the Family* 19, 2: 113–130.

Horst (1981) *Papers in Latin American Geography in Honor of Lucia C. Harrison*, Muncie, Indiana: Special Publication No. 1: Conference of Latin American Geographers.

Howe, W., Couch, D., Ervine, W., Davidson, F., Kirby, D. and Sparks, L. (1992) *Retailing Management*, London: Macmillan.

Hughes, J. (1990) *The Philosophy of Social Research* (second edition), London: Longman.

Husserl, E. (1970) *The Crisis of European Sciences and Transcendental Phenomenology: An Introduction to Phenomenology*, trans. D. Carr, Evanston: Northwestern University Press.

Huzinga, J. (1949) *Homo Ludens*, London: Routledge.

Institute of Leisure and Amenity Management (2003) *Breakdown of ILAM Membership by Grade and Gender* (ILAM Information Service), Reading: Institute of Leisure and Amenity Management.

Institute of Public Finance (1992) *The Impact of Compulsory Competitive Tendering in Sport and Leisure Services*, Croydon: IPF.

Institute of Sport and Recreation Management (1989) *Questionnaire Survey of Impact of Compulsory Competitive Tendering*, Melton Mowbray, ISRM.

Institute of Sport and Recreation Management (1992) *CCT: Sport and Leisure Management*, London: ISRM Information Forum.

Ireland, M. (1993) 'Gender and class relations in tourism employment', *Annals of Tourism Research* 20, 4: 666–684.

Iso-Ahola, S.E. (1982) 'Towards a social psychology of tourism motivation – a rejoinder', *Annals of Tourism Research* 9, 3: 256–261.

Itzin, C. (ed.) (1992) *Pornography: Women, Violence and Civil Liberties*, Oxford: Oxford University Press.

Jackson, J. (1998) 'Feminist social theory', in S. Jackson and J. Jones (eds) *Contemporary Feminist Theories*, Edinburgh: Edinburgh University Press.

Jackson, S. and Jones, J. (1998) 'Thinking for ourselves: an introduction to feminist theorising', in S. Jackson and J. Jones (eds) *Contemporary Feminist Theories*, Edinburgh: Edinburgh University Press.

Jackson, S. and Scott, S. (2002) *Gender: A Sociological Reader*, London: Routledge.

Jameson, F. (1986) 'Third world literature in the era of multinational capitalism', *Social Text*, 15, 1: 65–88.

Jeffreys, S. (1997) *The Idea of Prostitution*, Melbourne: Spinifex.

Jeffreys, S. (1999) 'Globalising sexual exploitation: sex tourism and the traffic in women', *Leisure Studies*, 18, 3: 179–196.

Jenkins, C and Sherman, B. (1981) *The Leisure Shock*, London: Methuen.

Johnson, T. (1972) *Professions and Power*, London: Macmillan.

Jones, M. (1992) 'Failure to promote women: a serious loss', *Caterer and Hotelkeeper*, 9, 12 January.

Jordan, F. (1997) 'An occupational hazard? Sex segregation in tourism employment', *Tourism Management* 18, 8: 525–534.

Jowell, T. (2002) Opening Plenary Address by Secretary of State for Culture, Media and Sport, The Culture Contribution: How Culture and Leisure Help Communities, Local Government Association Conference, 19th March, Leafric Hotel, Coventry.

Kanneh, K. (1998) 'Black feminisms', in *Contemporary Feminist Theories* S. Jackson and J. Jones (eds) Edinburgh: Edinburgh University Press.

Kanter R.M. (1989) *When Giants Learn to Dance: Mastering the Challenges of Strategy, Management and Careers in the 1990s*, London: Unwin.

Kaplan, M. (1960) *Leisure in America: A Social Inquiry*, New York: John Wiley.

Katz, C. (1994) 'Playing the field: questions of fieldwork in geography', *Professional Geographer*, 46, 1: 67–72.

Kay, T.A. (1996) 'Women's work and women's worth', *Leisure Studies* 15, 1: 49–64.

Kay, T.A. (1998) 'Having it all or doing it all? The construction of women's lifestyles in time-crunched households', *Leisure and Society* 21, 2: 435–454.

Kay, T.A. (2000) 'Leisure, gender and the family: the influence of social policy', *Leisure Studies* 19, 3: 247–265.

Kinnaird, V. and Hall, D. (1994) *Tourism: A Gender Analysis*. London: Wiley.

Kelly, J. (1983) *Leisure Identities and Interactions*, London: Allen and Unwin.

Kelly, J. (1987) *Freedom to Be?*, New York: Macmillan.

Knopp, L. (1995) 'Sexuality and urban space', in D. Bell and G. Valentine (eds) *Mapping Desire: Geographies of Sexualities*, London: Routledge.

Knopp, L. (1997) 'Gentrification and gay neighbourhood formation in New Orleans', in A. Gluckman and B. Red (eds) *Homo Economics: Capitalism, Community and Lesbian and Gay Life*, New York: Routledge.

Koopman-Boyden, P. and Abbott, M. (1985) 'Expectations for household task allocation and actual task allocation: a New Zealand study', *Journal of Marriage and the Family* 47, 2: 211–219.

Kuhn, T. (1975) *The Structure of Scientific Revolutions* (second edition), Chicago: University of Chicago Press.

Lauria, M. and Knopp, L. (1985) 'Towards an analysis of the role of gay communities in urban renaissance', *Urban Geography* 6, 2: 152–169.

Le Grand, J. and Bartlett, W. (1993) *Quasi-Markets and Social Policy*, Basingstoke: Macmillan.

Leach, S., Stewart, J. and Walsh, K. (1994) *The Changing Organisation and Management of Local Government*, Basingstoke: Macmillan.

Ledwith, S. and Colgan, F. (1996) *Women in Organisations: Challenging Gender Politics*, Basingstoke: Macmillan.

Leisure Manager (1989) *Editorial*, November/December, Reading: Institute of Leisure and Amenity Management.

Lencek, L. and Bosker, G. (1999) *The Beach: The History of Paradise on Earth*, London; Pimlico.

Lenskyj, H. (1986) *Out of Bounds: Women, Sport and Sexuality*, Toronto: Women's Press.

Lenskyj, H. (1990) 'Power and play: gender and sexuality issues in sport and physical activity', *International Review for the Sociology of Sport* 25, 3: 235–241.

Levi Stauss, C. (1968) *Totemism*, London: Penguin.

Lin, N. (2001) *Social Capital: A Theory of Social Structure and Action*, New York: Cambridge University Press.

Lin, N., Cook, K. and Burt, R. (2001) *Social Capital: Theory and Research*, Berlin: Aldine de Gruyter.

Linder, S. (1970) *The Harried Leisure Class*, New York: Columbia University Press.

Local Government Management Board (1995) *Salaries and Numbers Information*, London: LGMB.

Long, J., Melch, M., Bramham, P., Hylton, K., Butterfield, J. and Lloyd, E. (2002) *Count Me In: The Dimensions of Social Inclusion through Culture and Sport*, Leeds: Leeds Metropolitan University. Online (www.lmu.ac.uk/ces/lss/research/countmein.pdf) (29 July 2002).

Loomba, A. (1998) *Colonialism/Postcolonialism*, London: Routledge.

Lorde, A. (1984) *Sister Outsider*, New York: The Crossing Press.

Losch, A. (1940) *Die raumliche Ordnung der Wirtschaft (The Economics of Location)*, trans. W.H. Woglom and W.F. Stolper (1954) New Haven, CT: Yale University Press.

Lyotard, J. (1984) *The Postmodern Condition*, Manchester: Manchester University Press.

MacCannell, D. (1976) *The Tourist: A New Theory of The Leisure Class*, New York: Schocken.

McCarthey, J. and Lloyd, G. (1999) 'Discovering culture-led regeneration in Dundee', *Local Economy*, 4, 3: 264–268.

McClintock, A. (1995) *Imperial Leather: Race, Gender and Sexuality in the Imperial Context*, London: Routledge.

McCrone, K.E. (1988) *Playing the Game: Sport and the Physical Emancipation of English Women, 1870–1914*, Lexington, KY: University of Kentucky Press.

McCrone, K.E. (1991) 'Class, gender and English women's sport, *c.* 1890–1914', *Journal of Sport History* 18, 2: 159–182.

McDonald, D. and Tungatt, M. (1992) *Community Development and Sport*, London: Sports Council.

McDowell, L. (1990) 'Sex and power in academia', *Area* 22, 3: 323–332.

McDowell, L. (1993a) 'Space, place and gender relations: Part I. Feminist empiricism and the geography of social relations', *Progress in Human Geography* 17, 2: 157–179.

McDowell, L. (1993b) 'Space, place and gender relations: Part II. Identity, difference, feminist geometries and geographies', *Progress in Human Geography* 17, 3: 305–318.

McDowell, L. and Sharp, J. (eds) (1997) *Space, Gender, Knowledge: Feminist Readings*, London: Arnold.

MccGwire, S. (1992) *Best Companies for Women: Britain's Top Employers*, London: Pandora.

McKay, J. (1996) *Managing Gender: Affirmative Action and Organisation Power in Australian, Canadian and New Zealand Sport*, New York: State University of New York Press.

MacKinnon, K. (1983) 'Feminism, Marxism, method and the state: an agenda for theory', in E. Abel and E. Abel (eds) *The Signs Reader*, Chicago: Chicago University Press.

MacKinnon, K. (1995) 'Sexuality, pornography and method', in N. Tuana and R. Tong (eds) *Feminism and Philosophy*, Oxford: Westview Press.

McNay, L. (1992) *Foucault and Feminism*, Cambridge: Polity Press.

Madge, C., Raghuram, P., Skelton, T., Willis, K. and Williams, J. (1997) 'Method and methodologies in feminist geographies: politics, practice and power', in Women and Geography Study Group (eds) *Feminist Geographies: Explorations in Diversity and Difference*, London: Addison Wesley Longman.

Mannheim, K. (1952) *Essays on the Sociology of Knowledge*, London: Routledge.

Marcuse, H. (1964) *One Dimensional Man*, London: Abacus.

Marx, K. (1844) *Economic and Philosophic Manuscripts*, New York: International Press.

Mason, S. (1999) 'Beyond flow: the need for a feminist ethics of leisure', *Leisure Studies* 18, 3: 233–248.

Massey, D. (1984) *Spatial Divisions of Labour*, London: Macmillan.

Matheson, H. and Flatten, K. (1996) 'Newspaper representation of women athletes in 1984 and 1994', *Women in Sport and Physical Activity Journal*, 5, 2: 65–84.

Memmi, A. (1967) *The Coloniser and the Colonised*, Boston: Beacon Press.

Messner, M. (1998) 'The triad of men's violence: sport as pedagogy', paper presented at The Big Ghetto: Gender, Sexuality and Leisure, Leisure Studies Association International Conference, July 1998, Leeds Metropolitan University, Leeds.

Miles, M. (1997) *Art Space and the City: Public Art and Urban Futures*, London: Routledge.

Millet, K. (1970) *Sexual Politics*, London: Abacus.

Mills, C.W. (1957) *The Power Elite*, New York: Oxford University Press.

Mills, S. (1998) 'Post-colonial feminist theory', in S. Jackson and J. Jones (eds) *Contemporary Feminist Theories*, Edinburgh: Edinburgh University Press.

Mintel (1998) *Sponsorship*, London: Mintel.

Mirza, H.S. (1997) *Black British Feminism: A Reader*, London: Routledge.

Mommaas, H. (1997) 'European leisure studies at the crossroads? A history of leisure research in Europe', *Leisure Sciences* 19, 4: 241–254.

Morley, L. (1995) 'Measuring the muse: feminism, creativity and career development in higher education', in L. Morley and V. Walsh (eds) *Feminist Academics: Creative Agents for Change*, London: Taylor and Francis.

Morley, L. and Walsh, V. (eds) (1995) *Feminist Academics: Creative Agents For Change*. London: Taylor and Francis.

Morris, K., Woodward, D. and Peters, E. (1998) '"Whose side are you on?" dilemmas in conducting feminist ethnographic research with young women', *Social Research Methodology* 1, 3: 217–230.

Mort, F. (1996) *Cultures of Consumption: Masculinities and Social Space in Late Twentieth-Century Britain*, London: Routledge.

Mowl, G. and Turner, J. (1995) 'Women, gender, leisure and place: towards a more "humanistic" geography of women's leisure', *Leisure Studies* 14, 2: 102–116.

Munt, S. (1995) 'The lesbian *flâneur*', in D. Bell and G. Valentine (eds) *Mapping Desire: Geographies of Sexualities*, London: Routledge.

Myers, K. (ed.) (2000) *Whatever Happened to Equal Opportunities in Schools? Gender Equality Initiatives in Education*, Buckingham: Open University Press.

Nias, J. (1989) *Primary Teachers Talking*, London: Routledge.

Nicholson, L. (1990) *Feminism/Postmodernism*, London: Routledge.

Nicholson, L. (1995) 'Interpreting gender', in L. Nicholson and S. Seidman (eds) *Social Postmodernism*, Cambridge: Cambridge University Press.

Oakley, A. (1981) 'Interviewing women: a contradiction in terms', in H. Roberts (ed.) *Doing Feminist Research*, London: Routledge.

Oakley, A. (1998) 'Gender, methodology and people's ways of knowing: some problems with feminism and the paradigm debate in social science', *Sociology* 32, 4: 707–732.

Oakley, A. (2000) *Experiments in Knowing: Gender and Method in the Social Sciences*, Cambridge: Polity.

Oerton, S. (1996) *Beyond Hierarchy: Gender, Sexuality and the Social Economy*, London: Taylor and Francis.

Office for National Statistics (1998) *Labour Market Trends*, June, London: Office for National Statistics.

Ouston, J. (ed.) (1993) *Women in Education Management*, Harlow: Longman.

Ozga, J. (1993) *Women in Educational Management*, Buckingham: Open University Press.

Packer, B.P. (1995) 'Irrigating the Sacred Grove: Stages of Gender Equity Development', in L. Morley and V. Walsh (eds) *Feminist Academics: Creative Agents for Change*, London: Taylor and Francis.

Painter, J. (12998) Editors report, Area 30, 1, 5–6.

Parker, S. (1971) *The Future of Work and Leisure*, London: MacGibbon and Kee.

Parker, S. (1983) *Leisure and Work*, London: Allen & Unwin.

Parker, S. (1995) 'Towards a theory of work and leisure', in C. Critcher, P. Bramham and A. Tomlinson (eds) *Sociology of Leisure: A Reader*, London: E&FN Spon.

Parkin, F. (1979) *Marxism and Class Theory: A Bourgeois Critique*, London: Tavistock.

Parratt, C.M. (2002) *More Than Mere Amusement: Working Class Women's Leisure in England, 1750–1914*, Boston: Northeastern University Press.

Parson, T. and Bales, R.F. (1955) *Family Socialisation and Interaction Process*, New York: Free Press.

Parsons, T. (1949) *The Structure of Social Action*, London: Free Press.

Patmore, J.A. (1972) *Land and Leisure*, London: Pelican.

Patmore, J.A. (1983) *Recreation and Resources*, London: Blackwell.

Peake, L. (ed.) (1989) 'The challenge of feminist geography', *Journal of Geography in Higher Education* 13, 1: 85–121.

Peters, M. (1999) '(Posts-) modernism and structuralism: affinities and theoretical innovations', *Sociological Research 4*. Online (www.socresonline.org.uk/socresonline/4/3/peters.html) (14 May 2000).

Piaget, J. (1958) *The Child's Construction of Reality*, London: Routledge & Kegan Paul.

Plog, S. (1974) 'Why destinations rise and fall in popularity', *Cornell Hotel and Restaurant Administration Quarterly* 14, 4: 55–58.

Popper, K. (1959) *The Logic of Scientific Discovery*, London: Hutchinson.

Prakash, G. (1994) 'Postcolonial criticism and Indian historiography', in L. Nicholson and S. Seidman (eds) *Social Postmodernism: Beyond Identity Politics*, Cambridge: Cambridge University Press.

Pritchard, A. and Morgan, N. (2000) 'Constructing tourism landscapes: gender, sexuality and space', *Tourism Geographies* 2, 2: 115–139.

Pritchard, A., Morgan, N. and Sedgley, D. (2002) 'In search of lesbian space? The experience of Manchester's gay village', *Leisure Studies* 21, 2: 105–123.

Pritchard, A., Morgan, N., Sedgley, D. and Jenkins, A. (1998) 'Gay tourism destinations: identity, sponsorship and degaying', in C. Aitchison and F. Jordan (eds) *Gender, Space and Identity: Leisure, Culture and Commerce*, Eastbourne: Leisure Studies Association.

Putnam, R. (2000) *Bowling Alone: The Collapse and Revival of American Community*, New York: Touchstone.

Rapoport, R. and Rapoport, R.N. (1975) *Leisure and the Family Life Cycle*, London: Routledge & Kegan Paul.

Raymond, J. (1986) *A Passion for Friends: Toward a Philosophy of Female Affection*, Boston: Beacon Press.

Rendell, J. (1998) 'Displaying sexuality: gendered identities and the early nineteenth-century street', in N.R. Fyfe (ed.) *Images Of The Street: Planning, Identity and Control in Public Space*, London: Routledge.

Rich, A. (1977) *Of Woman Born: Motherhood as Experience and Institution*, London: Virago.

Richards, G. (1992) *The Nationwide Impact of CCT*, London: University of North London.

Richards, G. (1995) 'Politics of national tourism policy in the UK', *Leisure Studies*, 14, 2: 153–173.

Richter, L.K. (1994) 'Exploring the political role of gender in tourism research', in W. Theobold, (ed.) *Global Tourism: The Next Decade*, Oxford: Butterworth-Heinemann.

Roberts, H. (ed.) (1981) *Doing Feminist Research*, London: Routledge.

Roberts, K. (1978) *Contemporary Society and the Growth of Leisure*, London: Longman.

Roberts, K. (1988) 'A pluralist leisure theory', in A. Clarke and B. Bacon (eds) *Leisure Theory: Four Perspectives*, Sheffield: Working Papers in Leisure and Tourism, University of Sheffield.

Roberts, K. (1995) 'Work and its corollaries', in C. Critcher, P. Bramham and A. Tomlinson (eds) *Sociology of Leisure: A Reader*, London: E&FN Spon.

Roberts, K. (1999) *Leisure in Contemporary Society*, Wallingford: CABI Publishing.

Rojek, C. (1985) *Capitalism and Leisure Theory*, London: Tavistock.

Rojek, C. (1988) *Leisure for Leisure*, London: Sage.

Rojek, C. (1993) *Ways of Escape*, London: Macmillan.

Rojek, C. (1995) *Decentring Leisure: Rethinking Leisure Theory*, London: Sage.

Rojek, C. (2000) *Leisure and Culture*, Basingstoke: Macmillan

Rojek, C. and Urry, J. (eds) (1997), *Touring Cultures: Transformations of Travel and Theory*, London: Routledge.

Rose, G. (1993) *Feminism and Geography*, Cambridge: Polity Press.

Rose, G. (1995) 'Place and identity: a sense of place', in D. Massey and P. Jess (eds), *A Place in the World? Places, Cultures and Globalisation*, Milton Keynes: Open University Press.

Rose, G. (1996) 'As if the mirrors had bled', in N. Duncan (ed.), *Bodyspaces*, London: Routledge.

Rule, J. (1973) *Private Lives, Public Surveillance*, London: Allen-Lane.

Russell, D. (1996) 'Between a rock and a hard place: the politics of white feminists conducting research on black women in South Africa', in S. Wilkinson and C. Kitzinger (eds) *Representing The Other: Feminism and Psychology*, London: Sage.

Said, E. (1978) *Orientalism*, London: Routledge.

Said, E. (1993) *Culture and Imperialism*, London: Chatto & Windus.

Salisbury, J. and Riddell, S. (2000) *Gender, Policy and Educational Change*, London: Routledge.

Samuel, N. (ed.) (1996) *Women, Leisure and the Family in Contemporary Society*, Wallingford: CAB International.

Savage, M. and Witz, A. (eds) (1992) *Gender and Bureaucracy*, Blackwell: Oxford.

Schor, J.B. (1991) *The Overworked American*, New York: Basic Books.

Schuster, M. and Van Dyne, S. (1984) 'Placing women in the liberal arts: stages of curriculum transformation', *Harvard Educational Review*, 54, 413–428.

Scott, J. (1994) 'Deconstructing equality-versus-difference', in M. Hirsch and E. Fox Keller (eds) *Conflicts in Feminism*, New York and London: Routledge.

Scraton, S. (1994) 'The changing world of women and leisure: "post-feminism" and "leisure"', *Leisure Studies*, 13, 4: 249–261.

Self, P. (1993) *Government by the Market?*, Basingstoke: Macmillan.

Seller, A. (1994) 'Should the feminist philosopher stay at home?' in K. Lennon and M. Whitford (eds) *Knowing the Difference: Feminist Perspectives in Epistemology*, London: Routledge.

Selwyn, T. (1996) *The Tourist Image: Myths and Myth Making in Tourism*, Chichester: Wiley.

Shaw, J. and Perrons, D. (1995) *Making Gender Work*, Buckingham: Open University Press.

Shaw, S.M. (1985) 'Gender and leisure: and examination of women and men's experience and perceptions of family time', *Journal of Leisure Research* 17, 4: 266–282.

Shaw, S.M. (1988) 'Leisure in the contemporary family: the effect of female employment on the leisure of Canadian wives and husbands', *International Review of Modern Sociology* 18, 1.

Shaw, S.M. (1992) 'Dereifying family leisure: an examination of women's and men's everyday experiences and perceptions of family leisure', *Leisure Sciences* 14, 3: 271–286.

Shaw, S.M. (1994) 'Constraints to women's leisure', *Journal of Leisure Research* 25, 1: 8–22.

Shaw, S.M. (1997) 'Controversies and contradictions in family leisure: an analysis of conflicting paradigms', *Journal of Leisure Research* 29, 1: 98–112.

Shaw, S.M. and Dawson, D. (2001) 'Purposive leisure: examining parental discourse on family activities', *Leisure Sciences* 23, 4: 217–231.

Sheppard, D. (1989) 'Organisations, power and sexuality: the image and self-image of women managers', in J. Hearn *et al.* (eds) *The Sexuality of Organisation*, London: Sage.

Shields, R. (1991) *Places on the Margin: Alternative Geographies of Modernity*, London: Routledge.

Shinew, K.J. and Arnold, M. (1998) 'Gender equity in the leisure services field', *Journal of Leisure Research* 30, 2: 177–194.

Shinew, K.J., Floyd, M.F., McGuire, F.A. and Noe, F.P. (1995) 'Gender, race and subjective social class and their association with leisure preferences', *Leisure Studies* 17, 1: 75–89.

Shurmer-Smith, P. and Hannam, K. (1994) *Worlds of Desire, Realms of Power: A Cultural Geography*, London: Arnold.

Simmonds, F.N. (1992) 'Difference, power and knowledge: black women in academia', in H. Hinds, A. Phoenix and J. Stacey (eds) *Working Out: New Directions for Women's Studies*, London: Falmer.

Sibley, D. (1995) *Geographies of Exclusion*, London: Routledge.

Sinclair, T. (1997) *Tourism and Employment*, London: Routledge.

Skeggs, B. (1999) 'Matter out of place: visibility and sexualities in leisure spaces', *Leisure Studies* 18, 3: 213–232.

Skelton, T. and Valentine, G. (1997) *Cool Places: Geographies of Youth Cultures*, London: Routledge.

Skinner, J. (1988) 'Who's changing whom ? Women, management and work organisation', in A. Coyle and J. Skinner (eds) *Women and Work: Positive Action for Change*, Basingstoke: Macmillan.

Smith, D. (1978) 'A peculiar eclipsing: women's exclusion from man's culture', *Women's Studies International Quarterly*, 1.

Soja, E. (1985) 'The spatiality of social life: towards a transformative retheorisation', in D. Gregory and J. Urry (eds) *Social Relations and Spatial Structures*, Basingstoke: Macmillan.

Soper, K. (1990) 'Feminism, humanism and postmodernism', *Radical Philosophy* 55 (summer): 11–17.

Spencer, A. and Podmore, D. (eds) (1987) *In a Man's World: Essays on Women in Male-Dominated Professions*, London: Tavistock Publications.

Spender, D. (1980) *Man Made Language*, London: Routledge & Kegan Paul.

Spender, D. (ed.) (1981) *Men's Studies Modified: The Impact of Feminism on the Academic Disciplines*, Oxford: Pergamon Press.

Spivak, G.C. (1985) 'Three women's texts and a critique of imperialism', *Critical Inquiry* 12, 1: 243–262.

Spivak, G.C. (1987) *In Other Worlds: Essays in Cultural Politics*, London: Routledge.

Spivak, G.C. (1993) *Outside in the Teaching Machine*, London: Routledge.

Spoonley, P. (1995) 'The challenges of post-colonialism', *Sites* 30, 1: 48–68.

Sport England (2000) *Basic Facts About Sport*, London: Sport England.

Sports Council [n.d.] *Competitive Tendering and Sport for All*, London: Sports Council.

Sports Council (1982) *Sport in the Community: The Next Ten Years*, London: Sports Council.

Sports Council (1987) *Sport in the Community: Which Ways Forward*, London: Sports Council.

Sports Council (1988) *Sport in the Community: Into the Nineties – A Strategy for Sport 1988–1993*, London: Sports Council.

Sports Council (1993a) *Sport in the Nineties: New Horizons*, London: Sports Council.

Sports Council (1993b) *Women and Sport: Policy and Frameworks for Action*, London: Sports Council.

Sports Council (1993c) *Sport and Leisure Management: Compulsory Competitive Tendering National Information Survey*, London: Sports Council.

Sports Council (1995) *Sport: Raising the Game*, London: Sports Council.

Sports Council (1997) *England, The Sporting Nation*, London: Sports Council.

Sports Council (1998) *Women and Sport: From Brighton to Windhoek – Facing the Challenge*, London: Sports Council.

Stamp, L.D. (1948) *The Land of Britain: Its Use and Misuse*, London: Longmans.

Stanley, L. (1980) *The Problem of Women and Leisure: An Ideological Construct and a Radical Feminist Alternative*, London: Sports Council/Social Science Research Council.

Stanley, L. (1990) *Feminist Praxis: Research, Theory and Epistemology in Feminist Sociology*, London: Routledge.

Stanley, L. (ed.) (1997) *Knowing Feminisms*, London: Sage.

Stanley, L. and Wise, S. (1983) *Breaking Out: Feminist Ontology and Epistemology*, London: Routledge.

Stanley, L. and Wise, S. (1993) *Breaking Out Again: Feminist Ontology and Epistemology*, London: Routledge.

Stebbins, R. (1992) *Amateurs, Professionals and Serious Leisure*, Montreal: McGill-Queens University Press.

Stebbins, R. (1997) 'Casual leisure: a conceptual statement', *Leisure Studies* 16, 1: 17–26.

di Stefano, C. (1990) 'Dilemmas of difference: feminism, modernity and post-modernism', in L. Nicholson (ed.) *Feminism/Postmodernism*, London: Routledge.

Stockdale, J.E. (1991) 'Sexual harassment at work', in J. Firth-Cozens and M.A. West (eds) *Women at Work: Psychological and Organizational Perspectives*, Milton Keynes: Open University Press.

Stinchcombe, A.L. (1967) 'Formal organisations', in N.J. Selser (ed.) *Sociology: An Introduction*, Wiley.

Swain, M.B. (1995) 'Gender in tourism', *Annals of Tourism Research* 22, 2: 247–266.

Swain, M.B. and Momsen, J. (2002) *Gender/Tourism/Fun(?)*, New York: Cognizant Communications Cooperation.

Talbot, M. (1979) *Women and Leisure*, London: UK: Sports Council/Social Science Research Council.

Talbot, M. (1996) 'Gender issues, sport and physical education: stages of development', paper presented at Queen's University, Kingston, Ontario, Canada.

Theberge, N. (2000) *Higher Goals: Women's Ice Hockey and the Politics of Gender*, Albany: State University of New York Press.

Thompson (1999) *Faraway Shores*, London: Thompson Holidays.

Thompson, E.P. (1968) *The Making of the English Working Class*, London: Penguin.

Thompson, S. (1995) 'Playing around the family: domestic labour and the gendered conditions of participation in sport', *Leisure Research Series* 2: 125–136, Sydney: Australia and New Zealand Association of Leisure Studies.

Thrane, C. (2000) 'Men, women and leisure time: Scandinavian evidence of gender inequality', *Leisure Sciences* 22, 1: 109–122.

Toffler, A. (1971) *Future Shock*, London: Pan

Toffler, A. (1980) *The Third Wave*, London: Pan.

Tomlinson, A. (1981) *Leisure and Social Control*, Brighton: Chelsea School.

Tong, R. (1989) *Feminist Thought*, London: Routledge.

Turner, V. (1992) *Blazing the Trail*, Tucson, AZ: University of Arizona Press.

Turner, L. and Ash, J. (1975) *The Golden Hordes*, London: Constable.

Urry, J. (1990) *The Tourist Gaze*, Sage: London.

Urry, J. (1995) *Consuming Places*, London: Routledge.

Valentine, G. (1989) 'A geography of fear', *Area* 21, 4: 385–390.

Valentine, G. (1993a) '(Hetero)sexing space: lesbian perceptions and experiences in everyday spaces' *Environment and Planning D: Society and Space* 11, 4: 395–413.

Valentine, G. (1993b) 'Desperately seeking Susan: a geography of lesbian friendships' *Area* 25, 2: 109–116.

Valentine, G. (1993c) 'Negotiating and managing multiple sexual identities: lesbian time–space strategies', *Transactions of the Institute of British Geographers* 18, 2: 237–248.

Vamplew, W. (1988) *Pay Up and Play the Game: Professional Sport in Britain 1875–1914*, Cambridge: Cambridge University Press.

Vaughan, M. (1994) 'Colonial discourse theory and African history, or has postmodernism passed us by?', *Social Dynamics*, 20, 1: 1–23.

Veal, A.J. (1979) *The Future of Leisure*, London: Social Science Research Council.

Veblen, T. (1925) *The Theory of the Leisure Class*, London: Allen & Unwin.

Voase, R. (1997) 'The role of flagship cultural projects in urban regeneration: a case study and commentary', *Managing Leisure*, 2, 3: 230–241.

Walby, S. (1986) *Patriarchy at Work*, Cambridge: Polity.

Walby, S. (1989) 'Flexibility and the changing sexual division of labour', in S. Wood (ed.) *The Transformation of Work*, London: Hutchinson.

Walby, S. (1990) *Theorising Patriarchy*, Oxford: Blackwell.

Walby, S. (1997) *Gender Transformations*, London: Routledge.

Walker, S. and Barton, K. (eds) (1983) *Race, Class and Education*, London: Croom Helm.

Wallace, M and Hall, V. (1994) *Inside the SMT: Teamwork in Secondary School Management*, London: Paul Chapman.

Walvin, J. (1978) *Leisure and Society, 1830–1950*, London: Longman

Watson, B. and Scraton, S. (1998) 'Gendered cities: women and public leisure space in the postmodern city', *Leisure Studies* 17, 2: 123–137.

Waugh, P. (1998) 'Postmodernism and feminism', in S. Jackson and J. Jones (eds) *Contemporary Feminist Theories*, Edinburgh: Edinburgh University Press.

Wearing, B. (1996) *Gender: The Pleasure and Pain of Difference*, Melbourne: Longman.

Wearing, B. (1998) *Feminism and Leisure Theory*, London: Sage.

Wearing , B. and Wearing, S. (1988) ' "All in a day's leisure": gender and the concept of leisure', *Leisure Studies* 7, 2: 111–123.

Wearing, B. and Wearing, S. (1996) 'Refocussing the tourist experience: the "*flâneur*" and the "choraster" ', *Leisure Studies* 15, 3: 229–244.

Weber, M. (1949) *The Theory of Social and Economic Organisations*, New York: Oxford University Press.

Weber, A. (1909) *Uber den Standort der Industrien (Alfred Weber's Theory of the Location of Industries)* trans. C.J. Fredrich (1929), Chicago: University of Chicago Press.

Weber, M. (1922) 'The essentials of bureaucratic organisations', reprinted in P. Worsley (ed.) (1978) *Modern Sociology*, London: Penguin.

Weedon, C. (1997) *Feminist Practice and Poststructural Theory* (second edition), Oxford: Blackwell.

Weiner, G. (ed.) (1985) *Just a Bunch of Girls*, Milton Keynes: Open University Press.

Weiner, G. (1986) 'Feminist education and equal opportunities: unity or discord?', *British Journal of Sociology of Education* 7, 3: 265–274.

Weiner, G. and Arnot, M. (eds) (1987) *Gender Under Scrutiny*, London: Hutchinson.

Whyte, J., Deem, R., Kant, L. and Cruickshank, M. (eds) (1985) *Girl Friendly Schooling*, London: Methuen.

Wilkinson, S. and Kitzinger, C. (1996) *Representing the Other: Feminism and Psychology*, London: Sage.

Williams, R. (1961) *Culture and Society, 1750–1950*, London: Penguin.

Williams, R. (1965) *The Long Revolution*, London: Penguin.

Williams, R. (1977) *Marxism and Literature*, Oxford: Oxford University Press.

Wilson, E. (1995) 'The invisible *flâneur*', in S. Watson and K. Gibson (eds) *Postmodern Cities and Spaces*, Oxford: Blackwell.

Wilson, M. (ed.) (1997) *Women in Educational Management: A European Perspective*, London: Paul Chapman Publishing.

Wimbush, E. (1986) *Women, Leisure and Well-being*, final report to Health Promotion Research Trust, Edinburgh: Centre for Leisure Research, Moray House College of Education.

Wimbush, E. and Talbot, M. (eds) (1988) *Relative Freedoms: Women and Leisure*, Milton Keynes: Open University Press.

Witz, A. (1992) *Professions and Patriarchy*, London: Routledge.

Wollstonecraft, M. (1988: 1792) *A Vindication of the Rights of Women* (C. Poston, ed.) New York: W.W. Norton Press.

Women and Geography Study Group (1984) *Geography and Gender: An Introduction to Feminist Geography*, London: Hutchinson.

Women and Geography Study Group (1997) *Feminist Geographies: Explorations in Diversity and Difference*, Harlow: Addison Wesley Longman.

Women's Sports Foundation/Sport England (1999) *National Action Plan for Women's and Girls' Sport and Physical Activity*, London: WSF/Sport England.

Wood, R.C. (1992) *Working in Hotels and Catering*, London: Routledge.

Woodward, D., Green, E. and Hebron, S. (1988) 'Research note: the Sheffield study of gender and leisure: its methodological approach', *Leisure Studies* 7, 1: 95–101.

Wyatt, S. and Langridge, C. (1996) 'Getting to the top in the National Health Service', in S. Ledwith and F. Colgan (eds) *Women in Organisations: Challenging Gender Politics*, Basingstoke: Macmillan.

Wynne, D. (1992) 'Urban regeneration and the arts', in D. Wynne (ed.) *The Culture Industry*, Aldershot: Avebury.

Young, M.F.D. (1975) *Knowledge and Control: New Directions for the Sociology of Education*, London: Collier-Macmillan.

Yule, J. (1997a) 'Engendered ideologies and leisure policy in the UK, Part 1: gender ideologies', *Leisure Studies*, 16, 2: 61–84.

Yule, J. (1997b) 'Engendered ideologies and leisure policy in the UK, Part 2: professional ideologies', *Leisure Studies*, 16, 3: 139–154.

Yule, J. (1998) 'Sub-cultural strategies in patriarchal leisure professional cultures', in C. Aitchison and F. Jordan (eds) *Gender, Space and Identity: Leisure, Culture and Commerce*, Eastbourne: Leisure Studies Association.

Zuzanek, J., Beckers, T. and Peters, P. (1998) 'The harried leisure class revisited: a cross-national and longitudinal perspective. Dutch and Canadian trends in the use of time from the 1970s to the 1990s', *Leisure Studies* 17, 1: 1–19.

Index